MW01536243

The Box in the Closet

My journey to claim who I am

To Ainsley
Best wishes
Margaret Singleton

Margaret Singleton

Order this book online at www.trafford.com
or email orders@trafford.com

Most Trafford titles are also available at major online book retailers.

Printed in the United States of America.

ISBN: 978-1-4269-9000-7 (sc)
ISBN: 978-1-4269-9001-4 (hc)
ISBN: 978-1-4269-9002-1 (e)

Library of Congress Control Number: 2011914408

Trafford rev. 09/20/2011

www.trafford.com

North America & international
toll-free: 1 888 232 4444 (USA & Canada)
phone: 250 383 6864 • fax: 812 355 4082

To my daughter Christine,
with my love.

Contents

Preface

Athens, Ontario, 1950

Sobbing, she wedged her skinny frame behind the worn, plush covered chesterfield and curled into a ball between the back of the oversized sofa and the wall. She struggled to silence her crying lest the sounds reveal her hiding place, but every now and then her chest heaved, a sob lingered. She felt a longing and sharp, stabbing pains in her stomach. Her head pounded. Her vision or perhaps it was her tears and swollen eyes that made it impossible to see clearly through the thick lenses of her gold rimmed glasses streaked with salty tears. The backs of her legs ached and she had that stabbing pain in her back that she often felt because of her scoliosis. The floor was painfully hard, her mother would call her soon, and her brother might find her too. Still there was comfort with staying with her feelings now that they'd come blurting out. Her thoughts, a kaleidoscope of hot colors whirled in disarray in her head as she drifted into another level of consciousness.

Familiar sounds and smells from the kitchen wafted into the parlor where she hid and brought her back into the reality of her life. She heard the soft clanking of the rose covered dishes with the fine gold band around the edge as her mother lifted them carefully from the cupboard and placed them on the table, the clicking of the silverware being placed precisely at each place, the crackling of the thick beef steak frying in the old iron pan on the wood stove. She knew her mother would be there wearing a clean apron as she prepared the evening meal for the family, boiling pots of potatoes, carrots and parsnips on the woodstove in the kitchen. She hoped her mother would not call her to come and help because she wasn't ready to explain her tears and swollen eyes. She was never ready.

Her after school chores were completed for the day. First, before dark, she had thrown down the ensilage from the silo for the cows. She had climbed the ladder inside the old stone silo to the second window, slid back the wooden door that covered the opening, then crawled through and jumped down into the dark, damp, moldy, ensilage, grabbed the waiting fork and began throwing the fermenting corn through the small opening to the barn floor. She welcomed the dwindling day light as it filtered through the rotting shingles of the silo roof even though it created an eerie yellow glow and an ominous feeling that maybe something or someone was there, behind her. She threw furtive glances over her shoulder to make sure she was alone. Once she had the shivers when an overweight brown rat waddled along the silo wall and up the side, dropping out of sight through the sliding door. The pungent odor of rotting corn stung her nostrils. She felt ensnared like a caged, frightened fox and longed for the freedom to make choices in her life, choices that eluded her.

She often dreamed of flying free, endlessly swimming and soaring through the air over trees, daisy filled meadows and blue green water, searching for a destination. Once, she flew to the mountains and saw a woman perched amid the grey, craggy rocks high up towards the summit. A warm glow of love and caring came over her as she flew to the ledge across from the woman whose face she then realized was shrouded in mist. She stretched out her hand to touch this mysterious woman only to watch her dissipate into the air.

Sometimes in her dream she was terrified and cold. Her breathing labored, she thrashed around in her bed and cried out but she always escaped the unknown danger by flying away. She would wake up exhausted, scared and trembling; her pajamas soaked with perspiration, the sheets from her bed crumpled on the floor in a heap. Returning to reality, always took time.

Now, hidden behind the sofa in the front parlour, the feeling was coming again, a sort of déjà vu, as though she was suspended in a vacuum without sound, attached to thick elastic and would suddenly be snapped back to where she really belonged. But it was never clear where she had gone.

She didn't fit. She didn't fit here on this farm in this family; she certainly didn't look or act like anyone else and although she loved family picnics, walks in the woods, skating on the flats and sliding down hill in winter she wanted more. But she was adopted, born to a wealthy family from Toronto whose name and address even her mother, the one cooking potatoes for supper, didn't know. The need to know had been growing in her like a storm these past few months and now her normally good grades at school had slipped. She longed to go to the city, Toronto especially and she had been there a few times. At school she was the class clown to cover up her failing grades because she couldn't concentrate she was so absorbed in her inner thoughts, "daydreams" it said on her Report Card. She always felt alone. The Young People's Union in her church had lots of events and she would have liked to be president but that never happened. She was always passed over for the popular boy or girl in the group.

Two women whom she loved to be with were Thelma and Elsa and it was always special to be invited to their home for tea. She listened enthralled by their stories of traveling to England to photograph and write stories for newspapers and magazines about the wedding of Princess Elizabeth and Prince Phillip, the funeral of King George V1 and later the Coronation of Princess Elizabeth when she became Queen. She would choose an afternoon with Thelma & Elsa any day, over going to Diana Sweets Café in Brockville with the YPU.

Earlier, when doing her chores she had felt distraught as she climbed back up the side of the silo on the inside ladder, crawled through the opening and slid the square wooden door back into place and carefully climbed down the outside ladder. She was tired now and hungry too, but she still had to gather the eggs and fill the wood box before supper.

As dusk began to fall outside she walked through the barn in front of the cows, toward the ladder to the hay loft to gather the eggs. She had sprinkled oil cake on their hay and the cows licked it up the with their rough tongues and now relished their ensilage and stirred in their bails when she touched their heads and stroked their wet noses as she walked toward the ladder. The black and white Holstein cows stood in a long row in their bails. At the end of the row one tan coloured Jersey cow stood out as being different, just like her. The other cows would lower their heads and push the brown one out of the way as they were processing into the barn. The Jersey was always the last getting into the barn. She liked the gentle Jersey cow that provided the family with rich cream. Sometimes when there was a new baby born in the community her dad would take the rich milk and give it to the mother.

The hen house would be dark now and she dreaded going in. It wasn't the hens she feared so much, although some of them were not above pecking her hand as she slid it under them to get their eggs. It was the darkness and the unknown creature or person that might be there that caused her anxiety. Sometimes her brother would hide and jump out to scare her. Tonight she knew he was cleaning the stable and would not be a threat. She reached the top of the ladder and stepped on to the upper floor of the barn. The sweet smell of the hay in the loft was comforting. While she was climbing the ladder to the loft, her dog, Rover had run around the barn and up the ramp, squeezed his body under the door to join her and sat wagging his tail, waiting. It felt safer with Rover there.

She entered the hen house and spoke quietly to each hen as she slid her hand slowly under the warm black and white feathers and carefully removed the eggs. They cooed and crackled softly in a hen whisper, their heads drooping as they fell asleep. One by one she placed the brown eggs in the berry basket hung over her arm.

Strange, how the hens sat guardedly and were possessive of their individual nests, sort of like each having its own apartment. Strange too how they accepted her hand sliding into their nests to take the eggs. Every day, normally she did this. Most days it was something that steadied her; the dim light, the hay smell, the soft small talk of the hens. But today, she felt tears rising in her eyes, a raging torment rising in her chest.

Rover sat panting quietly by the door of the hen house waiting for her and when the last brown egg was placed gently into the basket, she opened the large barn door and they left the loft. Rover fell into step with her as they walked down the barn ramp into the darkening day towards the house.

She felt sadness, a longing for a different life but couldn't bring it into focus.

Yet still the wood box beside the kitchen door was waiting for her, its' gaping cavern mocking her hunger, her weary body and unhappiness. Tears had been brimming since she was in the silo and were now about to explode in an avalanche of distraught emotion. She concentrated on the mindless repetitive task, thinking of the homework still to be done and the poetry book she was so looking forward to reading. She trudged back and forth with heavy arm loads of sticks, from the woodshed, up four steps to the summer kitchen and dumped them into the wood box.

Angry and frustrated she tried to control the heavy arm load of maple chunks until she could fling them into the box. Her arms were scratched and a dramatic track of blood oozed on her upper arm. The unruly sticks protruded in all directions and one knobby, rough chunk fell from her arms with a thud, hit her big toe and made her cry out in pain. It flashed through her mind that her life was sort of like this pile of knobby sticks that were out of control.

The incongruity of her life was overwhelming but she couldn't explain or understand where these feelings came from. She had been delivered here to her adoptive parents in a chauffeur driven limousine from Toronto when she was seven months old. That's what kept coming back to her, the way her mom told her the story and she always asked for more details. How much did her mother and father know? What were they keeping from her? She tried to picture her grandmother and perhaps her mother too, carefully choosing all of the baby things they brought with them for her. The little dress and hand knitted sweater she was wearing that day were carefully folded away in the cedar chest. There had been other things too, but all of the wonderful gifts of clothing and toys had been rejected by her new parents. Why couldn't they have at least kept them for her? Of course they wanted to give the message to the birth family that they could take care of their new daughter but it must have added to her grandmother's pain. Anyway, who had the right to decide that she was better off on a farm feeding cows and filling a stupid wood box than living in the city surrounded by all of the glamour which she imagined was associated with that life. She longed for her birth mother and gave her imagination full permission to create the perfect person.

It wasn't that didn't love her adoptive mother, she did. Her mother did many special things for her, like cranking up her long, unruly straight hair in paper or rags to give it some curl, or have a dressmaker sew up a plaid skirt each fall for school. Her mother also saw to it that she had music lessons, books and sheet music. And there were other things, too. Her mother and father were always supportive and in the front row when she was in a musical at school, singing at a church service or reciting for the Women's Institute. But her mother constantly chided her to get better marks in math and French. And this year all of her marks were low, very low. How could she do well when she was so preoccupied?

Her mother's repeated reprimand was,

"Margaret, why don't you apply yourself better? You should be at the top of your class."

Her Dad would say quietly;

"Florence, leave the girl alone and give her credit for what she's done."

Yet here she was, her arms scratched from the bark, her hands rough as she trundles one more armful of wood into the box and arranged the sticks to be straight. Her brother would be sure to inspect it in his merciless way and tell on her if it wasn't done properly, not that she would be punished.

And then, on that very last load, something gave way in her and she heaved the last sticks of wood at the box letting them fall in disarray wherever they landed. Sobbing, she ran out of the door of the summer kitchen, around the house, letting herself in at the door that opened into the second parlor which was secluded from the rest of the house.

Now, crouching behind the chesterfield in agonizing pain, her tear streaked face and swollen eyes betraying her, she knew she had to come out of her hiding place and face her mother, father and brother but the words that she wanted to say stayed dumbed down, locked, and choked up in her throat and heart. It was so painful for her to express her feelings and try to ask more about her mother, the mother she longed for, the mother she desperately wanted to know. Someday, though she had to do something. Perhaps now.

"Margaret, come and help with supper," her mother's voice brought her back to the farm, in her hiding place, her slender body cramped and aching. It brought her back to the reality of her life, her life without her "real" mother.

It was another eighteen years before the time and circumstances in my life were right for me to begin my search for my birth mother.

2. Introduction

"Learn to get in touch with silence within yourself, and know that everything in this life has purpose. There are no mistakes, no coincidences, all events are blessings given to us to learn from."1

I want to share my story to give my birth mother a voice and a presence. The courage she lived in order to give me life, is astounding.

The story is also for my daughter; an account of her maternal and paternal grandparents. And it is my story as an adopted person, brought up on a farm by loving parents but always agonizing over who I was, biologically and trying to understand why I didn't seem to "fit." And I wanted to know if at all possible, the circumstances of the rupture of my being adopted away.

When I began to look for my birth mother it was illegal to do so and there were few resources available so I had to invent creative ways to find information. On many occasions I encountered obstacles and situations which blocked my search.

The journey of writing this story is a "coming home to myself," of sorts. It has given me the opportunity for deep reflection, to forgive where there was wounding and to grieve for my birth mother whom I was denied the joy of knowing. It has been the catalyst for me to develop a deeper understanding of who I am.[2]

There are still unknowns, but I have been able to uncover truth, solve a few mysteries and piece together what I believe to be a credible account of my birth and eventual adoption and of my birth mother's life up to the time of her reunion with my birth father.

My own passion for truth and wanting to know more about my biological mother and family was the motivation for the birth of this memoir. Writing the story has been a journey of learning and pain but also a life giving and healing experience.

3. The Limousine

Florence pulled her worn black woolen coat closer to her trembling body as the wind-driven leaves from the now naked trees blew around her. She could taste the dust from the street as it hit her face and stung her skin. The bitter November gusts were relentless. She raised her hand and pushed her plain turban hat firmly down on her head. If only there had been enough money for a new coat and hat. She wished too that she had worn her galoshes as they would have protected her feet and ankles from the cold. Florence allowed herself a fleeting moment to reflect on the years when she was a teacher with a slim figure and quite a fashionable wardrobe. Her mind must have been dizzy with her thoughts.

Did we come to the correct hotel?, she wonders.
I wrote the address on the back of an envelope. Where did I put it?

Florence plunged her hand into her pocket and rummaged for the creased envelope where she had written the address and held it close to her eyes. A furtive glance at what she had written reassured her that her husband Stewart had driven them to the correct address, *The Hotel Quinte*, 211 Pinnacle St., Belleville, Ontario.

She saw that Stewart looked comfortable and warm with his long, tan overcoat flapping around his legs in the wind. His heavy dark brown wool breeches and fisherman's sweater pulled over his shirt and tie gave him a sporty look. His large tweed cap was almost lost to one of the squalls but Stewart caught it just in time. He rubbed the sand out of his eyes and readjusted his cap jauntily on his thick wavy hair.

Florence moved closer to her husband for warmth from the cold and slipped her arm through his.

Even though Florence was freezing cold she experienced an inner warmth as her heart raced with excitement as she waited here in a strange city, on the unpaved road, outside an elegant, historic hotel, knowing her life was about to change forever.

Florence hoped the Bicknells would arrive soon so that they could leave with the baby and go home. Florence wondered what it will mean for them to support another child and Stewart has already expressed his concern. They are totally reliant on the farm income and if the crops fail or the cows don't produce enough milk they could be in financial trouble. Florence was also very aware that she was already forty-four and Stewart was forty- six and a new baby required additional work and energy. She watched her husband straighten his shoulders as a crooked smile formed on the side of his mouth and Florence wondered if he was thinking about how this all began. He and Florence began talking about having another child a year or so after their son Wallace was born. Florence wanted a girl who would be a playmate for Wallace but also a companion for herself in later years. Three and then four years went by and they gave up hope that they could have another child of their own.

The night she shared her vision with Stewart was vivid in her mind. They were lying in bed on a cold winter night, snuggled under the layers of quilts to keep warm because the fire had already gone out in the wood stove, when Florence whispered to him;

"Stewart, what would you think about adopting a little girl?"

"Adopting?"

Stewart was suddenly wide awake. He sat up in bed letting the cold air into their cozy nest.

"How would we do that Florence? You mean take in a child from an orphanage?"

"No, I wasn't thinking of an orphanage. I don't know how you go about it, Stewart. I think my cousin Evelyn can tell us, but let's just think about it. I would want an infant, not an older child, and from another city too, far away, so no one knows who she is. Evelyn is a nurse in Toronto and I think she's the person to ask."

"Florence," he said as he slid back under the covers beside his wife, "I want to discuss this with you but I'm dead tired. Let's go to sleep now and talk about it tomorrow."

The next morning at breakfast, Stewart shared a dream he had. As he drifted into a restful sleep he visualized a happy child running and skipping beside him trying to keep up, her braids flying behind her, as they went down the lane together towards the sugar bush.

The cold brought Florence back to the present momentarily but then, she continued her reverie. It had been a long four-and-a-half-hour journey in their old Ford car, over dusty, bumpy roads, through Lyndhurst and Morton, on to Brewers Mills and Joyceville. Finally they arrived in Kingston. By then the gas gauge was registering almost empty, although it was never very accurate, so Stewart stopped to put gas in the car. Another two and a half hours or so along Highway Two and they would be in Belleville. Stewart pushed the speedometer up to thirty- five miles an hour once, but Florence was scared and begged him to slow down.

The whole family had got up at five a.m. to do the milking and clean the stable, then have a substantial breakfast so Stewart and Florence could leave the farm at seven o'clock in the morning. Stewart had time to wash and change his clothes. Wallace wanted to go with them but they stood firm and left him behind with Florence's sister, Lavenia. Even though Florence was a worrier, she knew he'd be safe and have a good time with his aunt. Stewart's father used to look after Wallace when they needed to be away.

They were hungry and ready for a rest stop by the time they arrived in Belleville. As they drove along Front Street they saw *The Empire Grill* and considered going in there, even though Florence had packed a substantial lunch. They took stock of the situation. It was too cold for a picnic and the restaurant would provide bathrooms, but they didn't want to spend the money they had in a restaurant. Then Stewart had an inspired idea, they could go to the train station. They were very pleased with their decision when they found the Canadian National Railway Station as it was quite grand. Florence spread out the contents of the picnic basket on one of the seating benches. She carefully removed the wax paper from the sandwiches, two kinds, made with thick slices of homemade bread spread liberally with butter. One was filled with roast chicken and savory and her own mayonnaise and the other ham and homemade mustard. There were large chucks of new cheese made by Thalmage Stone at the Forfar cheese factory, a small jar of Florence's sweet pickles, homemade date squares and a hot thermos of tea to be enjoyed.

They freshened up at the station and asked the station master for directions to the *Hotel Quinte*. When they found the hotel, Stewart parked their old car around the corner from the front of the hotel but the couple was unsure of what to do next, so they decided to wait in front of the hotel, for the Bicknells to arrive.

The wind was incessant but it was not the blowing that caused Florence to gasp and clutch her handbag to her bosom. A tiny high-pitched sound escaped from her throat and she clapped one hand over her mouth. Florence watched in disbelief as a highly polished dark-green Cadillac Limousine, with a gleaming chrome grill and front bumper, emerged from a cloud of dust on the dirt road, slowed and crept toward them.

Stewart's eyes were fixed on the huge glowing headlights which were turned on, even in the daylight. He wouldn't run the lights in daytime because the battery would die. A headlight protruded from each side of the shiny metal grill. Stewart's eyes widened as the lustrous car, quietly rolled closer and the distinctive fender skirts, wide white-wall tires and wheels with sparkling silver spokes came into view. There was even a spare tire mounted in the tire well. Stewart had never even imagined such a car. It seemed like an eternity until the sleek, opulent limousine finally came to a stop as the dust settled.

Through the oval opera window, sitting deep in the plush-covered back seat, a woman's head was all that Florence could see. A feather moved from side to side as the woman leaned forward and strained to see the waiting farm couple.

As the front car door opened, Florence stared, rooted to the cold ground, numb and unable to speak as the chauffeur stepped out, resplendent in his well-tailored grey uniform. He reached for the back door handle and lowered his head in a bowing gesture toward Florence. With her heart beating wildly, her face flushed with excitement and no longer feeling cold, Florence had her first glimpse inside the car and could hardly take in what she saw. She was looking for a baby but her eyes were drawn to the window ledges of the car where magnificent, shining silver, cone shaped flower vases were mounted. Exquisite pink rose buds filled the vases. Rose buds, in November. How can it be?

As her eyes moved around the car Florence finally saw her. The woman was holding a bundle which must be the sleeping baby, but the child's face was obscured by clothing of the like Florence had never seen on a baby. Then, the parcels came into focus. The car was filled with packages of unknown contents, perhaps layettes. A large stuffed brown teddy bear with articulated arms and legs shared the seat with the woman and the baby and a floppy doll was propped up against the silver-coloured window crank which could have been mistaken for jewelry. There was a push chair with a blue, orange and white striped canvas seat and a hood to shield a child from the sun, folded and leaned against the back of the front seat. An ice box on the floor was labeled *Baby Formula.* The infant may have been fed recently as a baby bottle which was half full was lying on a soft looking, yellow, flannelette blanket. More packages and gifts were piled on the front passenger seat.

"Fred," said the woman inside the car, "please take the baby while I step out."

The chauffeur reached in and gently took the baby in his arms, then carefully wrapped the pink embroidered satin blanket around the infant to protect her from the cold wind. As he held her in his left arm he extended his other hand to help the woman out of the car. The baby was snug in an angora bonnet and coat. She kicked at the wrappings and her tiny feet adorned with white knitted booties and pink ribbons stuck out below the blanket. A soft, white wool scarf with a tassel was wrapped around the upturned collar of her coat and tied in the back.

"Mrs. Bicknell, let me help you."

"Thank you, Fred."

She grasped Fred's hand and he supported her as she stepped onto the running board of the car and then gracefully down to the ground. Mrs. Bicknell was stylishly attired in a long, black fur coat, which was unbuttoned revealing a fashionable grey suit with wide embroidered lapels. The jacket flared slightly over her hips and was belted at the waist. Her feathered hat and high, black buttoned boots finished her ensemble. She glanced toward the waiting couple as though she was acknowledging them reluctantly.

Florence heard an almost haughty voice say, "Come inside, please. I have reserved a room."

The warmth and shelter of the hotel beckoned and Mrs. Bicknell walked towards the door of the lobby, followed by Fred, holding the baby. Still not having spoken a word and feeling utterly out of place and very intimidated, Florence slid her arm through Stewart's to steady herself and they walked falteringly into the hotel behind the elegant woman and her chauffeur who was carrying the baby.

They entered the hotel through the large glass doors and emerged into the magnificent lobby with floor to ceiling green-grey marble columns and exquisite marble floor. Fine-looking dark oak armchairs and tables were placed around the lobby. Several of the chairs were occupied by well dressed men, some sipped tea and others chatted together or read the *Ontario Intelligencer*, Belleville's widely circulated newspaper. Mrs. Bicknell strode across the floor to the reception desk and spoke to the manager.

"Good afternoon, Mrs. Bicknell. I've been expecting you. Did you have a good trip from Toronto?"

"Yes, thank you, but it was a long drive."

"It will be my pleasure to escort you and your guests to your room, so you may rest."

The hotel manager picked up the key for room number 101 from the cubbyhole behind the reception desk, stepped out into the foyer and walked beside Mrs. Bicknell as they chatted quietly together. Florence let go of her husband's arm and everyone paraded down the wide corridor which was decorated with pictures of the history of the city. Mrs. Bicknell and the manager led the way, the chauffeur came next holding the sleeping baby, and then Florence followed in a heighted state of anxiety. Stewart walked two steps behind his wife and brought up the rear falling farther behind as he tried to take in the pictures of the city which were hung on the walls of the corridor. They came to room 101, the door was opened and they all filed in.

"I trust this will be satisfactory, Mrs. Bicknell. Will there be anything else?" asked the manager.

As Mrs. Bicknell unbuttoned her coat she replied, "This room is fine, thank you. Some tea would be very nice to take away the chill of the day. Could you please arrange for us to have some tea?"

"I'd be delighted, Mrs. Bicknell," responded the manager. He left the room and hurried down the hall to fill Mrs. Bicknell's request.

Although she was chilled to the bone, Florence thought, *Tea, I just want to get the baby and go home.*

A canopy bed dominated the room and Mrs. Bicknell removed her fur coat and casually draped it on the foot-board of the bed, then in a sweeping motion gestured to the others to sit in the upholstered arm chairs. Mrs. Bicknell chose a large sofa chair near the bed and as soon as she was seated, Fred carefully put the baby in her arms, then leaned into his employer's ear and spoke something softly to her. The elegant woman nodded her head and Fred left the room.

Florence unbuttoned her coat, pulled her arms out of the sleeves but kept her coat around her shoulders. Her plain wool dress wasn't new or fashionable but it felt comfortable and warm. She felt very self-conscious and ill at ease. The fingers on her right hand found the lovely, round gold wrist watch with the delicate gold band on her left arm, the watch that her father gave her when she left home many years ago to attend Normal School in Ottawa. Deftly, she pulled back the long sleeve of her dress to reveal the elegance of the watch. For some reason, the watch gave her confidence.

The silence was deafening.

Then, Mrs. Bicknell turned to her guests.

"Good afternoon Mr. and Mrs. Singleton. I'm Beatrice Bicknell. This is my daughter Betty's child whom you had hoped to visit at Sick Children's Hospital in Toronto a few weeks after her surgery. I'm sorry for the loss of your father, Mr. Singleton. I'm told that is why you were not able to come to Toronto."

"Good afternoon, Mrs. Bicknell, we are glad to meet you. Thank you for your words of sympathy," Stewart said, as he stood and took a step forward to greet Mrs. Bicknell who pulled her hand out from the elaborate wrappings around the baby and accepted the gesture with a weak handshake.

"Yes, my wife Florence and our son Wallace and I wanted to go to Toronto to see the baby. We were very concerned about her and wanted to see her." Stewart replied, precisely.

Mrs. Bicknell continued, "The baby is still quite frail, Mr. and Mrs. Singleton. This is a great worry for my daughter and me. It is very difficult for us to part with her, as I'm sure you realize, but even more so because she is so delicate. My husband James contacted your doctor and we are satisfied that Dr. Bracken will be able to assume the care of the baby."

"We have great faith in Dr. Bracken," Stewart responded.

Mrs. Bicknell lowered her eyes and gazed lovingly at the swaddled infant. It was as though she and the baby were the only two people in the room.

The baby wakened and stirred as Beatrice Bicknell began to remove the infant's outer wraps. The pink satin blanket swathing the baby was carefully folded back, corner by corner and Florence could see that the baby was enveloped in a white fur coat which seemed too large for her. As Beatrice began to unbutton the coat, Florence seized the opportunity, found her voice and overcame her shyness to say;

"May I help?"

In three swift steps she crossed the room, her arms outstretched, intent on taking the baby. The baby's coat slid to the floor as Beatrice grasped for a blanket to wrap her in, then picked up the child and cradled her.

Now standing close to the baby she longed to call her own, Florence saw the tears in Mrs. Bicknell's eyes as she clasped her granddaughter more tightly. The eyes of the two women met in partial understanding and Mrs. Bicknell, still not about to relinquish the baby, rose from her chair still clutching the child. Disappointed again, Florence lowered her outstretched arms as she followed Mrs. Bicknell to the bed where the baby was placed gently between them as they sat down. Beatrice untied the pink ribbons on the angora bonnet and removed it from the tiny head, which was sparsely dotted with wisps of blonde hair. The infant, now wide awake, looked up into the familiar face of her grandmother, began to smile and then saw the strange woman's face and looked from one to the other in complete bewilderment. The baby's countenance quickly changed as her tiny face was contorted into frowns and furrows. Her breathing changed to quick, short, open-mouthed gasps. Florence hovered over Mrs. Bicknell intermittently extending and retracting her arms in numerous attempts to take charge of the baby. Still ignoring Florence's futile attempts to take her grandchild, and hoping to avert the cries of a distraught infant, Beatrice scooped her up from the bed and buried her own tear stained face in the baby's blanket.

She cuddled her granddaughter in this new position and patted the tiny child's back as she spoke soothingly to her;

"There, there, Dorothy, let Grandma hold you, everything will be alright".

Dorothy, thought Florence, *I don't want to call her Dorothy.*

Baby Dorothy was now wide- eyed, held over her grandmother's shoulder where she could see the people in the room. Frightened by the strangers, an environment and the stuffy smells she could not comprehend, Dorothy used the only language she knew. She opened her mouth wide and a high pitched, unrelenting wail emanated from the center of the tiny being. Her thrashing arms and legs were synchronized in perfect rhythm with her cries of anguish which went on for hours and as Florence recalled later, intermittently for days. No amount of soothing, walking or rocking could console the anxious child.

There were things to be discussed between Mrs. Bicknell and the Singletons, perhaps papers to sign and a wretched parting to be accomplished but Dorothy continued to cry. The room dissolved into controlled chaos.

Over the wails of the crying baby Mrs. Bicknell explained that she had brought gifts, anything a baby might need for her first year.

"Mrs. Singleton, my daughter and I chose things for the baby which we would like you to take with you. It is difficult for me to give up my granddaughter, but it was even a more difficult decision for my daughter Betty, after she went to extreme lengths to give birth to Dorothy. She and the baby's father wanted to marry, but my husband and I prevented them from doing so. Now, after seven months, my husband James has made this arrangement with you. As Betty and I were forced to agree to this difficult decision it is helpful for us to send her away with gifts. We have brought clothing, a push chair, toys and other items and a formula written for Dorothy by Dr. Alan Brown, her pediatrician in Toronto. It is very important for the health of the baby that she is given this formula as prescribed by the doctor.

My husband and I are also prepared to offer financial support to you for anything our granddaughter may need."

To use Florence's words when she was telling her sister Lavenia later, "I was thunderstruck."

Florence was adamant as she found her voice to say,

"Stewart and I are able to provide for the baby and will not need any financial help or the gifts you brought."

Mrs. Bicknell looked crushed when she heard Florence's curt reply. There was silence for a moment while everyone took in what had just transpired.

Rethinking her words Florence softened her position because she knew they would never be able to afford to buy a push chair and it would be so handy.

"The teddy bear and doll would be nice to have and I could use the push chair when the baby is a little older. We have a lovely carriage that our son Wallace used that will be suitable for a year or so. And of course we want the baby formula," she said.

Florence silently worried; *will the formula spoil before we get home? But, on a cold day like this it will be cool enough in the trunk of the car, even if the ice in the ice box melts. I don't know anything about an ice box.*

Beatrice leaned forward and opened her mouth as though she was about to say something about Florence's decision not to take all of the gifts but she remained silent, and held Dorothy closer to her as she paced, trying to comfort her granddaughter whom she feared she would never see again.

A knock on the door was barely audible over the lamenting baby. The door opened slowly and a waiter arrived with the tea tray. Florence was ready for a hot cup of tea and was grateful too for the biscuits she saw on the plate. Mrs. Bicknell motioned to a table where the waiter set the tray down and began to prepare the tea.

"Milk, Mrs. Singleton? One sugar or two? Or do you prefer lemon?"

"Milk and one sugar please." *Lemon*, thought Florence. *I've never heard of lemon in tea.*

"Mr. Singleton?"

"Milk and two sugars, please."

"Mrs. Bicknell?"

"I'll have my tea with lemon, please. Just put it on the table as I can't drink it right now." *What I would really enjoy right now is a Scotch and soda,* she thought.

"I can hold Dorothy for you," *There I said it, 'Dorothy',* "and let you drink your tea," Florence offered, seeking whatever opportunity she could to take the infant in her arms. Beatrice ignored the prospective mother and continued to walk the distressed baby.

Florence became braver; "Maybe the baby has a diaper pin sticking into her."

"No, I checked that," Beatrice said with annoyance.

Undaunted Florence continued, "She may need to be changed. Let me check her diaper for you. You have your tea, Mrs. Bicknell; your tea is getting cold."

Oh, my, what do I have to do to get a hold of my baby, Florence agonized.

Clutching the distressed baby, Beatrice turned slightly towards Florence but didn't answer. Beatrice was consumed with her own thoughts.

Do I really have to give my granddaughter to this woman? She doesn't seem to understand my sadness and grief at all. What if I call for Fred and just leave with Dorothy? Why oh why didn't I bring Betty with me even though James forbade her coming. He felt if Betty came she might make a scene and upset the Singletons who might then decide not to take the baby or Betty might even walk out with Dorothy if something displeased her. Betty was so impulsive. Where was the poor dear today? Oh, I wish I hadn't left her alone or that Betty had agreed to stay with her Aunt Muriel. Muriel was so kind to Betty when she was pregnant, talking to her, taking her for lunch or just sitting with her and holding her when she was sad and needed someone.

Muriel, her husband's sister and Beatrice were very good friends and right now, Beatrice felt very alone and could use a friend.

Dorothy's crying was relentless, as though she was picking up the tensions all around her.

Florence looked over at Stewart, who was sitting silently and literally steaming in his chair. She could see that he was perspiring, with beads of sweat visible on his forehead and probably pooling in the small of his back. *Poor Stewart, why doesn't he take off his heavy sweater? He must be so uncomfortable and at a loss for what to do or say.* Florence considered whispering to him quietly to suggest that he take off his sweater but his shirt would be soaked anyway. His body odor was beginning to rise too and Florence was concerned about what Mrs. Bicknell would think.

A wave of love for her husband came over Florence, as she realized his discomfort and how ill at ease he was.

Stewart always feels so awkward when he's holding a delicate china tea cup in his large, rough hands. He must be starving too as the chicken sandwiches they had for lunch weren't his usual substantial farm fare.

Stewart remained heavy and damp in his chair.

The gold watch on her arm took Florence's attention and she pulled back her sleeve for the second time. She glanced at her watch and saw that it was already three o'clock and Stewart would be concerned about the long drive home and where they would find a place to have supper. It would be dark as they drove and sometimes the battery was too weak to run the lights on the car. What would they do then? They had friends in Morton and if they left soon they might get to Morton before dark. Their good friends, Harry and Nellie Wykes, would make room for them, Florence was certain.

They finished their tea and Florence began to tidy up the tea tray, mainly for something to occupy her. She desperately wanted to cradle the baby in her arms and wondered when that was going to be. Mrs.

Bicknell was definitely reluctant to part with her granddaughter. *What am I going to do if I can't take the baby home?*

Florence's reverie was broken by Mrs. Bicknell's wavering voice. "We must think about leaving soon." Still hanging on to the baby she reached into her purse and brought out a letter which she offered with quivering hands, to Stewart, as head of the family.

"My husband sent this letter and has prepared a document for you to sign, Mr. Singleton."

"Thank you, Mrs. Bicknell."

Stewart carefully unfolded the letter which had been typed on exquisite paper from the Toronto Law Firm of James Bicknell, the baby's grandfather and his law partner Bruce O'Brien. As Stewart read the letter in a kind of quiet monotone, mouthing the words as he read, his left eyebrow shot up in an arc which Florence immediately noticed and intuitively knew something was not right. Florence watched as he stood up and began to pace back and forth from the window to his chair. He had his back to her now, but Florence saw him reach into his pocket, pull out his striped handkerchief and wipe his face. Stewart returned to his chair and read the letter again as though he couldn't quite grasp what it said. He gave Florence a look of concern.

What can the letter say? Florence was worried.

As if to answer her silent request, Stewart leaned over, put his hand on her shoulder and placed the envelope in Florence's hands. He mopped his perspiring forehead with his handkerchief.

Florence carefully removed the pages from the envelope and took note of the names on the letterhead. She was reluctant to know the contents. She wished she and Stewart could be alone to discuss whatever was inside but didn't know how to ask for the privilege of doing this. Because of her poor eyesight Florence went over to the window where there was better light. She held the letter close to her face, closed her right eye and squinted to read the typed words with her other eye. The first page was an introduction to Mrs. Bicknell and a greeting to them. The second page was the document to be signed and she couldn't make any sense of it. She read what was on the paper again and yet again.

"In the matter of Dorothy Bicknell, registered as Dorothy Bicknell Watson, in the Province of Ontario in the City of Toronto in the County of York, on the tenth Day of May, 1935, and the request to adopt said child by Stewart Singleton and his wife Florence Singleton of Soperton, Ontario, it is agreed that they are to have custody of said child to care for and nurture for two years. In November of 1937 a review will take place and if at that time we are satisfied that compliance has been made with section 3 of the adoption Act, the adoption order will be authorized."

Her face turned ashen as the words began to sink in.

"Two years!" she almost shouted.

Now it was Florence who was distressed.

"How can we wait for two years? Who decides at the end of two years if we can adopt the baby? Oh, what will I do if I have to give her up? Oh Stewart, I want to name her Margaret Rose."

Stewart went to his wife and put his arm around her shoulder in an effort to comfort her, and whispered words of encouragement. Tears of disappointment streamed down Florence's cheeks. The stresses and anxieties of the day had taken their toll and Florence collapsed distraught, into a chair. In his quiet manner, Stewart took Florence's hand and in a sort of loud whisper said he thought they should accept the terms of the adoption. They would be able to take the baby home with them and they could talk about the legalities later. Stewart patted his wife's back in an attempt to comfort her as she sobbed.

"There, there, Florence, it will all work out."

Beatrice Bicknell didn't offer any answers to the questions or a response of any kind and continued to pace with the anxious baby. She had her own hurt and exhaustion to cope with and she wished her husband, James, was with her as he would know what to say and could answer all of the legal questions; after all, it was all his doing. It all seemed so inhumane.

Beatrice wondered how she could let the baby go to an uncertain future and totally unfamiliar environment. Why didn't she stand up to James and insist that they keep their granddaughter? Why did she allow James to pressure Betty and her too, to give the baby away? That's what it was, plain and simple. She was giving her granddaughter away to strangers. The thought was devastating.

Beatrice thrust a copy of the enclosed document at Stewart before she changed her mind.

"Please sign this copy, Mr. Singleton to close the agreement, so that I may take it to my husband."

Later, Stewart likened the request to negotiating a parcel of land.

A small desk with ornamental carvings and a fold down front to make a writing surface stood against the wall just inside the door of the hotel room. Stewart had a similar one at home so he walked with intention to the writing desk, pulled down the fall front, revealing six small drawers, a pewter inkwell with cover and a quill pen. One of the drawers had hotel stationery and envelopes, another contained blotting paper and wipes for the pen nib. Stewart sat straight on the chair, placed the letter on the desk surface, then picked it up and read it once again. Florence noticed him tugging at his collar as he hesitated. Has he had a change of heart? He ran his hands through his hair and looked intently at the letter. She knew it was a huge decision for him and Stewart liked everything to be orderly and clear. In this new development, there were many unknowns that could cause them so much grief if things didn't work out for them.

Florence sighed as her husband finally signed the conditions with a steady firm hand. His signature would be in his distinctive style, in old English script. Stewart carefully blotted the signature then held the signed page in front of his face and blew on it for good measure.

Beatrice watched him intently as he carefully replaced the top on the inkwell, wiped the nib of the pen with one of the wipes provided, closed the front of the desk, stood and then gently lifted the chair back into place in front of the desk. He smiled as he handed the signed document back to Mrs. Bicknell, agreeing to the conditions of the adoption.

Beatrice Bicknell decided that she liked this quiet, gentle man, that he possessed some gentility and that he would care greatly for her granddaughter.

With her eyes still fixed on Stewart, she dropped the paper which disappeared into the recesses of her purse.

The moment Beatrice Bicknell dreaded had arrived and she inwardly commanded herself to walk to the corner of the room and pull the braided cord to summon the porter. Too soon he arrived at the door of room 101. The porter was instructed to find Fred, her chauffeur and then take the Singletons to the limousine to get anything they chose to take with them for the baby. The porter and Fred could then transfer the items to the Singleton's car for them. The couple would have time to visit the lavatories and freshen up before beginning their trip home. It would also give Beatrice a few last minutes alone with the baby, her precious granddaughter.

When they had all left the room, Beatrice tearfully and lovingly changed the squirming, restless baby, talking softly to her and tried, through her tears, to sing a familiar tune.

> "Hmm, hmm, Rock-a-bye, baby
> In the treetop.
> When the wind blows

The cradle will rock. When the bough breaks
The cradle will fall
And down will come baby
Cradle and all."
It's a dreadful song and it makes me feel worse.

Beatrice stopped singing and humming the tune and talked quietly to the baby. Slowly she began to dress Dorothy in the clothes she and her daughter Betty, had carefully chosen for the child's long journey, not just to her new home but on unknown paths in a rural culture so different from her heritage. A journey that would mean that Beatrice's grandchild was out of their lives forever.

First a soft warm undershirt with two flaps which criss-cross over her tummy and ties on each side. The double thickness on the undershirt made a covering and protection over the horrendous scar, the result of surgery for pyloric stenosis when she was just two days old. Now seven months later, the baby was still very tiny and weighed only 11 lbs 6 oz. She appeared malnourished and had problems eating and digesting food. Dr. Alan Brown wrote a special formula and the baby was growing but was still underweight and size for her age. She might always be a very fragile child and that worried Beatrice.

She continued to dress the baby pulling on a cotton slip, then a delicate Madeira cotton embroidered dress with puffed sleeves. Finally, she guided the baby's arms into the sleeves of a white sweater, a blue ribbon at each wrist, a narrow blue edging around the sweater and delicate pink and blue rosebuds on the front and the collar. She wept as she thought about the love and hopes for the child that she had knitted into the sweater. Knitted leggings and booties tied with pink ribbons were carefully drawn on the baby's legs and feet to keep her cozy and warm. A bonnet was carefully pulled on the tiny head and tied under her chin. Beatrice opened the fur coat on the bed and gently put the baby on it, then buttoned the frog closings. All was ready.

Beatrice did not want a porter or anyone else to help her with what she had to do now. She wrapped the baby tightly in the satin blanket and with the baby's cheek pressed against her own their tears mingled together. Reluctantly, she began the walk from the hotel room, down the corridor to the lobby where they must go through the large beveled glass doors and outside to the cold street and the Singletons. It was heartening to see her chauffeur, Fred waiting for her at the large front door. She paused, to allow him time to push open the glass door. But instead of opening the door, Fred pulled off his glove then gently touched the baby's face to wipe away her tears. Then as he stooped to kiss her cheek, he tucked one pink rosebud into her blanket. Fred opened the hotel door and the glass reflected the tears welled in his eyes. Beatrice walked through the door into the late afternoon light, holding the baby tightly to her bosom.

Beatrice and the baby sobbed together as the grandmother walked toward the car where the farm couple waited impatiently for their new child.

One last kiss on the baby's wet cheek.

Beatrice Bicknell prayed for the happiness of her dear, precious granddaughter and also, that one day she would see her again.

4. *Separation*

Florence would always remember the moment.

The coveted infant, cradled in her grandmother's arms was sobbing, her breath coming in gasps, anxiety and fright emanating deep from within her soul. Beatrice stood in the street, a solitary, elegant figure with the wind whipping her long coat in frenzy around her. The grandmother was protecting and clutching the baby to her heart.

In the gloom of that evening, Beatrice took faltering steps towards Florence who was to be the child's new mother, a woman older than she. Florence reached out to take the bundled baby and the grandmother reluctantly released her grip and allowed her granddaughter to slip away into the hands of the stranger.

Beatrice hesitated, then turned away and walked tentatively towards her chauffeur, Fred, who was striding briskly towards her. Fred took Beatrice's arm and supported the grieving woman as they walked together to the limousine.

5. The Long Journey to Soperton
Hopes & Fears

Florence furrows her brow as she gazes at the pale, squirming bundle in her arms. All afternoon she ached to hold this baby so what is this wave of apprehension which has come over her? When she gave birth to her son, Wallace, her overwhelming love for him soon erased the memory of his difficult birth and the pain and trauma she had experienced. Florence anticipated a similar joy and excitement when she saw her new baby, but the whole experience today has been fraught with heartache and disappointment. Disappointment washed over the day because of the conditions of the adoption set out in the letter they were asked to sign from the child's grandfather; one of the stipulations which caused them anxiety was a two year wait before the final adoption. The wretched parting of the baby from her grandmother had brought tears of sorrow to Florence's eyes and diminished her joy when the infant was placed in her arms.

Florence is finally holding the daughter she longed for although she is filled with self doubts about her inadequacy to nurse the fragile baby and she is feeling a huge weight of responsibility. Her vision of the baby smiling and holding out her arms, eager to come to her new mother has been dashed. This unnerving situation of unrelenting crying and rejection has never crossed her mind. She and Stewart had driven to Bellville earlier in the day and during the trip and later as they waited in front of the Quinte Hotel she was excited and full of anticipation; now those emotions are a faint memory.

A gust of wind stirs up the dead leaves on the ground and startles Florence, bringing her back to the reality of the moment.

"Stewart, will you take her while I get into the car?"

He obliges holding the baby at arm's length and jiggles her up and down hoping in some way the movement will be calming. Florence sinks into the front seat and tucks her coat around her legs for additional warmth, then pulls her hat securely down on her head fearing it could be knocked off when the distraught infant is unwrapped and the baby's arms are free. Florence reaches out for the writhing, noisy bundle swathed in blankets which shield her from the cold and Stewart gladly gives her back to Florence, totally at a loss for what to do. The car door is closed and the new father checks, making sure it is latched securely before taking his place behind the wheel.

Florence speaks hesitantly, "Stewart, she's ours now. Isn't she?"

"Yes, Florence, she is." Then he said under his breath and in a voice momentarily lacking in enthusiasm, "For now."

"I wish I knew why she is crying, Stewart, and in such distress. There isn't any reason for her to be in such a state; she's been fed and changed and she's snuggled up warm in her blankets." Florence's voice betrays that she is almost in tears.

As Stewart pulls away from the curb he sees the Bicknell limousine preparing to leave. It appears that Mrs. Bicknell has buried her face in her hands. A sudden wave of compassion and uncertainty engulfs him as he absorbs the poignant moment.

There's still time… he pauses, then turns the car east towards Highway Two and home to Soperton.

Dorothy's crying is unrelenting and Stewart is beginning to show signs of weariness as he huddles over the steering wheel peering into the gathering darkness. Long shadows from the fence posts give the illusion of horizontal lines on the road that mingle with the cracks of broken concrete making it difficult to distinguish one from the other. Tree branches blowing in the wind create ghostly moving apparitions imitating animals darting across the road. Stewart swerves to avoid a raccoon but it is only a shadow.

"Stewart, what are you doing?" Florence chided.

"Flo, the crying is getting to me and I have to pay attention to my driving. It's hard to see the road in the dusk and I want to delay using the lights as long as I can to save the car battery. If I pull over to the side do you think you could sit in the back? Maybe she'll settle down if you put her on the seat. You can stretch out too. Okay?"

"Yes, of course, let's try that. Her crying is upsetting me too, Stewart, and upon my word, I don't know what else to do."

There are deep ditches on either side of the narrow, road and a stopping place has to be chosen very carefully. The car slows and gradually comes to a halt in a safe area on the roadside. Stewart depresses the clutch, grasps the knob of the floor-mounted gear-shift and pushes it into neutral, then pulls on the emergency brake. Confident that the car will not roll he steps out and comes around to the passenger door to assist Florence in getting settled into the back seat. They are soon comfortable in their new positions and for a few miles the tiny one is less agitated and almost falls asleep. The baby's eyes are red and swollen and her relentless wailing causes her make little noises as she sucks in her breath. Florence pats her back and talks soothingly to her.

"There, there, Margaret Rose."

Unresponsive to the unfamiliar name, she begins to cry even louder.

The road is narrow and rough and Florence remarks that other cars are few and far between. Stewart would have welcomed more road traffic in the event of car trouble which is a constant worry for him on a long trip. Service stations are not only sparse but closed at night. He calms his nerves by the thought that a garage owner would almost certainly come to his aid in an emergency. Finding a garage, if necessary, will be the problem.

They bump along in silence, each exhausted and in deep reflection.

Stewart looks in the rear view mirror at his wife and the new addition to his family. Florence is fussing over the baby, trying everything she can think of to mollify her. She has put the baby on her back on the seat, loosened the blankets and is gently stroking the little one's face. There are many thought going through Stewart's head. Will this tiny girl live? Does she usually cry this much? At the hotel she was quiet and she even smiled until she saw Florence. Was it Florence's glasses that frightened her? Florence is a wonderful mother to Wallace and she'll be a caring, loving mother to a little girl. Florence has always wanted a daughter so much. But, can Florence cope with a sickly child? Can he?

Running the farm alone takes much of his energy and time, and since his father's death Stewart misses the additional help to do some of the lighter chores that his father took care of. Father went to the pasture for the cows early in the morning which gave Stewart the additional time to prepare each of the cow stalls with oil- cake on a bit of hay. After Stewart finished milking the cows his father carried the pails of milk and poured them into the milk cans to be taken to the cheese factory, and then he washed the milk pails. Now Stewart would have to do these small tasks which are not very taxing on his energy, but they did take time. He wouldn't be able to help

Florence very much during the day and at night he's too exhausted. Next summer, Wallace might be old enough to bring the cows from the pasture at milking time but that doesn't resolve how to care for a fragile baby. Florence is a worrier and she is very emotional. He imagines her sitting in the rocking chair in the kitchen by the wood stove, rocking back and forth, back and forth patting, singing and soothing their daughter. He wonders if Florence will have time to do her own work. Will she have any time for Wallace? Is the care of the baby going to take all of her time? Is he going to have to help Florence as well as do his own work? Thank goodness Florence was able to do the canning and preserving before they got the call from Toronto that they could meet the baby's grandmother in Bellville and bring the infant home.

His wife's responsibilities flash through Stewart's mind. Dozens of sealers line the shelves in the cellar, ready for the cold winter days ahead. The glass containers look more beautiful than the coloured magazine pictures of preserves in the advertisements for Certo. Rows of canned pears, peaches, cherries and rhubarb are on the top shelves. They'll be wonderful desserts over the winter in addition to the pies, cookies, cakes, squares, apple desserts and candies yet to be made. Sealers of canned beef, corn, tomatoes and beets, along with jars and jars of pickles, jams and jellies fill the remaining wall of shelves. He can envision Florence the day she proudly showed her winter store to her sister, Lavenia, the sealers, bottles and jars organized just like they are behind the counter in Wilfrid and Lavenia's General Store. On the dirt floor of the cellar there are two large Stoneware crocks of salt pork in brine. Stewart has picked and stored several bushels of apples in the cellar. Over on the outside wall there's a door leading to the root cellar which can be accessed from outside through a trap door. Root vegetables fill the dark, cold area. Stewart recalls the pains in his back after harvesting and storing the carrots, potatoes, turnips, and parsnips.

How will Florence have time to care for the baby, for Wallace and for her husband? The washings alone are exhausting; they have a wringer washer now but Florence has to hang the heavy, wet clothes on the clothesline and in the winter that is an onerous task. The clothes are stiff when she brings them. Stewart has a light moment when he recalls how Wallace takes delight in leaning the frozen long winter underwear against the wall, with the trap door of the underwear sticking out at the back.

"Rock –a-Bye-Baby." Florence sings a song which used to help Wallace go to sleep when he cried. Perhaps it is because Dorothy has heard the tune many times before that she gradually relaxes, her heavy eyelids close, then open wide again. She fights to stay awake but sleep overcomes her; but a restless sleep with heavy breathing intermingled with gasps and sobs.

It is quieter in the back seat and Stewart glances in the rear view mirror again at his wife and their new daughter.

Stewart knows that they will become attached to the tot and if the Bicknells refuse to allow her adoption, what then? If they have to give the little girl up when she is two years old, it will crush them, Wallace too; he'll become fond of his sister. They can't afford a lawyer if it becomes necessary to go to court in order to keep the child. What if the girl doesn't turn out the way we hope for her? Have we made a mistake in taking this child?

Father's sudden death in June took our thoughts and time away from the final planning for the adoption and also going to see the infant. Father's illness was brief and he was bedridden only a week. Dr. Kelly called it a cerebral hemorrhage.

It surprised Stewart that his Father, usually on the frugal side, was so interested in them finding a daughter and that he offered them the money for the trip to go and see the infant while she was still in the hospital. Stewart regrets that they weren't able to make that trip and also that his father will never see this little girl, nor will their daughter have a grandfather or indeed, any grandparents. Florence's parents are both gone too. Father was probably hoping that this baby girl would grow up to be like Stewart's sister, Blanche, who was extremely talented. She was an accomplished musician, a gifted artist, good at all sports and outdoor activities and her bubbly personality drew many friends to her. Blanche was also a graduate of Queens University. Stewart still grieves the loss of his sister who died of tuberculosis at the age of twenty nine, shortly before she was to be married.

Then it suddenly crosses his mind that it is possible that this unsettled little being could grow up to be like Blanche. He smiles to himself and feels the burden of uncertainty lifted, momentarily, at least. Blanche's trousseau is in Florence's cedar chest; the beautiful hand stitched, monogrammed bed linens, the exquisite silverware, embroidered doilies of all shapes and sizes, knitted cushion covers and many other beautiful items. There are even two of her landscape paintings. Then he has an idea; when the time is right he'll talk to Florence about what she would think of saving Blanche's trousseau to give to their daughter when she is older; perhaps when she gets married.

Stewart has a private moment. He sighs, deeply and smiles to himself.

Car lights appear in the distance and Stewart pulls the lever with the white porcelain knob to turn on his car lights so that his car will be more visible on the dark road. As the cars pass in the night they honk a greeting to each other; "uh-ooga, uh-ooga."

"Stewart, don't, the baby!"

The warning comes too late. It was either the blast of the cars' horns or Florence's sudden outburst that frightens Dorothy and she opens her eyes wide. There is an ever so brief silence while the baby takes in her unfamiliar surroundings, the strange smells of the car and the couple and unfamiliar voices before her small, aching body begins to rise and fall again with the sobs of discomfort, heartache and fear.

"Florence, I'm so sorry."

"Stewart, I'm afraid something is seriously wrong. How far are we from Morton?"

"Probably a half an hour or so. Why?"

"We could stop at Harry and Nellie's and feed the baby there. I can't feed her in the car because the formula is in the ice box and it would be too cold. We can warm up a bottle at Wykes' house. I think she is hungry."

"I'm hesitant to go there unannounced; Nellie has four children and isn't she expecting another soon? But I don't have another suggestion. Let's see what they say when we get there, Florence."

"This one is going to be sick if we don't get the crying stopped soon, Stewart."

The baby continues her mournful cry without interruption as the car moved carefully along the dark road.

The sign, "Village of Morton," glows in the beam of the headlights and Stewart sighs with relief. Harry owns the General Store in Morton and the family lives at the bottom of the hill, just on the edge of the village. The two couples have been friends since their courting days and were each others' wedding attendants. Now, the distance between their homes and family responsibilities prevent them from seeing one another often. Stewart steers the car onto the oil-stained grassy patch which defines the parking area beside the house.

"You go to the door, Stewart, and see if it is alright to come in."

The weary man is glad to stretch his legs and steps out into the night. The clear black sky is studded with millions of twinkling stars. The wind has ceased and the air is crisp and cold. He pauses to take in the beauty and then slowly inhales the night deeply into his soul before approaching the door.

He knocks several times before the door opens, slowly, and a diminutive silhouette appears.

"Stewart! What in the world are you doing here at this time of the night?"

"Nellie…" He doesn't have time to finish as she hears the crying baby and is already flying down the steps of the verandah towards the car which appears to be the source of the sound.

"Florence, what have you got there? For goodness sake get out of the car and come in. You can explain when we get inside. It's freezing out here. Give me the baby."

Nellie takes charge and guides her friends into the kitchen.

"Come in by the stove and get warm."

Dorothy screams, and then once again, settles into a steady, monotonous cry.

Harry appears and he and his friends exchange greetings, and then Stewart and Harry retire to another part of the house away from the commotion to have their own conversation and get caught up on their respective lives.

"Flo, you must be exhausted."

Nellie places the unhappy infant over her shoulder."Shush, shush," she whispers as she walks and pats her back.

The three boys had followed their father but Mary, who is seven years old, lingers in the kitchen with her mother in order to be closer to the baby. She knows about babies because her little brother is only three and she has helped with his care.

"Mary, bring a blanket to put on the table so I can change the baby."

Questions pour out of Nellie as she tries to understand why Florence has this baby.

"Now, Flo, tell me about this child. What's her name? Where in the world did you get her? Is she yours?"

Florence hesitates, and then begins her story with the child's name, leaving the other details for later when the baby has settled down. "Her young mother named her 'Dorothy' and that's the way her birth is registered. I want to call her 'Margaret Rose'. Stewart likes 'Eleda,' after a favorite cousin of his."

"How old is she Flo?"

"She was born last May."

"It's the end of November now, Flo. Let's see, May, June, July," Nellie counts out the months on her fingers.

"August…. well, Flo, she's almost eight months old and she's familiar with the name 'Dorothy'. It will take her awhile before she understands that you are talking to her when you say, 'Margaret.' You may want to give changing her name more thought, Flo."

Mary brings the blanket for her mother to fold to make a soft surface on the table and while Nellie undresses the wriggling infant, Florence begins the long story of their search for a daughter. She talks about the letters from Evelyn, the children she was offered and how she came to decide on this one. Nellie is a nurse and Florence asks her friend what she knows about the operation and how it might affect the baby's growth. The illness and Mr. Singleton's death as well as the Bicknell's indecision about giving up his daughter's child have delayed their being able to bring her home[3]. Nellie listens while Florence pours out the details of the stressful meeting with Mrs. Bicknell in the Belleville hotel, and now her heart-sick worry over the incessant crying.

Stewart brings a bottle from the icebox in the car and Nellie places it in warm water on the stove to heat. Harry comes into the kitchen and moves the kettle to the front of the wood-stove to boil for tea.

Gentle hands wash Dorothy's swollen eyes and face, and then dress her in fresh clothing and a dry, cotton diaper from the cupboard that holds the clothing of Nellie's own four children. The diapers were carefully stored in the event of another arrival. Mary sits in the rocking chair and asks if she can hold the baby. Her mother brings her the bottle which has been warmed to the correct temperature. Drops from the bottle are shaken on the inside of Nellie's wrist to test that it is tepid and not hot.

Florence rummages in her purse for the card with the formula written by Dr. Alan Brown which Mrs. Bicknell had given her from the Hospital for Sick Children, in Toronto.

She reads, "Four ounces of barley flour, corn syrup, evaporated milk and water cooked ½ hour, to be given every four hours, or at 10, 2, 6, (Day) and 10, 6, (Night)."

Florence continues, "On the back of the card there are instructions for giving her orange juice. "Give 1 tablespoon with a little sugar, once a day.' "

"My goodness, Flo, that's an unusual formula. Barley flour, I've never heard of barley flour in a formula. I guess that's why there's such a big hole in the nipple on the bottle. I would think it would be difficult for her to pull the thick liquid through the nipple. I wonder if she is getting enough nourishment."

"Apparently the pediatrician, Dr. Brown, doesn't believe in giving cow's milk to babies. He's also invented a food for babies called *Pablum.* [4] I wasn't given any of that food. It may be for older babies."

As Mary rocks her, Dorothy sucks erratically on the nipple, fighting to keep her eyes open. Finally, sleep wins and she closes her eyes. The exhausted infant takes in a deep, unsteady breath before sinking contentedly into the Mary's arms and falling asleep.

"Flo, you and Stewart haven't had supper. I'll warm up some potatoes with onions and scramble some eggs. With some cheese and bread will that do, Florence? "

"That would be wonderful Nellie. Don't go to any trouble, now."

"While I'm doing this Flo, you call your sister who is looking after Wallace and tell her you'll be home tomorrow. You can't head out tonight with a sick baby, and besides, Stewart is too tired to drive any further. The boys can double up in their beds and there'll be room for everyone. Now, don't say anything Flo, just call Lavenia and then eat your supper. You and Stewart have some quiet time and Mary can rock the little one. Harry and I will join you later. There's some cake left. I'll get my boys into bed and then come back."

As Stewart and Florence begin their supper, Nellie hurries off to inspect the older boy's homework and put her three-year-old to bed. Her brown hair is pulled tightly away from her face and twisted into a smooth bun at the back. She pins the untidy strands at the sides with two stray hairpins as she hurries upstairs to attend to her children and then make up the beds for her friends.

Stewart is worried about the farm chores but after a discussion with Florence about staying overnight they decide it is the best thing to do.

"Florence, I need to call Willy Howard and see if he can do the milking again in the morning. I'm sure he'll help out for another day. Willy and Robena don't have a phone but I'll call his dad and Charlie can go next door and ask Willy if he'll do the morning milking and we'll be home as soon as we can get there tomorrow."

"Stewart, I'm sure Willy will do the chores. I'll give you the phone as soon as I call Lavenia. I'm worried about Wallace, too. He has never stayed overnight with Lavenia and Wilfrid without us being there."

Arrangements are completed and Florence and Stewart are just finishing their meal when Nellie and Harry come into the kitchen to join them for dessert and tea. Dorothy wakens and wide-eyed takes in the scene before continuing her song of lament. Nellie takes the distressed baby from Mary and suggests her daughter have some cake and milk and then "off to bed." Florence showers praises upon Mary for the tender care she gave the child so that they were able to enjoy their supper.

The sounds of distress continue, making meaningful conversation impossible. Nellie suggests they all turn in and then heats another bottle for Florence to take upstairs with her. She wraps it in towels to keep it warm and leads the couple to their room. Nellie has laid out night attire for them; a pair of Harry's pajamas and one of her nities for Flo. The crib recently vacated by her youngest is already in the room.

"The bathroom's just down the hall, Flo. I put out towels. Make yourself at home and use whatever you need. Goodnight."

"Goodnight, Nellie. Thank you for your kindness, you have no idea how much we appreciate it. I feel badly though that we are putting you and your children out."

"Florence, don't say another word. We're glad you stopped. It is so good to see you. Now, try to get some rest. Things will look better tomorrow."

It is a long, restless night with Florence and Stewart taking turns pacing with their new daughter who fusses and cries intermittently until dawn. They prepare to leave soon after breakfast.

The children have gone to school and Harry is opening the store as they pack up the car and say their "goodbyes." The longest part of the journey is behind them and, barring any problems, they will soon be home in Soperton.

They drive in relative silence with each thinking their own thoughts but they have brief forays into conversation accompanied by the intermittent wail of their daughter.

Two hours later, Stewart turns the car into their long, tree-lined driveway.

Florence heaves a sigh of happiness to be home, safely. Their collie dog, Ring races to greet them barking loudly and wagging his tail in a joyous doggie welcome. The baby is not amused and sends up a scream of terror, frightened by the dogs' jumping around as well as the unfamiliar barking sounds and dog smells. Ring is about to run away when Stewart calls to him and puts his arms around the dog's neck in a reassuring gesture.

"Here, boy, good dog. This is a new addition to our family. You'll get used to her; she's just a little hungry now. Good dog, good dog." He pats the shaggy, thick white and black coat as he soothes the dog.

They enter the house with Ring bumping against Stewart's leg and pushing his nose through the door opening, eager to be included in this new happening in the family.

"I wish Wallace was here. He needs to meet his new sister."

"He'll be here soon, Florence. Let's get the baby settled if we can."

They have borrowed a lovely English wicker pram from Stewart's brother Stanley, and his wife Edith, and it is ready to receive the baby. The house is cold and while Stewart gets the fire going in the kitchen stove, Florence fusses over her baby, trying to get her "settled in."

Ring stations himself sitting beside the pram in a guard-like stance, every now and then raising his paw and letting it rest on a wheel.

In the afternoon Lavenia steers her distinctive, dark blue, Essex Terraplane car into the laneway at Soperton. Wallace bounds out of the car and into the house to see his mother and father.

"Would you like this baby for your sister, Wallace?" Florence asks, holding the crying baby for him to see.

"Yes," he says, grinning. Wallace stands close to his sister, takes a brief look at her, and then quizzically up at his mother, before dashing off to play with Ring.

"Oh, Flo let me see the baby. May I hold her?" Lavenia asks as she reaches out her arms to take the child.

Florence and her sister settle in for an afternoon of chatting and sharing. Florence is so grateful for her sister, who is her best friend.

By the end of the next week, Florence is weary because there is little relief from the crying and fussing of the restless, unhappy child. On Saturday afternoon she hears the sound of a car coming down the laneway. A visitor is the last thing she needs or wants in her life right now. She opens the door in response to the gentle knock and is greeted by her cousin, Helen Johns, who is a teacher in Ottawa. Helen explains that she has come to visit her Aunt Sarah Johns in Brockville for the week-end and thought she'd drop by and see Florence and Stewart. Helen has not heard that Florence was expecting a baby or about any addition to the Singleton family and was very surprised to hear crying when she came into the kitchen.

"Oh, Florence, what have you there?"

Margaret Rose greets Helen with her customary howl and her distraught new mother picks her up from the pram and tries to sooth her, "There, there, Shh, shh."

Helen, ever truthful and accustomed to stating her thoughts, says, "Well, Florence, where did you find this baby? She isn't a pretty child, is she? And she's so tiny."[5]

Tears begin to well in Florence's eyes. She is exhausted and worried about her baby. She doesn't understand Helen's humour and so she finds the comment hurtful. Helen quickly realizes her error and apologizes for her ill chosen words.

"There are no ill feelings, Helen. I'm glad you came. Would you like to hold the baby, Helen, while I make some tea?"

"A few minutes would be alright, Flo. I'm never sure what to do with a baby."

Florence puts her little girl in Helen's arms and the baby gazes at this new person with interest and stops fussing.

When the tea is ready, Florence takes Margaret, from Helen's arms. The baby has finally fallen asleep. Her mother gives a gentle sigh as she gently lowers her daughter onto the feather mattress in the pram and tucks a blanket around her.

With some prompting from Helen, Florence pours out the story to Helen about how she found the baby. For the remainder of the afternoon, through both tears and laughter, Helen and Florence enjoy their tea and each other's company.

6. Don't you know who I am?

Betty flew down the long winding staircase of her Rosedale home in Toronto, her long wavy blonde hair flying behind her, and her manicured hand resting lightly on the railing as she descended, her feet barely touching the highly polished steps. She had heard voices and was on her way to the foyer to check it out. Her father James was a prominent lawyer in Toronto and often had very interesting visitors of the male persuasion. The stairs fanned out into a beautiful foyer of soft pink and grey Italian marble. A magnificent crystal chandelier dominated the space and hung directly over a huge inlaid marble circle, outlined in gold. The prisms of the chandelier sparkled as they caught the light from the windows on either side of the double door creating wonderful dancing rainbows on the walls and ceiling.

Betty came to an abrupt stop when she saw the young man talking to her father. He was tall, straight and so handsome. He wore a long, tan coloured overcoat with the belt undone so the coat hung loosely from his broad shoulders over a well tailored beige suit. He held fine brown leather gloves and a brown felt hat sporting a wide band with a jaunty blue feather. His slightly untidy hair caught her eye as it fell casually over his forehead on the left side. As she glided closer to him she noticed his intense blue eyes, tanned skin and chiseled features. Altogether it made him the most handsome man she had ever seen.

Their eyes met.

Betty caught her breath; she thought the young man did the same.

Her father introduced them.

"Betty, this is Clyde Elder from the *Toronto Star*. I am the prosecutor in a murder case, and Clyde is covering the story for his newspaper.

Clyde extended his hand which Betty took and held on to as long as she could. Clyde smiled and acknowledged the exchange between them with a penetrating look.

James was anxious to get on with the interview and a nod signaled to Fred, their butler and chauffeur, to attend to Clyde's outer clothing. An ornate Victorian Hall Tree was placed temporarily in the foyer while the closet was being painted and Fred helped Clyde out of his coat and hung it on one of the hooks, then carefully placed Clyde's hat and gloves on the bench below. James then ushered Clyde into the library off the foyer leaving Betty standing alone, her eyes following Clyde until he disappeared behind the door. She wondered if she would ever see Clyde again.

James carefully reviewed the notes from the trial with Clyde and added some detail that had been missed in his newspaper story printed in *The Toronto Star* that day and which James felt was important for the public to read. With the interview completed, James, ushered Clyde quickly out without summoning the butler. Clyde stepped into the crisp, late fall evening air and breathed in the homey smell of the smoke from the logs which Fred had lit in the fireplace. He pushed his hands deep into his pockets and smiled as he walked away, a new spring in his step.

No one noticed the finely stitched, brown leather gloves left behind in the foyer.

The next day Betty skipped school. Her Branksome Hall School uniform for the day, a white midi and navy blue skirt was hanging in her closet when her mother, Bea, looked in her room later in the day. Bea was surprised that Betty would miss school today as it was Branksome Hall's annual Physical Training Demonstration at Varsity Arena and Betty was looking forward to the event. She excelled in sports of all kinds and had developed broad muscular shoulders and arms and powerful legs from swimming, rowing and tennis. In the summer when the family went toPresqu'ile she practically lived outside.

Each fall Betty came home to Toronto, strong, tanned and full of energy. Betty could have been an Honour student but she just didn't seem to have the interest in studying that her father had hoped she would. Perhaps if there had been programs and incentives for the recognition of athletic ability Betty would have been more interested in school. Theatre and music were also strong interests and to some degree were supported at Branksome Hall but only as extra-curricular activities, not full time study.

As Bea stood in Betty's bedroom, she reflected on her daughter's interests and free spirited personality. It was always fun to be with Betty and her spontaneous nature left you guessing as to what might happen next. Bea wondered what her daughter was up to today. It was Friday, so she wouldn't be at the Theatre. The Bicknells owned the Lowe Theatre and Betty often attended the Saturday afternoon matinee with her friends. As she and her friends joked and talked together, Betty walked boldly into the theatre, ignored the ticket stand and with the usher in hot pursuit strode down the aisle with her friends following behind her and they settled into front seats. When confronted by the usher and asked to buy tickets or leave,

Betty stood up, placed her hands firmly on her hips with her palms facing back and announced to all within hearing range,

"Don't you know who I am?"

Bea smiled to herself as she recalled her daughter's mischievous actions. James enjoyed his daughter's pranks and without her knowledge arranged to pay for the tickets Betty and her friends used, keeping up the matinee drama.

Betty was up early, dressed in a casual pink wool sweater and dark blue pleated skirt, had a quick breakfast with the maid in the kitchen, then quietly left the house by the side door and walked briskly along the expansive, winding, tree-lined streets from Cluny Drive to Park Road. Betty loved exploring the charming, quiet streets of Rosedale and let her thoughts wander to what she might do today as she admired the architecture of the mansions and the beautiful gardens. She waved to a policeman, perched jauntily on a gleaming black horse and he returned her greeting. Betty walked down Mount Pleasant Road, with a feeling of happiness and freedom, enjoying the bright morning sunshine. She crossed Bloor Street and came to Jarvis St. where her friend Annie German lived and hoped she could convince Annie to take the day off school and go to a coffee house or restaurant, then maybe to the island in the afternoon. As she passed her grandfather Watson's house at 182 Jarvis street Betty briefly considered going in there. She could go to the Watson Candy Factory with her grandfather for the day, rock in the huge black leather swivel chair behind the oak desk in the office and help him with the candy orders. The smells flashed through her mind and gave her pleasure; the wood of the paneled office mixed with the sweetness of the candies being stirred, rolled and molded. She enjoyed being with her grandfather and working around the factory, joking with the men and women who worked there and, of course, sampling the candy.

She decided, she would go to Annie's house and if Annie wouldn't skip school she would surprise her grandparents with a visit.

Betty arrived at the German residence. Annie German's uncle, Bruce O'Brien was a partner in Betty's father's law practice, Bicknell & O'Brien. Betty's friends were scrutinized very carefully but her friendship with Annie was given wholehearted approval. As Annie attended Jarvis Collegiate and Betty was enrolled in Branksome Hall the friends didn't see each other every day. Today Betty had news for Annie and she hoped Annie would spend the day with her. She wanted to tell Annie about the handsome young man who had come to visit her father.

Betty sprinted up the steps of the sprawling red brick mansion on Jarvis Street, the street known as the Champs-Elysee of Canada, and pressed the illuminated button which activated the clear sound of the Westminister chimes. The butler opened the heavy oak door and invited her in.

Annie appeared from the kitchen and the two friends greeted one another in a warm, laughing embrace. Annie picked up her school bag and they left the house through the front door and ran down the wide wooden steps. The two friends chatted as they walked along Jarvis Street towards Jarvis Collegiate. Betty put her arm around her friend's shoulders as she said,

"Annie, let's not go to school. Why don't we go to the Paris Café instead? We can stay there for the morning and then go to the Island for the afternoon. Come on, it will be fun."

Annie stopped walking and looked at Betty in dismay.

"Betty, we can't just skip school. Our parents will find out and my father will be cross. And I don't want to miss baseball practice."

Jarvis Collegiate recognized Annie's skill as a pitcher and her team photo hung in the entrance with their most recent trophy.

"Come on, Annie, let's go to the Café."

Betty linked her arm with Annie's and their pace slowed as they approached the school. Betty felt Annie relax a little and took the opportunity to steer Annie into a quick right turn on Wellesley St. towards Yonge. The Café was just a few blocks away. They giggled as they strode together in perfect step.

Betty led the way into the café and a booth at the back where they could talk discreetly. The waitress wore a white frilly apron over her French blue dress and took their order promptly.

"I'll have a scone with jam and coffee please," said Betty.

Annie ordered the same thing and they settled in, leaning forward towards each other as Betty described in meticulous detail the interesting young man who came to Cluny Drive. Annie listened as Betty tried to explain the excitement she felt in their handshake. She hoped she would see him again soon.

The sun was high in the sky when Betty and Annie left the café and headed for the streetcar to take them downtown and to the Island Ferry for the afternoon. Betty had a fleeting thought that she would call their chauffeur, Fred, to take them to the wharf and *The Bluebell*, but dismissed the idea quite quickly when she realized Fred would probably drive her home.

This was an ideal kind of day for Betty with independence, adventure, the great outdoors and time with her friend Annie.

She would worry about explaining her absence from Branksome Hall tomorrow.

7. The Paris Café

The Paris Café was becoming Betty's after school haven. As she waited for Clyde, her thoughts went back to the day they first met when Clyde came to interview her father. Later, Fred found Clyde's gloves, purposefully left behind which provided him with another opportunity to come to their home and meet her, or so he hoped. When Clyde came for his gloves, Betty was there in the foyer, just about to leave for a rendezvous with Annie. Clyde grinned broadly when he saw her. The memory of the moment sent shivers of delight through her body.

"Hello again," he had said as he extended his hands and clasped hers warmly.

"Hello Clyde," she stammered, uncharacteristically at a loss for words. Betty was rooted in time and place, her hands held tightly between his.

"Your gloves, sir," the thrall was broken by Fred's voice.

Betty and Clyde had been seeing each other secretly ever since that day, even though James had forbidden his daughter to see the young reporter for two reasons: Clyde was not in their social circle and, James reasoned, Betty needed to concentrate on her Christmas examinations at Branksome Hall. Once, Betty skipped school and she and Clyde had a blissful morning sipping sodas in an ice cream parlour, chatting, laughing, talking, and then in the afternoon, roller skating at the Strathconna Rollerdome. Betty arrived home at her usual time, but the head mistress had called and reported her absence. Betty was very creative in her explanation to her father as to why she was absent, saying she had helped out in the library and missed the attendance sheet in her home room, which had actually happened on another day, and he accepted it without question.

It made Betty feel proud to be with Clyde, even if they were alone. Since she wasn't supposed to see Clyde, she had to be careful about inviting someone along who might spill the beans to her father. She trusted Annie who joined them for coffee occasionally and once Clyde invited Betty to a restaurant with a few of his reporter friends. Betty thought it was a strange place, dark and smoky. It was not at all like the restaurants that her family would go to for dinner. Clyde was handsome, older, almost twenty-three and much more mature than the young men she met in her parent's social circle. She had interesting conversations with Clyde on a wide variety of topics. His work at the newspaper was fascinating to her because of the people he met and the news items he heard, before anyone else. He was in the news room when it came over the wire that Bonnie and Clyde had been killed. They both liked to dance and the emerging new big band sound with Glenn Millar playing the trombone set their feet tapping. There was frightening talk of war and they discussed what that might mean for them if Clyde had to enlist.

Clyde talked of how he enjoyed hunting and fishing. Betty loved animals and the idea of hunting seemed so cruel. She didn't approve of that sport. Betty was a superb swimmer, loved boating and just being beside or on the water. She had her own fishing pole in her row boat and was skilled in its use. Perhaps they could go on a fishing trip together next spring. If Betty was able to win her father's approval of Clyde, her father might let them have the motor launch. Betty was planning ahead.

Clyde wore Betty on his arm, placing his right hand on hers as she snuggled closely to him, clutching his left arm at his elbow. Sometimes he leaned down and kissed her forehead as they walked along the street. Very definitely a couple, Clyde and Betty were two young people from very different backgrounds, which mattered to her parents but not to them. They adored each other.

Betty's sudden new interest in school had nothing to do with the content of her lessons. She bragged about her new boyfriend in the locker room and the dining hall. Her friends listened, some with envy while others cautioned her. She loved being the centre of attention. Her grades improved with her new attention to study and her regular attendance at school. James was overjoyed because of Betty's new successes, and to celebrate, arranged for the family to have dinner at the Royal York Hotel, and after, to attend an organ concert on the new Casavant in their concert hall. They all loved music and the new hotel was magnificent.

In the spring, when Branksome Hall started casting for a new play, *Alyson's House*, by Susan Glaspell, Betty surprised and delighted the drama teacher by arriving at the rehearsal hall to read for a part and she was successful. Rehearsals could be a good excuse for her lateness in arriving home after school, but her big plan was to invite Clyde to attend the production. Her father and mother would be there applauding her and it would be the perfect time for Clyde to appear and show his interest in the play and in Betty.

Clyde planned to approach Betty's father and ask his permission to invite Betty to attend a concert at Massey Hall. Betty played the piano and happily practiced her piano lessons. The performer was to be Miss Harriet Cohen, from New York City, a renowned pianist known as the greatest interpreter of Bach of her time. It all seemed perfect.

The applause was loud and long as the cast stood, arm in arm onstage, glowing with their success. Betty's heart raced not only with the excitement of her achievement, but the anticipation of Clyde's meeting, and talk with, her father. Her parents, younger brother James and her grandmother Watson, were all there to admire and support her. Betty felt tightness in her heart as she remembered her grandfather Watson and wished he were there too. At that moment she longed for her grandfather's warm embrace and approving smile. His wonderful Irish brogue was sharp in her memory. She missed her grandfather since his recent death.

The principal, Miss Edith Macgregor Read, appeared on the stage and received her appreciative applause, and then the director of the play took her place. Finally one last bow with all of the cast and the curtain slid to the floor. Betty ran to the dressing room to remove her theatrical make-up, change into her well tailored, linen evening suit and then appear at the reception.

The girls talked and giggled as they rushed down the corridor toward the hall to accept the congratulations of parents and friends and to enjoy the buffet which had been set out. Betty came to an abrupt halt and Llila bumped into her.

"Betty, watch where you're going."

"I'm sorry, Lila."

He was so handsome, standing there talking to her parents. Betty thought her looked like one of the Greek Gods she read about in history. How could her father not accept Clyde as a suitor?

Betty danced up and embraced her father as she threw a glance and broad smile in Clyde's direction.

"Oh Daddy, did you like the play?'

"Yes, Princess, it was wonderful and I was very impressed with how you played your role of Elsa. I'm proud of you, Betty."

Betty hugged her mother and grandmother, received their enthusiastic congratulations on her performance, and then glided over beside Clyde.

"Daddy, I see you've met Clyde again. Remember, he came to the house when he was writing an article for *The Star*?"

"Yes, Betty, I remember. We've been talking about the play."

Clyde turned his attention to Betty.

"You are an accomplished actress, Betty, and your portrayal of Elsa was brilliant. I enjoyed your performance very much. Betty, I was telling your father about my work at *The Star*. Just today, I was given an assignment to go to the Royal York Hotel to interview Miss Cohen, a renowned pianist, who is giving a concert in the city next week."

"I've heard of her Clyde. Did you know that Betty, too, is a very accomplished pianist?"

"Oh, is she? I'd love to hear her play sometime."

"Betty often plays for her mother's afternoon teas. The women enjoy a little entertainment. She has been invited to play at teas in other homes too."

"The women never stop talking when I'm playing, so I wonder if they listen at all."

"Betty, Mrs. Gooch and Mrs. Hanna have often said what a beautiful touch you have and how much they look forward to hearing you."

"Do they, Mama?"

"Clyde, what other interesting assignments have you been given?"

"As you know, Mr. Bicknell, there is an increase in crime in the city, mainly gambling and betting parlors, and I've had a few assignments covering the police raids on illegal gambling and betting parlors. I'm sure you heard of the scandal in Trenton, Ontario, where the police chief was in on the worst corruption scandal in their history. It ripped the cover off the underworld ties to law enforcement, and there's a court case going on now."

"Yes, Clyde, I do know of that case. With the end of prohibition and a limited number of alcohol permits, combined with the increase of speakeasies in the city there's bound to be graft."

"Your work sounds fascinating, Clyde. Is it dangerous?" asked Mrs. Bicknell.

"Bea, perhaps we should go in now. Shall we approach the buffet?" James said as he put his arm across his daughter's shoulders and skillfully moved her away from Clyde. Clyde said something that made young James laugh, and then chatted easily with Betty's mother Beatrice and Mrs. Watson as they all walked toward the beautifully prepared tables to enjoy tea, sandwiches, sweets and other delicacies.

Clyde felt reassured after his conversation with Betty's father and would soon ask Mr. Bicknell if he could escort his daughter to the Concert Hall to hear Miss Cohen perform.

Betty's reverie was broken when Clyde came through the curtained door of the Café and strode over to the booth that had become theirs. He bent down and kissed Betty on the cheek as he lowered his tall frame to the seat, and then took Betty's hands in his. They sat silently grinning at each other.

James had agreed to the evening concert and asked their chauffeur Fred, to escort them to Massey Hall and wait for them. Clyde sat proudly in the back seat of the limousine close to Betty. Fred looked in the rear view mirror and grinned as he saw their fingers intertwined.

"I'm so looking forward to the concert, Clyde."

"Me too, Betty. Most of all, I'm enjoying being with you, and with your parent's permission. I hope they have changed their minds about me, Betty."

"I think they have Clyde, as they let you take me to the concert. I'm excited and a little nervous. This is the first time we've attended a concert together and there's sure to be some of daddy and mother's friends there. I can hardly wait to introduce you."

Clyde was looking forward to meeting friends of the Bicknells too, as he thought if he could impress them it would increase his chances of being with Betty. Clyde didn't articulate it, but apart from being mad about Betty, he would enjoy the prestige and attention that came with his association with the Bicknell family.

Betty reached into her evening bag and pulled out a fine leather case and opened it, revealing a fuchsia coloured velvet lining and exquisite mother of pearl opera glasses.

"Daddy loaned me grandfather's opera glasses, inscribed with his name, *James Bicknell.* See, aren't they grand? Grandfather bought them in Paris. We can take turns looking through them, Clyde."

The limousine rolled to a stop in front of Massey Hall. Fred stepped out and opened the door for Betty and the love of her life. Clyde's chest swelled as they alighted at the concert hall.

They were ushered to their front row seats. The muted buzz of the voices of the audience faded as the renowned pianist appeared on the stage, bowed slightly then took her place on the piano bench. The audience was hushed. Slowly, Miss Cohen's beautifully shaped fingers were curved over the keys, poised, in anticipation of the intricate notes of Bach flowing through her body and out to the audience. Her fingers danced over the keyboard communicating the crisp, clear tones. Tears trickled down Betty's cheeks as she absorbed the runs and intricacies of the music. Miss Harriet Cohen played Bach brilliantly. The beguiling music and being there with Clyde filled Betty with happiness.

The applause was warm, long and appreciative as Miss Cohen acknowledged her audience with appropriate bows, her hand resting gently on the piano. In another time and place Betty might have displayed her skill of whistling through her teeth just to stir things up, but tonight she was quiet, wanting the strains of Bach to linger as long as possible.

Betty clasped Clyde's arm as they walked into the reception room to meet the pianist after the concert. Miss Cohen greeted them and Betty knew she was in the presence of someone very special. Her father's partner, Bruce O'Brien came to be introduced to Clyde, whom Betty thought, made a favorable impression. They lingered, talking, discussing the music and greeting others they knew. Betty wanted the evening to last forever.

When they left the hall and stepped into the warm air of the spring night, Fred was standing beside the car waiting for them and ready to escort Betty safely home. For Betty, this was part of her everyday experience but for Clyde, it was a whole new way of living and he reveled in the attention and respect it brought.

"Clyde, will you come in and have a night cap with Daddy and Mamma?"

"I'd love to sweetie. We can tell your parents about the concert and the people you introduced to me."

"I do hope daddy has changed his mind about our going out together."

The limousine drew up to the decorative door of 37 Cluny Drive. Fred helped Betty out of the car, giving her a quick wink as she stepped from the running board to the ground. As Betty and Clyde approached the front door it opened and James was silhouetted in the evening light. He had been watching for their arrival. Clyde and Betty stepped into the foyer and before Betty could remove her evening wraps, James extended his hand to Clyde and shook it.

"Thank you for escorting Betty to the concert Clyde. It was not possible for me to attend tonight so it was good of you to go with her. I knew my daughter would thoroughly enjoy Miss Cohen's playing. Fred, would you kindly drive Clyde to his home?"

Clyde was taken aback, but he managed to stammer,

"You are welcome Mr. Bicknell, it was my pleasure. Thank you for offering to have Fred drive me home."

Clyde briefly took Betty's hands in his, hesitated for a moment not sure of his next move, and then bid Mr. Bicknell good night. It was clear that for now at least, he was viewed only as a casual companion for Betty. He would have to find a way to change that.

Fred opened the door for Clyde and motioned for him to go through. The door closed behind them.

"Daddy, I invited Clyde to come in for a night cap. I wanted Clyde to stay for awhile and tell you and Mama about the concert. Miss Cohen was brilliant, Daddy."

"Betty, it was very generous of Clyde to escort you to the concert, but he is not a suitor I want to encourage. Your mother and I do not approve of him."

"But daddy, he is so intelligent, and fun to be with, and we have wonderful conversations. If you just got to know him daddy, you would like him too. Bruce O'Brien met him tonight and I think he liked Clyde."

"Betty, my dear girl, it is not just about liking him. He and his family are not in our social circle. It would be courting unhappiness and embarrassing situations for you to get involved with this young man. Although his parents may be wonderful people, they would not fit into our lifestyle and circle of friends. Our experiences are so different. And, Betty, if you continued to see him and it led to marriage, he could never provide for you in the way you are accustomed."

Betty could not hide her disappointment and was close to tears.

"Oh, Daddy, how do you know that? Where is Mama? I want to talk to her."

"She's in the library reading, Angel, but she feels the same way I do."

Betty walked through the foyer to the library door which was ajar. Her mother was sitting in the overstuffed chair nursing a sherry, her open book overturned on her lap.

"Hi Mama, the concert was so beautiful. You would have loved it too." Betty threw her arms around her mother's neck and hugged her warmly, then wedged herself into the chair beside her mother.

"And Mama, Clyde loved the concert too and I had such fun with him. I wanted him to stay and say hello to you, but Daddy sent him away. Daddy says I can't see him, but I want to Mama."

Tears escaped down Betty's cheeks and fell on her collar.

Beatrice wrapped her arms around her daughter and held her close as she gently pressed her lips to Betty's head.

"Oh Betty, dear, I'm so sorry. I don't like to see you so sad, but it's for your own good. Your father makes these decisions and I agree with him to a certain extent. Clyde's family would feel out of place with our friends, playing bridge, attending or hosting afternoon teas or even attending your coming out party. It wouldn't work Betty, even though you are fond of him."

"Mama, those things are not important to me and I don't want a stupid coming out party, with all those wimpy boys ogling at me. Clyde is different. He knows about things going on in the world. We talk about important things."

"Betty, it sounds to me as though you've spent more than one evening with this young man", Beatrice confronted her.

"Sometimes we meet after school and have a soda, mama, but please don't tell daddy, not yet anyway."

"Betty, I wouldn't feel right about keeping things from your father. I'll talk to him and we'll see what he says. Maybe he'll relent a little."

"Thanks, Mama."

Betty took out her embroidered handkerchief and wiped her tears.

"Would you like some cocoa before bed dear? Ask Marie to take it upstairs to you. It's quite late and you should go to bed. Good night, sweetheart. I'll see you in the morning."

Bea kissed her daughter and gave her an adoring smile.

Betty raised herself out of the warmth and security of cuddling with her mother and walked toward the long winding staircase towards the haven of her own bedroom, without asking for the cocoa. She performed her ablutions in her private powder room, then quickly undressed and slid between the crisp sheets, then pulled the satin comforter up under her chin and closed her eyes.

As she fell asleep, the haunting strains of Bach were still intensely alive, helping her to cope with her sudden feelings of anxiety and loneliness.

The spring term was almost over and Betty's average was high enough that she would continue in Middle School at Branksome Hall, working toward the Diploma program the following year.

In July the family would move to their cottage at Presqu'ile and Betty and Clyde were already feeling lonesome as their meetings would be limited to the times that the Bicknells came back to Toronto for brief visits, teas or functions involving Betty's father.

In between meetings it would be a long, lonely summer for each of them, but the anticipation of being together would be joyous.

Betty's dream of boating, fishing and fun at the cottage with Clyde would have to wait.

As they sat across from each other in their little Paris Café, they talked about how they could be together in the summer. With Betty in Presqu'ile and Clyde in Toronto working for *The Star*, it would be difficult, but, they were sure they could find a way to see each other. Neither was lacking in imagination or determination.

8. The Locker Room

"Betty, what's wrong with you today? You missed two baskets. You're the best shooting guard on our basketball team." Lila admonished.

"I don't know Lila; I guess I was just a little preoccupied. My boyfriend is away on an assignment with the newspaper," she offered somewhat wistfully, not exactly true but close. Gordon Sinclair, his boss, busy himself with his pending trip to South East Asia, was keeping Clyde so busy covering the city news that she and Clyde didn't see each other as often as they would have liked.

"Tell us more about your boyfriend Betty. Is he the one who came to our play in the spring? I haven't seen him at any more events." Lila moved closer to Betty who was standing in front of her locker, about to change into her street clothes.

"That's because I don't trust you girls. I want to keep him all to myself. I have a picture in my purse. Want to see?" She pulled a photograph and waved it in front of her friends. "Here, good looking isn't he?"

"Oh, he's so handsome; look at him Lila. What paper does he work for Betty?" asked Georgina.

"He's a reporter for the *Toronto Star* and meets all kinds of fascinating people, even gangsters. Once he was in on a police raid of a gambling house. There was even shooting," she bragged. "Clyde also goes to the court house to write about murderers who are on trial. That's how I met him. Clyde came to our house to interview Daddy about a case he was trying. The man Daddy was prosecuting was on trial for killing a man."

"Well, you'd better be careful Betty," Lila offered, "He looks older than you and mother says we have to beware of older men."

The girls all laughed.

"We're having a special dinner tonight, so I have to change and go home," Betty said, glancing once more at the photograph before she put the picture back in her purse.

She turned to face her locker with her back to the other girls and fumbled with her gym uniform. First she pulled off the short skirt with attached bloomers, and then quickly put on her school Huntington Stewart tartan skirt and fastened the buttons on the side. It was tight on her muscular body and she hoped the girls didn't notice. She had rolled up the sleeves of her gym blouse which made it more difficult to remove, but she peeled it off and swiftly slid her midi over her head, taking more time than usual to adjust the collar and tie. Lastly, she pulled up her long, black stockings which had been rolled down to her ankles, to the horror of the basketball coach.

She thrust her arms into her coat and pulled open the door.

"Goodbye, Lila, goodbye, girls," she called over her shoulder as she strode out of the locker room. She addressed Lila separately as it was astute to be on the good side of Lila. Lila would be the one to lead the teasing and scorn and make life very unpleasant if the girls found out about her condition.

"See you tomorrow," chorused the team.

She walked out of Branksome Hall into the Elm St. courtyard and toward Mt. Pleasant Road in the cool fall air. Her usual quick steps faltered and a salty tear or two escaped and ran down her cheeks. Betty had stopped skipping school as she wanted to be as inconspicuous as possible. During class, sometimes she was so deep in thought about her plan that she missed the questions being asked and blushed when she was called upon for an answer. She recalled the incident in class today and it was embarrassing.

"What was the question, Miss?"

"Miss Bicknell, please stop daydreaming and pay attention."

"Yes, Miss."

She was about to pass by a little coffee shop and felt a pull to go in. There was time to stop here and try and think, before their maid, Marie, would have dinner on the table. Not many people were in the shop and she glanced quickly around to see if she knew anyone. She was grateful that they were all strangers so she wouldn't be expected to carry on a conversation. Betty would have given anything if Annie had been there though, and she might come in yet as Annie often came to this coffee shop with her friends from Jarvis Collegiate. Betty reached into her pocket for her Players package and tapped a cigarette out of the carton. Methodically she put the cigarette between her lips, lit a match and cupped her hands as she pulled the smoke into her lungs, held it and then exhaled. She repeated the action several times, taking comfort from the familiarity of the aroma and routine.

"May I take your order?"

"Yes, please, I'd like a jelly roll and coffee."

Her mind wandered back to the day in August that Clyde borrowed a friend's car and came to Presqu'ile while her parents were in the city attending a cocktail party. Only Marie was there with her and Marie had her own things to do. They took the boat out on the lake and enjoyed a day of boating and later, sunbathing on the beach. It was wonderful to be together. That evening on the beach she and Clyde talked about how they might get her father's approval for their marriage. Did Clyde suggest it or did they come up with the idea together? She didn't remember exactly, but because they loved each other so much, she thought it was a splendid one. She knew she would be giving up her privileged lifestyle but it would be worth it to be with Clyde.

"Your coffee and jelly roll, Miss."

"Thank you."

Betty squashed her cigarette in the ashtray on the table, grinding out the last spark and then lit another. After a long, slow drag, she placed it on the ash tray and sipped her coffee, holding the cup close to her mouth after each sip, her elbows on the table as she continued her reflection.

When would she tell her parents? It had to be soon as the signs couldn't be hidden much longer and her mother had already found her vomiting in her bathroom early one morning.

"It must be the flu, Mama," she had said, "Some of the girls at school are sick."

School was worrisome, having to be on guard to mask her secret. She feared it would be unwise to continue with basketball, badminton and swimming, which she loved. Should she see a doctor? Whom could she consult? Her own doctor would tell her parents, but they had to be informed soon anyway.

She first missed her "time' in September and now, it was she who had morning sickness, whose clothes didn't fit and whose life was changing dramatically each day. Clyde was going along with his normal life and nothing had changed for him. For the first time she felt anger toward him.

"Damn it Clyde, what are you giving up?" she said out loud. Heads turned, and then the low buzz of conversation continued.

Betty obliterated another cigarette.

It's time to tell Annie, she decided. She would call her tonight and suggest that they meet here at this coffee shop after school tomorrow.

The waitress brought her check, and placed it on the table. Betty finished eating her cake, put her cigarette package into her purse and walked to the cash register to pay her bill.

As she left the coffee shop, her usual light, quick step was replaced by a slow, methodical walk down Mount Pleasant Road toward her home.

Betty put her hand inside of her coat and felt her growing waistline. So far, that's all it was, weight gain and discomfort. She didn't feel any connection to the life developing inside of her and even though she tried to imagine the baby but no picture emerged. She pulled her well tailored coat more tightly around her to keep out the biting cold.

It was dusk when she approached the short walkway leading up to the door of her home. Warm lights glowed through glass side panels of the door. Betty rang the bell and with a flourish their butler and chauffeur, Fred opened the door to welcome her home. As she stepped into the foyer she felt the warmth and homey aroma of the recently lit fire in the fireplace.

"Hi, Princess," her father called, approaching her with a scotch in his hand. He kissed her affectionately on the cheek. "Come into the Library and tell us what mischief you got into today."

"Not much Daddy. We had a basketball game and I missed some baskets. The girls on the team were upset with me."

"Don't let it bother you my dear, tomorrow you'll do better. What would you like to drink, some Coca Cola?"

"Okay, Daddy."

Fred took her coat and books and she followed her father into the library where the colourful, orange and blue flames danced behind the decorative fireplace screen. Her mother Bea was sitting in the overstuffed chintz covered chair sipping a gin martini.

"Hello Dear, were you cold walking home? You could have called Fred to pick you up."

"I was fine Mama. Is Jimmy home yet?"

"I think he had a meeting of his rowing club after school, dear. He'll be here soon, I'm sure."

Her father brought her Coca Cola over ice in a tall crystal glass and they settled into conversation about their various activities and the tea Bea was hosting next week.

"James, dear, did you put the announcement in *The Star*? Mrs. Jameson has a secretary to do that sort of thing and I wonder if I should have one on staff, or at least available. Betty will be having her debutante tea in a year or two and I'll require help with invitations, choosing musicians, ordering flowers and so on. I thought we might have a small orchestra playing in the sunroom upstairs."

"I put the announcement in the paper Bea and soon you'll have a parade of ladies at your door. Ha, Ha." James' loud laugh filled the room.

"We'll think about a secretary to help with the arrangements and invitations for Betty's party when the time comes. You would like an orchestra Bea? Well, I guess my mother had musicians playing in the sun room, but there's lots of time to think about that. I'll bet Betty would prefer a pianist. What do you say Princess?"

Betty squirmed in her chair, nursing her Coca Cola. There would not be a Coming Out Party but she decided not to challenge the discussion this time. A small wedding was her dream and soon.

"I love the piano Daddy," she said with less enthusiasm than usual.

Betty was relieved when her brother Jimmy came into the Library from his day at Upper Canada College. He was handsome, full of spirit and fun and Betty loved to be with him. She allowed a brief reverie of their fun together. In their younger days they had written and put on plays together for their parents and their guests, with themes of Pirates, Animals and Folk Lore. A favourite of the family and also Betty and Jimmy, was their version of *The Cat Who Went to Heaven*, not one of their own plays, but one written by Elizabeth Jane Coatsworth. They had also played outrageous tricks on their parents and the household staff. The siblings' swimming prowess and their love of playing tricks on people, combined to create what could have been a tragedy. One summer when they were in Presqu'ile, Betty and Jimmy invited their nurse out on the water in the row boat. When they were far from shore, Betty and James both dove into the water and swam back to the cottage, leaving the poor woman, who was quite inept in boating skills, to row to safety. Betty shivered when she thought about what could have happened.

"Jimmy, Daddy said you had a meeting of the Rowing Club. What does the Rowing Club do in the fall and winter?"

"Well today, one of the boys gave a paper on the world famous sculler, Edward Hanlan and it was extremely interesting."

Then, Jimmy stood up and with a sweeping bow announced,

"And, meet the new President of the Club."

James jumped to his feet and clapped his son on the back as he loudly congratulated him. James, himself an athlete of some note, was always delighted to hear about the accomplishments of his children in athletics.

Marie appeared at the door and announced that dinner was ready to be served. The remains of the drinks were left behind as the family proceeded to the dining room.

James pulled out Bea's chair and caressed her shoulder as she sat down. Jimmy seated his sister, and then the men took their places, James at the head of the table and Jimmy across from Betty. With pride, Marie served her wonderful dinner. First scalloped oysters followed by lettuce with tart dressing, roast beef, Yorkshire pudding, scalloped parsnips, five-minute cabbage, pickled beets and jellied fruit. Fred was there to attend to the champagne glasses. The table was cleared and the desserts were offered; the chocolate drop cookies and Washington pie were almost too much.

The family retired to the library for their final course. Marie brought in the sterling silver tray with the coffee pot, cream and sugar and a small dish of after-dinner mints. The rich coffee was poured into exquisitely hand-painted Limoges demitasse. Each white translucent cup was painted with a gold band along the rim and in old English script the initial "B" was inscribed on the curved side of the cup.

They enjoyed their coffee and each other's company, although Betty wasn't fully present. How could she be, with so many thoughts whirling through in her mind? They chatted about the superb dinner, Marie's culinary skill and how fortunate they were to have her. Bea revealed that Mrs. Gooch said her maid could scarcely boil water and she was looking for a new employee. James told them about a crime boss from a speakeasy he was prosecuting.

Marie gathered up the tray and cups, and the family dispersed to their customary places in their home. James retired to the library for a cigar and Scotch, and Bea went to the kitchen to thank Marie again for the wonderful dinner and to chat about the daily shopping for tomorrow. Later she joined her husband in the library. Jimmy ran up the stairs to his room to study and write a paper, and Betty phoned Annie. They arranged to meet after school but not at the coffee shop. Annie suggested they meet at the Glen Road Bridge, which was the usual meeting place for their Rosedale friends, and they could go somewhere from there. Betty hung up the phone and climbed the stairs, to the shelter of her bedsitting room. No homework for her tonight. She reclined in her chaise-lounge; her swollen feet stretched out straight, and then let her head fall back on a soft down pillow. Betty pulled the colourful knitted coverlet that her grandmother Watson had given her over her tired body. She rested until the house was quiet and everyone had retired, and then quietly slipped down to the Library to find the volume of the encyclopedia that described the details of pregnancy.

The next day, after school, Betty walked toward the Glen Road Bridge to meet her dearest friend, Annie; she arrived first and waited impatiently for Annie. Betty knew a little more about what it meant to be pregnant after reading the chapter in the *Encyclopedia Britannica* the night before. There were several pages of diagrams and overlays on cellophane which were very informative but also frightening. She made some notes and stuffed them into her pocket.

Annie was late and explained that she was held up by her basketball practice. Annie had won trophies for basketball and baseball and her practice always came first. The two girls embraced when they met and then walked with their arms entwined, along the path.

"Betty, what's this about?" Annie dove right in.

"Annie, what do you know about having a baby?"

Annie stopped, rooted to the path. Then Betty heard her gasp and "Oh, my God!"

Annie wheeled around abruptly, brought her face close to Betty's and placed her hands firmly on Betty's shoulders.

"Ouch", Betty exclaimed.

Annie's voice rose as she said, "Betty, you didn't go and get yourself in the family way, did you? You're not pregnant are you? Betty, you didn't do that. Tell me you didn't do that."

"I'm pregnant Annie. Clyde and I are going to have a baby. We talked about it and planned it this way. It wasn't an accident, Annie. We think daddy and mama will let us get married if I'm pregnant."

"Hell, Betty. What's wrong with you? Are you crazy Betty? Clyde should know better. Damn it Betty, this is terrible. What are your parents going to say?" The deep concern she had for her friend came through in Annie's voice.

"I don't know Annie. I hope they say we can get married. I found some information last night in the encyclopedia but I don't know very much about being in the family way. I thought you might, Annie, because your cousin just had a baby."

"Betty, you knew how to get yourself pregnant, so you should know something about what's going to happen. A baby, Betty, I still can't believe it. What about school?"

"Annie, let go of me please. You're hurting me. Don't be angry, I just want to talk to you. I wanted to tell you."

"Sorry, Betty, I'm just very upset with you. I'm scared for you too Betty. Aren't you scared?" Annie lowered her arms and Betty readjusted her coat and rubbed the places where Annie had grasped her arm. Annie continued without waiting for Betty to answer.

"Okay, I'll tell you what you are going to do. You call Clyde and take him to your father, that's what you are going to do. Betty, you've sometimes thought I was a sissy, and I'm pretty naïve about the boys, and you've said so, but I don't think I would get myself into a mess like this."

The friends went a few steps further but Annie's stinging words hurt Betty deeply and brought tears to her eyes.

"Come on Betty, you'll always be my friend, no matter what. I don't know much about babies and I probably won't be any help to you at all, but let's go to the coffee shop. What do you mean 'you planned it'? I don't believe this. You can tell me what this outrageous plan is about."

Annie put her arm around Betty and felt her expanding waistline for the first time, then pulled her closer as they walked together. In the coffee shop they took out their cigarettes and found comfort in inhaling deeply as they sipped their coffee and talked. Betty agreed to arrange that she and Clyde would meet her father soon. Annie made Betty promise to call Clyde as soon as got home, then squeezed Betty's hand as they parted.

Betty hastened her step so that she would be home first and be able to make an uninterrupted call to Clyde. The house was quiet when Betty entered the foyer. She went directly to the library and dialed *The Star*, then asked for Clyde Elder. Luckily he was at his desk and answered in his usual cheery, nonchalant way.

"Hall.oo, this is Clyde Elder speaking."

"Hello Clyde, this is Bet. . ."

"Well, Sweet Pea, how are you?" He interrupted when he heard Betty on the line. "What a nice surprise to hear your voice and not one of my cranky readers who didn't like the news."

"Clyde, be serious. Clyde honey, we have to talk to Daddy and Mama and soon. I don't want to talk about the details on the phone. Can we meet tomorrow and talk a about it?"

"Okay, Betty. Let's get together tomorrow and talk about what we will say to your father."

"I'll meet you at the Paris Cafe after school, Clyde. I can hardly wait to see you."

"Me too. Goodbye Honey. See you tomorrow."

"Bye, Clyde," she said, almost in a whisper.

Betty put the phone on the cradle slowly, reflecting rather sadly on her brief conversation with Clyde, partly because it was so short and Clyde wasn't as serious about the whole situation as she had expected him to be. Confronting her father would be difficult because not only had she disappointed him, but she had also disobeyed. What her father's reaction would be to the disclosure that she was pregnant, she wasn't sure. One thing she knew, she could accept his reaction, whatever it was if it meant that she could be with Clyde. Betty was almost sure he would agree because with his social position, he wouldn't want the embarrassment of having an unwed, pregnant daughter.

The Paris Café was the scene of a dramatic and joyous reunion with Betty and Clyde. It had been a week, which seemed like an eternity since they had been able to meet. They talked nose to nose, with Clyde holding Betty's hands in his as they planned every word of their discussion with James. Clyde was articulate and clever with language and that gave Betty hope for her father's approval. It was Wednesday and Betty would arrange their meeting for Friday night after school. She would tell her father and mother in the morning, just as she was leaving, that there was something she wanted to talk to them about.

They left the Café arm in arm and Clyde walked with Betty to the corner of Rosedale Rd. and Cluny Ave. He would have taken her to the door but Betty insisted that they not "rock the boat", to use one of Bea's expressions. He put his arm around her waist and squeezed her then planted a kiss on her head before he strode away.

"See you Friday, Bonnie."

"Okay Clyde. Don't shoot anyone," she laughed.

They often joked about how they were a little like Bonnie and Clyde whom they read about in the newspapers. They were somewhat like outlaws, especially Betty, breaking away from the expectations of her position in society and throwing caution to the wind. The consequences of their actions carried punishment of a sort too, for each of them. But they thought only of the fun and outrageous similarities between themselves and Bonnie and Clyde.

Friday it rained. It rained cats and dogs as Marie would say. Fred drove Betty to school and arranged to pick her up at 4:15 PM. Betty had planned to meet Clyde and they would walk home together, so with this change in plan, she asked Fred to drive directly to *The Star*. Fred parked the car at the front door and went inside and asked that Clyde come out to meet Miss Bicknell, a request that was promptly honoured.

Her father and mother knew only that their daughter had something to tell them.

Fred turned the car up Mt. Pleasant Road. Betty and Clyde sat nervously in the back seat holding on to each other's hands.

"Just think Clyde, we'll soon be married," Betty whispered as she cuddled closer to Clyde, but shaking nonetheless. "I just know Daddy will give in when we tell him I'm pregnant. But I'm a little scared Clyde."

"I am too. I hope your father will listen to us, Betty," Clyde sounded apprehensive.

Fred turned his head abruptly and looked at Betty in the back seat when he overheard the conversation and as he did, jerked the car to the right, and was heading for a telephone pole.

"Fred, what are you doing?" Betty called out, already in a state of fright.

"Sorry, Miss," Fred said as he jerked the car back onto the street again.

Thundering rain was coming down in sheets, hitting the puddles and bouncing up towards the sky again only to hammer down in another torrent. It was impossible for the windshield wipers to keep the windshield clear. Fred pulled the limousine as close to the entrance as possible, then stepped out to open the door for the couple in the back seat. Betty and Clyde stepped down from the car about to face her parents. Fred tried to hold an umbrella over their heads as they sprinted to the door. He opened the door for them, and once inside helped them remove their wet coats then left them alone in the foyer while he took away the dripping garments to hang them to dry.

"Okay Clyde, let's find Daddy and Mama. I expect they are in the library."

Fred appeared from the direction of the closet after hanging up their outer garments and intervened for Betty.

"This way Miss, Sir, I believe your parents are in the library." He led the way and opened the door to show them in.

James and Bea were enjoying their afternoon cocktails in front of the fire and James bounced to his feet when he saw his daughter. When Clyde came into view behind her, James was completely taken aback. He went to his daughter and kissed her lightly on the cheek, and then as briefly as was possible he acknowledged Clyde's presence.

"Betty, you didn't say Clyde would be with you this afternoon. What's this all about? Hello Clyde." James' social graces overcame his surprise and he offered a brief handshake and acknowledged Clyde grudgingly.

Betty didn't answer but greeted her mother with a hug, then went back to stand beside Clyde. It all felt so awkward, as though she was a stranger in her own home.

"Sit here Betty," her father motioned for her to sit in a chair beside her mother, and then pointed to a chair on the other side of the sofa for Clyde.

Clyde took Betty's hand and led her to the sofa where they sat side by side.

"Mr. Bicknell, we want to talk to you. We have something important to tell you."

"Daddy and Mama, Clyde and I want to get married," Betty quickly added.

"Married," her father exploded. "What kind of crazy idea is that?"

"Oh, Betty, no," her mother objected, "You are much too young."

"How do you expect to support my daughter, young man?" James sneered.

"I have a good job as a reporter with *The Star* and I've worked there for four years."

"You can't provide for my daughter on a reporter's salary. What are you thinking?"

Bea had something else to say. "Betty, why do you want to get married now, dear? Why not wait a few years? You have to finish school. You are too young. Oh, Betty dear, think this through a little more. You have your whole life ahead of you, time for travel and lots of other things before you settle down."

"Young man," said her father quite sternly, "You seem very personable and you are certainly well spoken. I know my daughter likes you but you can't possibly understand her social responsibilities or provide for her so that she can maintain her social standing. It's a lifestyle Clyde, something one is born into."

"Daddy, I don't care about the lifestyle. I love Clyde and he loves me. Mama, Daddy, I've got to tell you." Betty paused, afraid to say any more. Then very softly she said, "I'm pregnant."

James' face quickly showed the level of his anger as his flesh turned bright red.

"Good God, child," James bellowed, "What were you thinking?" James jumped to his feet and confronted Clyde. "Young man, I hold you totally responsible for this. I can have you thrown in jail, and I might."

"No, Daddy, no."

Authorial Interjection

There is a drama technique in which the actors suddenly freeze in their positions and hold that pose for a length of time. I want to freeze this scene, take a time out, so to speak. It is very difficult for me to write about this, to go deep into the emotions, the tragedy and heartbreak in my parents' life. I feel deep pain when I allow myself to go there and be wholly present, to acknowledge that I was there with them, their unborn child. I'm overwhelmed by this now and I need to step away from the library and take a break.

So we'll leave the library for a while and go to my kitchen. I'll grind some French Roast beans and make a bodum of coffee. It smells so good.

I remind myself to take a deep breath and release it slowly. Breathe in another long, slow breath and let it go, Ahh, hmm. The coffee is just right.

This would be so much easier to write if it was fiction and I could control my characters to some degree. I want to go back and rewrite the scene and create a courtship that flows into a happy marriage. But this is real. Betty and Clyde are real people. They are my parents. Out of love and a desire to be married, they hatched this crazy, outlandish plan that for some reason my mother at least, thought would win the approval of her father for her marriage to Clyde. The stories I have heard about my mother don't paint her as a naïve person, but this act of getting pregnant to attain the approval of her father for her marriage, does indicate naivety. I think my mother was a rebel; someone who rejected the codes and conventions of social norms. At the very least she was a strong person with a mind of her own.

As I wrote about it Clyde didn't seem to be quite so positive that the plan would work, but neither did he speak up and say he didn't think it was a good idea. I have some questions for Clyde and Betty, some things that are troubling me.

So, Clyde, I have to wonder what your motivation was to come up with this plan in order to marry Betty. Was it your love for her, which I don't doubt in the least, or was there an additional motivation? Were you eyeing the lifestyle and social position you would have if you were part of the Bicknell family? Was this solely your idea Clyde? Did you convince Betty that this was a good plan?

Aunt Muriel told me that the pregnancy was planned.

As I write this scene, I want to meet you in the Paris Café, Betty, sit across the table from you and maybe reach out and touch your hands. Even though I never smoked, I might have a cigarette with you if that would bring us closer and help me to convince you to wait a few years. Wait a minute, I can't rewrite the scene in which you hatched this plan, can I? That scene was probably written in Presqu'Ile many years ago. To rewrite the scene would be to write me out of your life, and I am very much a part of your history. Throughout my life I loved and longed for you, Mother, and I feel cheated that the last time I saw you I was seven months old.

When I began searching for you, I placed an ad in the Toronto Globe each year on my birthday which read:

"I was born on May 10, 1935. I am grateful that Mother showed the courage necessary to give me life. It has always been my desire to meet my mother. The present minister of her girlhood church knows where to contact me."

Little did I know when I placed that ad what courage you lived to bring me into the world, only to lose me.

It is heart-wrenching Betty, that you were the one who carried the entire burden of the pregnancy; morning sickness, hiding the truth, coping with school and friends, leaving school, the shame that went with out-of-wedlock pregnancy, the disapproval of your parents, especially the anger of your beloved father who adored you. I think of what it meant then, to give up your life of privilege and be burdened with the scorn, whispers and rejection of society throughout your life.

Clyde, where were you when Betty fled to the Victor Home for Girls for safety, to avoid having the abortion her father arranged? You abandoned her, perhaps not by choice, but she was left alone in an institution to fend for herself. Could that have been the time for you to run away together?

When I finally found my wonderful family and met my great-aunt Muriel, the first thing she said to me was: "Your mother was a bad girl." Aunt Muriel was very fond of you, Betty but carried that image of you, one of being a bad girl. "Bad" does not describe the mother I have come to know through writing this path to truth.

I want to share something with you. As I have been writing this story with the scenes of my parents and grandparents, it as though I am there. I hear their voices and their conversations; I feel their emotions. I see the room, the streets and the people clearly. I can smell the distinctive aromas of the leather chairs and the wood paneling in the library. It's as though I was there, a muffled witness to this story.

My mother lived her life carrying a stigma. I have lived my life carrying a stigma.

My coffee is finished, and I am ready to return to the library and continue the story. I need a tissue. There.

Bea gasped and the colour drained from her face; she looked as though she might faint. Her words were almost incoherent as she uttered her mournful thought. "Betty, Betty, my little girl. Betty, you're not pregnant, you can't be pregnant. You are just a child yourself. Oh, Betty. What will we ever do? What will our friends think?"

James continued in great distress, trying to control his temper. "Whose idea was this? This is the most ridiculous thing I've ever heard."

"Mr. Bicknell, Betty and I love each other very much. We could have eloped and we talked about that but we respect you and Mrs. Bicknell and we wanted your blessing. We talked about it together. We planned it together."

"You planned it. What do you mean you planned it?"

"Daddy, we thought if I was pregnant you and Mama would agree to our marriage."

Red-faced, James bellowed, "Respect us? You dare to say you respect us? You call what you've done respecting us? You want our blessing? Well, you sure as hell are not getting my blessing. Betty, I thought I forbade you to see Clyde. And, Clyde, I thought I had made it very clear to you that you were to stay away from my daughter. Betty, you've never disobeyed me before. This makes me so damned angry."

Bea had recovered from her near fainting spell and was now concerned about the frightening level of her husband's anger." James, dear, watch your temper and let's talk this through. I'm very upset with you too, Betty, and I want what's best for you, but marriage doesn't seem like a good idea to me."

"Mama, think about our baby? I'm going to have our baby and Clyde and I want to be together. We have to get married." Betty was in tears, totally unprepared for her parents' reaction to learning that she was pregnant. She had never seen her father so angry.

"Betty, have you seen a doctor?"

"No, Daddy."

"Well, Clyde, that is a further indication that you are not a suitable husband for Betty. Any man worth his salt would have taken her to a doctor by now."

"James, we must call Dr. Brown tomorrow. Allan can examine Betty and advise us as to her health and the baby's. Oh Betty, Betty, this is such an unfortunate thing."

"Mama, I told you, Clyde and I planned this baby. It wasn't an accident or unfortunate. Mama, we want to get married. Please try to see it our way."

James paced the floor, his hand cupped over his mouth, thoughts racing through his mind. What could he do? Betty had brought disgrace to the family and he couldn't let his friends and clients know about her condition. Neither could he allow her to marry this young reporter with a questionable future, just to save face.

Clyde and Betty sat clinging to each other. Betty was wide-eyed with fright and disbelief that their plan had been totally rejected. Feelings of anxiety were new to Clyde but they engulfed him. He truly thought that Mr. Bicknell would at least consider the idea of their marriage. Now, he was terrified that he might even go to jail, given Mr. Bicknell's anger and the influence he had in his position in the judicial system in Toronto.

James Bicknell stopped pacing and stood in front of Clyde and Betty.

"Young man, I want you to leave now," he said abruptly.

"No, Daddy, please."

"We'll talk about this later Betty. For now, he must leave and quickly before I do something that I might regret."

Clyde was on his feet swiftly, pulling Betty up too. Betty threw her arms around her beloved and wouldn't let go. Clyde started moving toward the door with Betty still clinging to him, sobbing. It appeared that the lovers tried to leave together, in spite of James' threats, but James grasped his daughter's arms and pulled her away from Clyde. Clyde stood frozen. His usual confidence and charm washed away by tears, fright and uncertainty. Bea put her arms around her hysterical daughter and held her as she sobbed and sobbed.

"Go," James demanded and pointed towards the door, "Go, before I call the police. I won't expect to see you here, ever again. Do you understand?"

"Mama, please don't let Daddy do this. Please, Mama."

Clyde started toward the door but made a quick turn and put his arms around Betty and her mother. He kissed Betty quickly and then grabbed his damp overcoat from Fred, before hastening blindly out into the rain.

The next day, Betty stood in front of her locker for the last time. The girls were snickering behind her. She didn't mind leaving school, as a matter of fact, she had no other choice. The issue was that her classmates were humiliating her and that was terrible for Betty. She expected them to feel happy for her and to support her but she didn't feel much happiness, just a heavy feeling of abandonment. They didn't understand that this was no sleazy accident, her baby was planned. It wasn't like Emma. When she left school, her parents said she had gone to a Spa in Switzerland for a holiday, but the girls suspected there was another reason.

Only Lila came to speak to her.

"I'm sorry Betty. I hope everything turns out alright for you. I hope the Head Mistress lets you come back to school Betty, but whatever happens come back and see us after. I'll be glad to see you."

Lila gave Betty a hug, something she had never done before. Betty returned the hug and gazed at Lila for a moment. She felt new respect and appreciation for her friend.

One by one the girls left with their book bags, some turned toward her, smiled and acknowledged Betty, but most left with no more than a fleeting glance.

Betty was all alone in the locker room, the hub of the school. Usually a place where secrets were shared, stories told, apologies made, teachers assessed, dates with boys discussed, and homework passed around, and yes, even where one could be shunned; now the only sound was the occasional creak of the lockers.

Her father would be waiting for her, standing quietly beside the closed office door of the school. The hearty laugh within him silenced, his voice suppressed for now. She imagined the Head Mistress who would have no intention of coming out to say "goodbye", seated very straight on the chair, her hands folded properly on her tidy desk.

Betty looked around the locker room for the last time, remembering the cheers of the staff and students when she gained points for her school the day her skill in shooting baskets helped the basketball team win a trophy.

Slowly, Betty stood, took in a deep breath and with a long slow sigh she breathed out her days at Branksome Hall. The locker room door closed quietly behind her.

9. The Man in the Shadows

The office was bathed in the muted light coming through the dust covered windows. The flickering bulbs in the hanging fixtures created an eerie feeling as the diffused light descended on the empty desks and silent typewriters. Clyde cleared his desk, and then carefully placed the brass paperweight on top of the notes to be dealt with tomorrow. Today he couldn't concentrate, his thoughts were scattered so his work had been criticized. He didn't know how long he had been sitting at his desk in deep thought after his colleagues had left.

"Are you coming to the Beverage Room, Clyde?" they had called as they donned their hats and long coats.

"No, not tonight, thanks. I've got something I have to do."

But, what could he do? James Bicknell had the whole legal system behind him and Clyde knew he was no match for that powerhouse. Clyde ached to be with Betty and he had to find a way for them to be together. He felt a tug of sadness in his gut. Was it only yesterday that they had confronted Betty's parents? It seemed like an eternity.

Clyde approached the rack in the corner of the office and reached for his hat and overcoat. He thrust his arms through the sleeves as he walked towards the door. He left the building at 80 King Street, buttoning his coat and fastening his belt as he walked. It was cold so he yanked up his collar and pulled it tightly around his neck.

The darkness engulfed him as he walked along King Street towards Yonge. The white globes on the sparsely placed lampposts offered dusky light and cast shadows on the sidewalk. The store windows were darkened and the recessed doorways could hide shadowy figures that were up to no good. Sometimes Clyde felt nervous walking along this lonely strip at night. A streetcar rumbled by traveling in the opposite direction, with only a few passengers. The people sat with their heads leaning against the unwashed windows straining to see out into the night. If a streetcar comes along in my direction, I'll jump on, Clyde decided, but at night they were few and far between.

Betty was never far from Clyde's thoughts and heart. It was as though a film was playing in his head as he imagined her now, running down the staircase, laughing. He pictured her throwing herself into his arms and felt her body against his stirring emotions of love and longing. He could see her in a beautiful gown, turning heads at the ballet. What was she doing now? Did he dare go to the Bicknell home and confront her father again? He stopped to light a cigarette and cupped his hands around the match to shield it from the wind, then took a long drag and filled his lungs, savored the feeling, then breathed the smoke out of his nostrils. As he looked up again he thought he saw a figure step into a doorway further up the street. Perhaps it was just something blowing in the wind, but he'd be alert as he continued along the deserted street. The neon sign for TUCKERS, a small lunch bar, beckoned from a block away and Clyde hastened his step to go in there. As he passed by the doorway where he thought he saw someone step off the street into the darkened recess, he glanced in but didn't see anyone. Now he felt as though he was being followed, so he hastened his step, but he didn't look back.

The lights were on in the lunch bar and Clyde quickly pulled open the door and went in. He welcomed the aroma of coffee and the warmth of the little place. He swung his leg over the seat of one of the red padded stools at the counter and slowly began to relax, unbuttoning his coat and loosening the belt.

"What will it be, sir?" asked the waitress, handing him a menu.

"Let's see," he said, glancing over the top of the menu at the waitress, "I'll have a coffee, please and something else." Clyde smiled and kept his eyes on the waitress as he rummaged in his coat pocket for his cigarettes.

The waitress put a cup on the counter in front of Clyde, then turned away to get the coffee pot. She's about Betty's size but older, maybe my age, he mused.

As the waitress picked up the coffee pot she paused to glance at him in the mirror over the back counter.

"He's very handsome and a charmer. Well dressed too," she thought. Sometimes I'm nervous alone, but he's okay. I'll enjoy his company.

Slowly she poured the steaming coffee into the cup creating bubbles on the top.

"They're good luck, sir. You can make a wish."

Clyde closed his eyes as he blew gently on the hot coffee and wished with all his might that at that moment Betty was beside him. He poured in some cream from the counter jug and added sugar and stirred, tracing the pattern of the cream mixing with the coffee.

"Anything else, sir?"

"You know," he said, "I think I'll have a sandwich."

"What kind of sandwich sir?"

"What kinds do you have?" he asked, still holding the menu and staring at the list.

"Egg salad, chicken salad, grilled cheese or ham and cheese," she recited. "You can have your sandwich plain, toasted or grilled. We still have some chicken noodle soup too."

"I think I'll have the ham and cheese. Not many people out tonight," Clyde said, as he put the menu in the black metal rack beside the salt and pepper shakers.

"Too cold, I guess, and the wind is terrible," the waitress said as she wiped the counter.

"It's hardly worth keeping the lunch room open on a night like this."

"I'm not the owner sir, so I do what I'm told."

"I'm glad you were open for me." Clyde beamed his charm.

"Would you like your sandwich toasted or grilled, sir?"

"I'd like it grilled, please. On a night like this a hot sandwich will be comforting."

"I'll make your sandwich, sir."

Clyde dragged on his cigarette as he watched the waitress. She had a good figure and her uniform was clean and tidy. Her hair was neatly tucked under a little uniform cap. Clyde followed her every move as she slapped butter on two slices of white bread then turned them over with the butter side down and put mustard on one slice, then plopped on the ham and cheese. She put the other slice of bread on top, butter side up and pushed it down with her hands.

The grill was at the other end of the counter and the sandwich was soon sizzling with greasy smoke rising and permeating the air. She flipped the sandwich over with a flourish and when she was satisfied that it had browned enough she scooped it up with the lifter and placed it on a plain white plate. The young woman reached into an enormous jar of dill pickles and pulled one out with her fingers. The brine dripped from the pickle onto the hot sandwich as she topped her creation with the green garnish and plunged a toothpick through it to hold it all in place. She smiled at Clyde as she slid the plate across the counter in front of him.

"Thank you, Miss. That smells delicious."

"The name's Bertie, sir. What's yours?"

"I'm Clyde. It's nice to know you, Bertie."

Clyde sipped his coffee and nibbled on his sandwich while he and the waitress made small talk about how long Bertie had worked at TUCKER'S, Clyde's work at *The Star*, movies that were playing at the Lowe Theatre, skating at the Rollerderm and the never ending stories about Bonnie & Clyde.

"More coffee, Clyde?"

"Yes, thanks, Bertie, one more then I have to go."

Clyde was grateful for this oasis in the night before continuing the lonely journey home and facing his and Betty's dilemma. He finished his sandwich and reluctantly slid off the stool.

"Goodnight, Bertie. I enjoyed the coffee and sandwich and the conversation. It was nice to talk to you and have your company."

"Goodnight, Clyde. See you again sometime."

Once again he fastened his coat against the cold and stepped into the night. He walked briskly along King toward the streetcar stop that would take him home. Suddenly a man came out of nowhere and grasped him by his lapels.

Claude was terrified and was certain he was going to be robbed, or worse. This was a rough part of town and he had covered muggings and robberies for *The Star* which had taken place here.

"Are you Mr. Clyde Elder, the reporter?" The burly man asked in a raspy voice.

"Why do you want to know?"

Clyde heard his own trembling voice. How did the thug know his name? What does he want with me? Was this one of the gangsters he had written about? Recently, a man was murdered and his body thrown into the Don River and Clyde was there when the police dragged the body out. This man could be the murderer. All kinds of escapes flooded his mind. Would he plead for his life or just run for it. He was a fast runner and this guy looked too overstuffed to run very fast. In the dim light, Clyde could see that the man was well dressed so probably not a robber but worse, perhaps a member of the mob, someone in organized crime. He felt the man loosen his grip and instinctively Clyde made a dash for the approaching streetcar. The large man grabbed him before he got away and tightened his vice-like hold on Clyde.

"I've been sent with an important message and an envelope from a Mr. James Bicknell, through my boss."

"James Bicknell."Clyde's voice rose.

The burly man delivered his message without benefit of the King's English, punctuating his words by shaking Clyde so hard that Clyde bit his tongue and lip and his hat fell to the ground. Blood dripped out of the corner of his mouth.

"Yes, Mr. James Bicknell. I think you know his daughter. Maybe a bit too well eh? Ha, Ha," he laughed in an unnerving way.

"Let go of me." Clyde tried to wrench himself out of the man's grasp.

The man loosened his grip and Clyde wiped his mouth on the back of his hand, and then brushed his sleeves as though brushing away the incident, but it was not over.

"Listen you, my boss said to tell you to get out of town and don't come back. And, don't ever try to contact Mr. Bicknell's daughter. He said to give you this envelope. Oh, yes, I'm to tell you that you don't have a job anymore. My boss had you fired."

The stuffed envelope was thrust into Clyde's hands as Clyde stammered, "What do you mean I don't have a job?"

"My boss said you're not to go back to the newspaper office. If you do, there'll be consequences."

Clyde was perspiring. He was usually a strong, persuasive man, but he felt his knees turn to jelly as he tried to comprehend what he was hearing. His life was crumbling around him and he feared for his safety.

"Consequences, what consequences?" he stammered.

"You don't want to know, sir. Just get out of town. We know where you live on Wineva Ave., Mr. Elder, and we've got a guy watching you and so you better follow the orders. Then, there's the matter of Mr. Bicknell's daughter and whether or not you would go to jail 'cause you got her in the family way."

That was the last straw and Clyde lunged at the man who easily defended himself and knocked Clyde to the sidewalk. The intimidating figure stood over Clyde, hitting his fist into his hand as he spit out,

"GET OUT OF TOWN. Do you hear? That's an order."

The figure strode quickly away leaving Clyde sprawled on the sidewalk.

Clyde slowly raised himself from the ground and brushed off his clothing. He was shaking violently and had difficulty lighting the cigarette which he hoped would help him calm down. Walking a few steps to the building the terrified man leaned against the wall for support and remained there until his cigarette was burned down to the last ash. Still shaking, Clyde lit another then walked slowly along King St. wondering what to do or where to go. He remembered the envelope and assumed it contained money, but how much? He pushed the thick package deep into his pocket and began to walk quickly towards Yonge Street where he would get a streetcar to Queen and home to the safety of his apartment in the Beaches. The long ride home would give him time to think things through.

The wheels squealed on the track as the streetcar came to a stop at the corner of Queen St. and Wineva Ave. Clyde stepped down and looked furtively around to make sure he hadn't been followed, before half running down the rough concrete sidewalk to his apartment. He fumbled with his key in the lock and then pushed open his door to the safety of his home. Closing the door, he secured both bolts, and then ran upstairs to his second floor flat where he sank into an arm chair and sobbed.

When the sobs ceased and his body stopped shaking, he unbuttoned his coat and let it fall to the floor. Clyde walked to his small kitchen where he opened the cupboard door underneath the sink and with his hands still trembling he reached for his bottle of Scotch and poured himself a double. The well stocked Bicknell bar in James' library flashed into his mind and contrasted with his one bottle under the sink. His despair deepened.

He sipped and nursed the drink as he tried to come to grips with his situation. He retrieved the envelope from the pocket of his coat on the floor. As he opened it hundreds of dollars fell into his hands, all fastened in packets with rubber bands. Clyde had seen these packets before during a police raid on a gambling house and he realized the full implications of being paid off. What choice did he have against the mob? He didn't think James Bicknell's instructions were just as they had been delivered. He was sure whomever James had asked to contact him had overstepped their authority and instructions by sending a thug. Betty's father would never have wanted to be associated with the mob or be involved with them in any way. Clyde saw James as a reasonable man and wondered how things might have changed if he and Betty had done things differently; perhaps if they had taken more time for James to accept Clyde as a suitor and then waited a year or even two before suggesting marriage. At least for now, Clyde knew he had to leave town, but he would be back.

"God, I'm in a mess," he said out loud to the shadows in the corner and the mice scampering in the wall.

His eyes were swollen from crying and his body ached. His tongue was damned sore too. Clyde poured another double.

His thoughts continued in search of a swift solution.

Where can I go?

Who could he call in his family? His mother lived in Toronto and would take him in but that was dangerous because he was told to leave town and he knew he had to comply or suffer some unknown consequence. Better not to think about what that might be. Clyde was very aware of the cold-blooded actions and ruthlessness of mobsters. He had covered stories about men with broken arms and legs as a result of disobeying mob orders. Even the members of the gang were not safe if they talked too much. *The Star* carried a story a few months ago about George Ziegler, a mastermind in the Barker gang in Illinois, who was shot and killed by a fellow gang member for bragging about his accomplishments.

Who could he turn to? Where could he go? With the money in the envelope he could go away to Montreal or Halifax for awhile. Montreal would be a better choice to be inconspicuous than a smaller city like Halifax.

His siblings went through his mind, one by one, Gordon, Wilf, Jack. He and brother Wilf were close in age. When they were growing up Wilf had helped him out of a few scrapes in his school years. They had hunted and fished together and he remembered how he had enjoyed those trips. They always got along well together. Since Wilf married and moved to Sudbury to work in the mines he didn't see him often. He liked Ruby, his brother's wife, too. He could pay them rent and that would help them out. They just might go for the idea of a boarder for a few months, at least.

"I bet Wilf would help me get a job in the mines. I'd do anything right now," he told himself.

He picked up the phone and dialed his brother in Sudbury.

10. The Man in the Shadows
Postscript

That night Clyde slept in his chair.

Thoughts and dreams of Betty flowed in and out of his mind as he sank deeper into an alcohol induced sleep. Clyde was unaware that the woman he loved, secretly left home tonight, feeling scared, alone and that he had abandoned her. He didn't know that her father had demanded that she have an abortion and that Betty had sought refuge at the Victor Home for Girls to save their child, nor that right now Betty was spending her first night in that Home, longing for him.

11. Three Forty One Jarvis Street

Betty put one foot on the rung of the stool and boosted herself onto her perch in the kitchen of three forty one Jarvis Street. She grimaced when she looked at the worn, unattractive, grey battleship linoleum with the wavy areas where the glue had not adhered to the floorboards. She planted her elbows firmly on the table and stared at her challenge; a bucket of potatoes to be peeled with a dull paring knife, a menacing job which taunted her.

"Here, peel them", Matron said, as she plunked down the potatoes. She didn't say, "Please," nor, "Would you be willing?" Just, "Peel them."

The Bicknell's maid, Marie prepared all of their meals so Betty had never peeled potatoes in her life, or done any other domestic task, except occasionally she arranged the pillows on her bed and tidied her dresser.

Reluctantly she picked up a dirty, brown potato and held it in her left hand. She gazed at the unfamiliar object. Covered in dark brown dust and punctured with black indented spots, to her it looked grotesque. A green shoot grew out of one of the caverns and she flipped it back and forth with her finger. Surely this isn't what Marie uses to make her scrumptious mashed potatoes. She brought the knife to the surface of the knobby foreign object and awkwardly began the daunting task. The knife found its way into the flesh of the potato as she slowly cut a thick swath. Most of the potato was cut away. The white flesh became a gritty brown as the dirt on the skin mingled with the moisture inside and the two smeared together. She heaved a heavy sigh and continued her task. The only sound was the cutting and scraping of the knife, the quiet swish in the dirty water and the plunk as she dropped it into the cooking pot.

Betty felt her baby move, a tiny kick inside of her. She put down the knife and placed both wet, soiled hands on her abdomen and felt the faint nudges. A wave of happiness and love came over her; her child would be born, in spite of her father. But she carried resentment and indignation that she, Betty Bicknell, daughter of James Bicknell, one of Toronto's most prominent lawyers, had to be in this horrible place of confinement.

"Don't they know who I am?" she thought.

When she fled here to avoid an abortion she expected to be treated as a young woman of her social standing. Her Aunt Muriel had attended Ontario Ladies' College in Whitby and had recounted wonderful stories about living there. She expected the Victor Home for Girls to be something like the Ladies' College or perhaps like a hotel.

Nothing had turned out the way she expected the night she and Clyde told her father and mother that she was pregnant and they asked for approval of their marriage. She had anticipated raised voices and some objection, but not this outcome. Her father had gone into a rage and threatened Clyde that he was going to call the police and put him in jail. Clyde tried to pull Betty out of the house with him but her father intervened and told Betty to go to her room. She had obeyed her father, had gone to her room after Clyde left, and sat frozen, not able to fully comprehend what had happened. Betty recalled her mother weeping quietly into her hands and repeating over and over,

"Oh dear, oh dear. What are we to do? My darling Betty."

Betty heard the front door close and then footsteps into the library. For what seemed an eternity she heard the muffled voices of her parents in animated discussion. Then a gentle tap on her bedroom door and their butler, Fred's voice,

"Betty, your parents would like to see you in the library. May I escort you downstairs Miss?"

"I will come down alone Fred, thanks."

Her father was an imposing sight, tall and stately in front of her still in his formal court attire.

James had made a decision which he deemed was the best one for the family. It was all very simple, really. James knew of a doctor who would perform an abortion even though Betty didn't fulfill the requirements of the law for the procedure. [6]

He would make the appointment tomorrow, the abortion carried out as soon as possible and the matter would be put behind them.

Betty fled from the library sobbing and ran up the winding staircase to her room. Her mother followed her and took her daughter in her arms trying to comfort her as they sobbed out their anguish together. Bea sympathized with her daughter but thought she was powerless to override her husband's decision.

Her baby kicked hard against her abdomen and brought her back to the task of peeling the dirty potatoes. She hated it here but she and her baby were safe. She wanted this baby that she and Clyde had planned together. Betty longed to be with Clyde, but he had disappeared and she couldn't find him. When she called *The Star* the desk clerk said Clyde no longer worked there.

Oh, Clyde, where are you? Why don't you call? What has happened to you? My heart is breaking Clyde. I miss you so much.

Betty decided she would do what was best for herself and for her baby. She didn't give a whit about what people would think, but it was necessary to act quickly, before her father took her baby away. The Victor Home for Girls was on Jarvis Street close to the homes of Annie and her grandmother Watson. She often passed by the house and knew it was a residence for wayward girls, girls in the family way who weren't married. Although she didn't know the implications of living there, she would go the Victor Home for Girls.

The day after James had taken her to Branksome Hall for her belongings, and to explain to the principal why she would be leaving, she had packed a small bag with a few cosmetics and some essential clothing as well as her favorite sweater and skirt, a book of short stories, the November issues of *Movie Classics* with Jean Harlow and *Screenland* featuring Greta Garbo. She put her hand to her throat to feel the cross that she always wore, a gift from her mother. Lovingly she picked up a small blue, velvet box hidden in her dresser drawer, brought it to her lips, and then tucked it into a secret pocket in her bag. She kissed her mother and her brother and said she was going to Annie's for dinner. She and Annie often pored over movie magazines, so she took *Screenland* out of the bag and tucked it under her arm. She then asked Fred to drive her to Annie's house. Fred was instructed to come back for Betty after dinner. Betty had written a brief note for her parents telling them only that she was in a safe place and would get in touch with them soon. She was not going to have an abortion; she was going to give birth to her baby. When the car was out of sight, Betty put her arms around Annie and the two friends stood in the foyer in a long embrace. Betty said goodbye to Annie and let herself out. Slowly and hesitantly Betty began the long three block journey alone, to the Victor Home for Girls and an unknown future.

Later that night, when Fred arrived at the German residence for Betty, Annie gave him the note to take to her parents.

She reached into the bucket and pulled out the last soil encrusted potato and began to peel away the skin as though she was peeling away the life of privilege she had known until now.

Matron strode into the room, forbidding in her long black dress, buttoned up to her chin. She inspected the mangled potatoes and scolded Betty for the poorly done job. Betty attempted to explain that she had never before peeled potatoes, but she was hushed into silence and told to clean up the mess. Betty's thoughts were her closest companion these days and as she reflected on the events leading up to the present moment, she hadn't noticed the dirty water splashed on the table and the floor, the bits of peeling and soil on her clothing and worst of all her broken, dirty fingernails. Two wet, dirty handprints added to the ugly design of her worn, ill-fitting, hand-me-down skirt. The kitchen mirror flashed an image and even her hair was a mess from running her fingers through it to push back the strands that fell on her face. Betty's sense of humor overcame her urge to cry and she burst out laughing. If her family or friends saw her they wouldn't believe how she looked. It was as though she was in a costume for one of the many theatrical productions she had been in at Branksome Hall.

This drama was very real.

Matron scowled at Betty as she left the room and it was a relief to see her go.

Deaconess Sweetman came into the kitchen to inspect Betty's clean-up and patted her back gently.

"That's fine dear; you've done a good job. Perhaps you'd like to go and wash up now." Deaconess Sweetman was middle-aged and was kind and pleasant, not like Matron who was old, at least fifty, and cranky.

The days at the Victor Home for Girls were all very similar with daily routines which had to be carried out: scrubbing floors, dusting, washing dishes, doing laundry, and setting tables, preparing meals, walks in the garden, quiet times and on Sunday, going to church. A mid-week lecture by ministers of various faiths was dreaded by all of the residents at the Victor Home. The men-of-the -cloth lectured Betty and the other girls on sin and how to mend their evil ways.

On one particular week, the United Church minister, whose turn it was to visit the Home, came dressed in his customary black suit and stiff white clerical collar. Matron ushered the girls into the dining room where they assembled around the table. The minister stood at the head of the table to deliver his message to the girls. Betty, who loved fun, jokes and laughter, listened, and wondered about how his sermon could be helpful in any way, as he preached stone-faced, just as though he was in the grandest pulpit in the city. The Rev. rambled on and on about the sin of high fashion and makeup, the immorality of fast living and going into beverage rooms which undoubtedly led to their present condition. Betty thought about how that applied to her family. She had never been in a beverage room and she doubted anyone in her family had either. Her parents went to the Cricket Club or the cocktail lounge in the Royal York Hotel or the King Edward, when they wanted to socialize away from home. Certainly, her mother and grandmother loved fashion, and she did too, but how was that sinful?

The minister's reasoning is outrageous, Betty thought. He not only makes me angry, he also frightens me with his tirade and hitting his fist on the table.

The girls cowered in their chairs and Edna covered her face with her hands, as he ranted on, to make certain that each girl understood that she was an embarrassment to her family and a burden on society in these difficult times.

God, will he ever shut up? Betty agonized as she squirmed on her hard chair. She wanted to yell at him that he had it all wrong, that he didn't understand anything about her life. Betty and her family attended church every Sunday at St. Paul's where Dr. Cody was the rector and she had never heard him preach in this way. Betty tried to tune out the Rev. as she let other more pleasant thoughts come into her mind.

Another ritual dreaded by Betty and the other residents at the Victor Home, was the monthly visit to the hospital. The girls were accompanied by a staff member to the Toronto General Hospital where, as Betty described him, "A lecherous old doctor examined her." As she lay on the examining table he leaned over her, his cigarette dangling from his mouth, the long ash glowing at the end held together by some mysterious means and she feared it would drop on her at any moment.

"When will my baby be born?" she asked.

No answer, just more smoke.

"If I smoke will it hurt my baby?" Not that she was able to sneak a cigarette. They had been confiscated long ago. *Maybe I can get one from the doctor*, she mused to herself with a wry smile.

A look of disdain was thrown her way.

"What food can I eat?"

"Is it dangerous to stretch my arms over my head?"

No sound except the clang of the cold metal instrument as it fell onto the tray.

"How long will I be in labour? What will that be like? "

The doctor refused to answer any of Betty's questions as he puffed on his cigarette.

After the examination Matron called a taxi and they rode together in silence back to the Victor Home.

Phone calls and visitors were forbidden. In a way that was a good thing because Betty had overheard Matron talking on the phone to someone and she was sure it was James, her father.

"I am sorry, sir," Matron had said, "None of the girls are allowed visitors, not even Betty."

"Matron, was that my father?"

"Finish your chores, child, and never mind," Matron snapped.

It was late November so an abortion was not out of the question, and it would be risky to see her father. Betty longed for her mother though, and wished there was a way she could talk to her.

The house on Jarvis Street was spacious and elegant, with stained glass in the transoms over the large windows. The sunlight streamed in, bathing the rooms in dancing rainbows reflected off the coloured glass. In other circumstances Betty would have been quite happy in this environment as the house was not unlike her grandfather Watson's, although some of the carpets here were worn because of so much use and the kitchen needed fresh paint and new linoleum.

Most of the young women shared bedrooms, which although sparsely furnished were kept spotless, not by a cleaning staff but by the girls themselves. One bedroom at the end of the hall was reserved in the event a young woman returned with her baby to the Victor Home after giving birth, although this was discouraged.

Betty had arrived unannounced and was assigned a single room as all of the shared rooms were taken. She had a dresser and night stand which were inspected daily, lest she bring in a forbidden item, cigarettes, a magazine, chewing gum or some candy. The Bible and a book entitled, *What Every Young Woman Should Know*, by Margaret Sanger, had been placed in the drawer of each night stand. Betty's magazines were considered unsuitable reading and disappeared on the first day of her arrival. Soon after, other cosmetic items were missing from her dresser. Matron felt it her duty to remove all personal items not considered to be essential. Face powder was tantamount to evil and no doubt as having contributed to the downfall of each young woman.

Betty always wore a delicate, silver cross on a chain which had been a special gift from her mother on her tenth birthday. When she first arrived at the Victor Home for Girls, Matron asked her to remove her cross as this was a protestant home and in Matron's view, only Catholics wore crosses.

The Bicknell family had been members of the Anglican Church for many generations, and wearing a cross was totally acceptable to their family and faith. Betty's sliver cross was still in her dresser drawer and she was grateful that the matron had respected this particular personal item and allowed her to keep her treasured gift.

Betty and Lucy were standing in front of the window in the upstairs hall when they noticed a car approaching and come to a stop in front of their house. A man helped a woman out of the car, and then placed some parcels in her arms before driving away. Betty had seen this routine before and ran down the hall in great glee alerting the other girls that they were about to have a visitor.

"The missionaries are coming, the missionaries are coming", she laughed.

Matron heard the commotion and spoke sharply to Betty and her friends.

"Betty, please don't stir things up; and girls, conduct yourselves properly and be grateful for this visit. We really need the help of these church women."

The doorbell chimed and Matron wiped her hands on her apron as she approached the door and welcomed Mrs.Banford, from Erskine United Church, into the foyer.

"Good afternoon Matron."

"Good afternoon Mrs. Banford; how very nice of you to come."

"Thank you, Matron. It is a pleasant day for a drive and my husband, Mr. Banford, drove me here and will pick me up shortly. At our Women's Association meeting your superintendent, Miss Ainkenhead gave a talk on the splendid work you are doing here. The women in the W.A. had a shower for the girls and I have brought the gifts," Mrs. Banford gushed. "Our shower this month was used clothing which we thought the girls might like."

Betty leaned toward Lucy and whispered in a taunting tone, "Do you remember being invited to a shower Lucy?"

"No, I wasn't invited to a shower Betty." Lucy responded in a harsh whisper.

Matron frowned at the girls.

Mrs. Banford continued, "I have a daughter about the same age as that girl over there," she said pointing to Edna, "and my daughter graciously gave up a skirt she is very fond of."

Edna responded with, "My name is Edna," and seethed as she thought, we are people, not just 'that girl over there.', but didn't say anything for fear of reprisal from Matron.

"How do they know what I might like?" Betty was incensed and wanted to scream and demand respect. Every month the well meaning women from at least one of the United Churches had a shower for the Home and delivered the gifts to the girls.

Betty wanted a shower, a wedding shower or a baby shower. She wasn't keen on a jam and pickle shower.

After Mrs. Banfield's husband arrived to pick her up, and the aroma of her strong perfume was fading, the girls began to unpack the unlikely shower gifts; jams and pickles, cups and saucers, knitted mitts and sweaters, candy, dishes, cutlery, layettes, used uninteresting and irrelevant books and second hand clothing. Betty pulled a worn, brown woolen coat out of a *Robert Simpson* box. She had opened many *Robert Simpson* boxes and *Birks* boxes. When she pulled off the lid a wonderful surprise would be revealed. A new red coat with a matching leather belt, black leather gloves, an elegant pearl necklace and ear rings and a green taffeta dress in the princess style, were some of the gifts she remembered, all chosen by either her mother or father and given to her spontaneously.

Betty tried on the coat and tugged it around her. It barely fastened but it would do.

Every month the girls repeated the depressing routine and then wrote a thank you note to the church which sent the gifts and to the woman who delivered the so-called gifts.[7]

"Writing thank you notes is a wonderful practice," Matron told them. "You need to know how to do these things."

We will leave the young women to write their thank you notes while I, the author, step out of the picture. As I go deeper into my mother's life, my heart aches for her as I realize what she gave up and what it meant for her to live at the Victor Home for the safety of her baby, me. One can argue that she didn't have any other choice, but she did. She could have had a discreet abortion and then continued with her life as before; attending school at Branksome Hall, going to concerts and sporting events, enjoying her privileged family life, travelling, among numerous other activities. I am very grateful that she didn't make that choice. Another choice could have been for her to elope and marry Clyde. That choice would have legitimized my birth in the eyes of society and the law. My first birth certificate had, "Illegitimate," typed on the back, a demoralizing term to have associated with oneself. I muse about how my life might have differed if my parents had married before I was adopted away.

Another source of my indignation is my father, Clyde. Where was he when Betty decided that the only way to save her baby's life was to run away? If Clyde was so much in love with my mother, why did he abandon her? Was it by choice or was he forced by some means? I shared a plausible theory in the chapter, "The Man in the Shadows."

I think Betty showed great strength and tenaciousness when she continued with her pregnancy. Alone, seemingly abandoned by her lover, the father of their planned child, and separated from her close family unit, she was living in less than ideal circumstances.

In 1935, to be pregnant and unmarried meant shabby, vilifying treatment. Young women who were secretaries, teachers, domestics, nurses, students and others from all walks of life were shunned, called abusive names, looked down on and stripped of their dignity and self worth. Not all women became pregnant out of wedlock because of an indiscretion. There were also cases of women who had been raped by their fathers, their employers and other family members. My research shows that most teen age girls under the age of fifteen who were pregnant had been raped by their fathers. They then, had an abortion or they were forced to leave home until after the birth of the child. The Victor Home for Girls was a respectable institution and the girls were safe there, although still victims of the prevalent attitudes and practices of the time.

My mother chose to give me life in spite of the appalling attitudes she endured. She may not have anticipated the consequences and life-long stigma for herself because she gave birth to a child before she was married. She gave up a lifestyle of privilege and freedom to live in an institution under strict Victorian principles so that she might bear the child that she and the love of her life had planned together. Was she a courageous, strong young woman? You bet she was!

Now, I tell myself to take a deep breath and let it go slowly. I will continue with my story.

*

Betty missed music in her life and although there was a console radio in the hallway, it remained silent.

Reading was restricted to the books in her night stand, some ancient books in the library and weekly religious tracts supplied by the ministers and the staff. Rarely was there a newspaper brought into the house.

The formal dining room boasted a glistening chandelier dripping with crystal prisms and gold candles topped with chandelier bulbs. The table was set for twelve and the straight backed chairs stood ready to receive the young women who were expected to sit silently throughout the meal. Matron presided at the head of the table and offered the long prayer which preceded each meal. When conversation was allowed, the matron provided the topic which they could quietly discuss. Betty longed for some useful knowledge about her pregnancy or how to care for herself, but they were instructed endlessly on manners and proper etiquette. Betty's manners were exemplary. She missed the fun and conversation her family had around the table at dinner. This way of living was foreign and cruel; it was as though the girls were being punished for being pregnant, not supported and helped which one would think was the purpose of their being there.

Christmas in 1934 was different from all others. Betty longed for Clyde most of all, but also home, the excitement of Christmas, making the Christmas pudding, shopping for gifts for her parents, her brother and her friends, wrapping the presents, keeping secrets and even anticipating Branksome Hall parties. She missed being with her friends, especially Annie. Had Annie tried to contact her she wondered? They were never told if someone came to see them. It was like being in prison.

Tears escaped from her eyes as she thought fondly of her family. There was an emptiness and longing in her heart. But, next Christmas she would have her baby and she hoped Clyde and it would be wonderful.

Marie would be baking all kinds of Christmas cookies and sweets. The smells of ginger, cloves, evergreens and baking would be wafting through the house. Would James, her brother have chosen a special gift for her? She was positive he would have chosen something, the perfect gift. Betty closed her eyes and tried to imagine what it would be, perhaps a new tennis racquet. James's voice was changing and she could hear him teasing her mother, saying,

"Hey, Maw, what did you get me for Christmas?"

Betty loved her brother James and she missed him terribly. What would he think of her now? Would she and James still be close or would her pregnancy cause a rift between them? Betty didn't believe it would.

In the days before Christmas the girls were given a few ornaments and Christmas boughs to decorate the front hall of the residence. It was wonderfully festive. There was a day that they all made Christmas cookies which was fun as they mixed the cookie batter, rolled it out and cut it into star shapes. Then one afternoon, Jesse Sweetman invited them to come into the kitchen to make gingerbread men. They were allowed to talk and laugh and there was a feeling of Christmas. Perhaps it was her experience as a traveler's aid worker at Toronto Union Station that helped Deaconess Sweetman to be compassionate and kind.

On Christmas Eve some of the staff and the residents of the Victor Home all walked to the service at St. Luke's United Church, which was one of Toronto's most beautiful examples of religious architecture. Betty had visited the church with her father and loved the imposing stonework and turrets that made it look like a castle. Beautiful stained-glass windows had been donated by the wealthy businessmen and their families who attended the church. Tonight, the colours glowed from the light behind the windows. Matron and the girls trouped into St. Luke's and sat in a pew together. It was magical with the candles flickering on the altar and the pine wreaths below the windows giving off a wonderful fragrance. To Betty's delight, a beautiful medley of Christmas music filled the air. When the minister invited them to stand and sing some of the Christmas carols, Betty's strong, clear voice rose above the others as she sang every word of every carol from memory. It was joyous. Her baby stirred as she sang and Betty bonded with the life forming in her womb. She knew it was a girl. At last that special Christmas feeling crept into her being and filled some of the empty places.

Gigantic fluffy snowflakes fell, silently, glistening, shimmering, in the glow of the streetlamps along Jarvis St. as they walked back to the Victor Home. No one spoke as they walked, each with her own thoughts, each wishing she was somewhere else tonight.

The spell was broken as they walked up the wooden steps to the large verandah of 341 Jarvis Street. A broom was leaning against the wall to sweep the snow from their shoes and boots. They swept, stomped and shook off the snow with great delight. Matron announced that cocoa and cookies would be served in the dining room as a special treat. The girls gathered laughing and talking, as they each found a place at the table. It seemed that the rules were relaxed for Christmas Eve. The expectant mothers enjoyed their treat and then, one by one, excused themselves and found their way to their rooms, some to sleep, some to weep. Betty was awake late into the night thinking many things but mostly wishing Clyde was there with her.

Christmas morning Toronto looked like a fairyland, with white glistening snow covering rooftops, trees and fences. The residence was quiet, except for the kettle whistling in the kitchen. Betty and the others scurried down to Christmas breakfast at 7:00 am, an hour later than usual. As they finished a special breakfast of squeezed orange juice, muffins, and coddled eggs and coffee, Matron invited them to gather around the radio for his Majesty, King George V's Christmas broadcast. The radio came to life and they all listened intently, some because it was better than going to their room and a few because it was their family tradition on Christmas morning. Betty pulled her chair closer and imagined her family listening to the same broadcast on Cluny Drive. She felt close to her parents.

When the broadcast finished there was another surprise; Christmas mail had arrived and the girls held their breath in anticipation of their name being called. Betty clutched her three letters to her heart and ran upstairs to the privacy of her room. After staring in disbelief at the envelopes, from her parents, her brother James and her friend Annie, she tore open the first one, without using the letter opener as she had been taught to do. It was from her parents. They missed her and were concerned about her. Her father had tried to see her but had been refused. He had sent money to the Victor Home for her room and board so she didn't have to worry about being asked to leave. Betty hadn't even thought about payment. Christmas would be lonely without Betty and they hoped she was in good health.

Then, a question that took her breath away.

"Have you signed the adoption papers?"

"Adoption papers," she said out loud, "I don't want adoption papers. I'm keeping my baby."

Her heart sank. Was this another hurdle to go through? Not today. She read to the end of the letter and her mother had written a few lines too, full of love and concern and longing for her daughter.

The second letter was from her brother James with news of his parties, his friends and Christmas preparations and asking her to come home soon.

"I miss you sis, and I've got a great present for you."

"Love, James."

She opened Annie's lengthy letter last and savored every word. Annie wrote about their friends, what she was doing in school, about roller skating with a boy named Bill, and going to a coffee shop on Bloor Street with the baseball team, just to keep them together until spring. She also said that sometimes she walked past 341 Jarvis street hoping to see Betty. Could they find a way to meet and talk?

Betty wondered if there had been other letters delivered for her. Why hadn't Clyde written? He wouldn't know where she was, she reasoned.

Betty lay back on her pillow, her letters in her hand and closed her eyes. She had a lot to think about. Happily, she drifted off to sleep.

She was awakened by the smells of Christmas dinner. Cook had prepared the meal so the girls had Christmas Day without responsibilities.

The table was resplendent with candles, sprigs of Holly and glistening Christmas balls in gold, silver and red. Serving dishes brimmed with mashed potatoes, carrots, cranberry sauce and sweet pickles. A beautifully browned turkey with chestnut stuffing was the centerpiece of the meal. Matron sat at the head of the table and carved, giving each one a generous helping. Conversation was light, lively and unimpeded. Lucy told about her family Christmases at home and Hilda half whispered that she didn't have any traditions but when she and her baby found a place to live, she was going to start some. Jane said her family didn't have any traditions and Christmas was like any other day except that her father didn't go to work.

"I missed making the Christmas pudding, this year," Betty told her friends. "It's an English tradition that the Bicknell family have continued since my great grandfather James came to Canada with his family in 1872. Daddy always invites my Aunt Muriel because she's lots of fun. Marie, our maid, has everything ready and we gather in the kitchen to stir the ingredients and add special items to the pudding like a shiny quarter or a shin plaster wrapped in wax paper. Then we make a wish and put the money in the pudding. The lucky person who finds the prize will come into money. After we stir the pudding we all go to the library and Fred brings in hot cider or hot rum. Daddy always invites Fred and Marie to join us for rum and cider."

"Thank you, Miss Bicknell. That was quite a long story."

"You have a maid?" asked Lucy? There was a murmuring amongst the girls.

"That's enough girls." the matron scolded.

The telling of her story helped Betty feel a connection to her family even if some of the girls at the table were bewildered.

After dinner, everyone pitched in willingly with the tidying up. It had been a happy day for most of the young women.

The day after Christmas it was back to strict rules and routines.

High winds and driving rain brought in January, 1935 and continued throughout the month. The newspapers reported the worst storms on record in Toronto. Betty was content to be safe inside.

The winds were howling on the night of January 16th when Edna Damude, one of the young women soon to give birth, went quietly to Nurse Barclay's bedroom door and knocked gently. Miss Barclay opened the door and knew at once that it was time to call a taxi and go with Edna to Toronto General Hospital. Several hours later Edna gave birth to a dear baby boy whom she named James Robert Damude. Edna cradled her newborn and kissed his soft, pink cheeks before he was taken away to the nursery. She lay back on the bed to rest and savor this new happiness. It was Edna's hope that she could find work and raise her child herself, but she knew it would be difficult. Unwed mothers were scorned, as were their children. Edna and James Robert had an uncertain and difficult future.

When James Robert was a week old, Edna arrived back at the Victor Home with her son bundled up in blankets to shield him from the cold. With the eager assistance of the girls who met her at the door, he was soon unwrapped to reveal his tiny body cozy in a layette which was one of the gifts from the Women's Association. The girls cooed over their new resident. A feeling of joy and hope crept into three forty one Jarvis Street.

Edna and her infant son were moved into their own room at the end of the corridor where they were expected to remain most of the time. She could bring her baby out into the corridor for walks from time to time as long as no one was disturbed.

The Superintendent of the Victor Home was encouraging the soon- to- be -young mothers to give up their babies for adoption. It was better that Edna and her child stay out of sight as the other girls could get attached to the baby. It was feared that some young women who had given in to the adoption idea might change their minds and not sign adoption papers for their babies if they became fond of James Robert.

After two weeks or so, there were whispers around the residence that Edna was having problems. She didn't seem happy and cried much of the time. The girls heard James Robert crying but no one was allowed to go in and visit Edna and her baby. Edna remained behind the closed door of her room and stopped bringing Robert out for walks. Everyone at the Victor Home was very worried and spoke to Miss Barclay of their concerns. Neither the nurse nor the matron seemed to have the same concern.

On the morning of February 16th there was a commotion in the hall. Above the sound of the wind, sirens wailed. Two speeding police cars drew up outside of three forty one Jarvis Street. The officers jumped out and ran to the door of the Victor Home. Matron opened the door and pointed up the stairs. Hurried, heavy footsteps down the corridor brought the girls to their doors.

"Go inside and shut your doors." Matron shouted orders. "Close your doors and stay in your rooms until you are told you can come out."

Betty left her door open as much as she dared so she could see what was going on. Her room was closest to the activity. One by one the other bedroom doors along the corridor were nudged open quietly, and eyes peeked out.

Soon the door bell rang again, long and loudly. Black suits in clerical collars rushed up the staircase and down the corridor. Heavy footsteps were heard, back and forth, back and forth. Muted voices discussed and gave directions. Commotion, confusion and chaos punctuated the morning. The nurse, Miss Barclay, was distraught weeping into her handkerchief. Betty heard Matron scold her,

"Pull yourself together. The press will soon be here."

Betty's heart pounded and her breathing was difficult. She was frightened and wanted to know what was happening in Edna's room. Gently she moved her hands over her expanded abdomen and then let them rest there in a protective way. Betty's back ached as she stood straining trying to take in what was going on.

The doorbell rang again and a man carrying what looked like a doctor's bag ascended the stairs and strode down the hall to Edna's room. Next, Betty saw a tall man in a black suit arrive and he disappeared into the room. After what seemed like an eternity Betty saw the man with the doctor's bag and the tall man come out of Edna's room. The tall man was carrying something. Was it a bundled up sheet? It was difficult to see through the small opening of the door.

Edna's door opened again and Betty quietly pushed her own door wider to be able to take in the fullness of what was happening. She gasped when she saw a disheveled, confused Edna, escorted and helped by two policemen, one on either side, holding her up, half carrying her as she tried to walk down the long corridor.

"Edna." Betty found a constricted voice. "What's happened? Where's little James Robert?"

As Edna shuffled by, Betty saw her glazed over, vacant eyes as her head dropped. The girls watched, feeling helpless and frightened as the policemen supporting Edna between them, continued their long walk down the corridor to the staircase. They descended the stairs slowly to the verandah and to waiting reporters with the incessant pops and flashes of their cameras. The reporter's questions went unanswered.

Betty's heart skipped a beat when she thought she saw Clyde on the street with the reporters. This was the kind of assignment he would have been given but she had been told Clyde didn't work for *The Star* anymore. It was a momentary lapse and then she was jolted back to Edna.

The policemen and Edna emerged from the house and Edna was directed to a police car where she was helped into the back seat to sit alone.

Betty expressed her concern. "Lucy, wouldn't you think that Matron would go with Edna? Why is Edna being left alone? Oh, girls, poor Edna. What's going to happen to her?"

"Betty, it looks as though Matron and the superintendent are getting in the car with the ministers, or priests or whoever they are. They're wearing those funny collars."

"They're clerical collars, Lucy."

Suddenly Agnes rushed away. "Where are you going Agnes?"

"I'm sick to my stomach, Betty. Oh, this is so awful." The bathroom door slammed.

The girls watched as one by one the cars fell into line and left in procession up Jarvis Street towards Bloor St.

Eleven bewildered faces at the upstairs window with their arms entwined around each other and tears of anxiety and compassion streaming down their cheeks, watched helpless, as their friend was taken away.

Jesse Sweetman took charge in the absence of Matron who was on her way to an unknown destination in a car with two ministers of the cloth and the superintendent. The nurse, Miss Barclay was there to help too. The girls were invited to come to the dining room where they could talk freely and release some of their fears although there were no answers forthcoming about the tragedy. The cook brought in tea, hot bread and jam.

For a few minutes they sat silently, each young woman with her own thoughts.

"Miss Sweetman, what happened to Edna?" Lucy was the first to break the silence.

"Lucy, I don't know. Perhaps she was feeling very sad and didn't know what to do. Maybe she was worried about how to care for her son. I just don't know Lucy."

"Miss Sweetman, when the police were taking Edna down the hall she was in a daze as though she didn't understand what was happening to her or why the police were taking her away. Do you think she knew what she was doing? How could anybody do what she did?

"Oh, that dear, sweet boy." Betty's voice broke as she spoke.

Miss Barclay joined the conversation. "Sometimes women develop mental illness when they have a new baby. It doesn't happen very often but I have seen cases. It could be that was what happened to Edna."

"I'm really scared," said Betty clasping her arms around her own body, "I don't want that to happen to me but I don't know how to prevent it. The doctor we go to is useless, he doesn't tell us anything."

Then Betty, thinking of her own family and what they might do in such a situation, asked, "Will someone tell Edna's parents? Do they know? Can they come and be with her?" How she wished she could talk to her father because he would know what to do.

"I don't know," Miss Barclay said in a quiet voice.

"You know", said Jesse Sweetman as she stood and prepared to leave the room, "We may never know the truth."

The next morning when the girls came for breakfast there was a newspaper on the table.

They all huddled around to read the brief account of Edna Damude in the *Court News.*

Court News

"Edna Damude, 21, unmarried mother, charged with murdering her three week old baby son, was remanded one week to be sent to the psychiatric hospital in the meantime. She is alleged to have strangled her infant child in a room at the Victor Home for Girls, Jarvis Street, yesterday. She came to Toronto from Silver Bay, near Port Colborne. She is said to have told police she had no money to raise her child properly."

Taken from, *The Toronto Star*, February 16, 1935.

A pall fell over the residents of Victor Home for Girls.

In the following days, the girls watched as cars slowed and the occupants pointed as they drove by the Victor Home. At church on Sunday, the women shook hands with Matron and whispered their shock and surprise. They fumbled for words to offer their condolences and moved on. The young women residents huddled together, waiting, yearning too for words of comfort and caring. They waited in vain.

Life plodded on for Betty. Uncertain about her own future, she was grateful for her good health. It was early March and Betty had begun to assert herself more. She bravely challenged Matron and intervened for other girls whom she felt were being unfairly treated. Deaconess Sweetman recognized Betty's compassionate nature and felt a bond with her. She would watch over Betty.

Betty had changed since her arrival at the Victor Home. The lives of the less privileged had never been of interest, but now she understood how it felt to go without the luxuries she was accustomed to having. Forced, through circumstances to swallow her pride and wear second hand clothing, Betty felt gratitude and not shame. The young women who had become her close friends would not be approved of by her parents or her Rosedale social circle, but the similar circumstances of their coming together in the Victor Home provided a basis for developing special friendships.

Betty's determination and strength carried her through the days as she began her seventh month.

Lucy, the young woman in the room beside Betty's, made her regular trip to the doctor and on her return, reported to the others that her baby would soon be born. She wanted to keep her baby and would return to the Victor Home with the child for a few weeks, until arrangements were made for her to go to Fergus to live. Soon after, Betty heard a disturbance one night and peeked out of her door to see Lucy leaving with Matron. At breakfast they learned that Lucy had gone to the hospital to have her baby. Most of the girls were excited and looked forward to Lucy's return. She could tell them what it had been like to be in labour and to give birth. There was apprehension too, as they remembered poor Edna. Two weeks later Lucy arrived back in a taxi with the matron and ran straight to her room. No one saw a bundle in her arms. The sobbing from behind the door of Lucy's room continued for hours. Betty did the forbidden and went to Lucy's door and knocked softly.

"May I come in Lucy? It's Betty"

"Yes," was the faint reply.

"What's happened Lucy? Where's your baby?"

"Betty, they took him away. I never saw him. I didn't know I signed papers for my baby's adoption. They said it was a boy, but I don't know, I never saw the baby. Oh, Betty, it's so awful. Betty, be careful if you want to keep your baby. I don't trust that doctor and Matron wouldn't help me. She said I signed the papers. What papers Betty? I don't know what to do."

Lucy's tears soaked Betty's faded green blouse as Betty tried to comfort her in whatever way she could. Matron, doing her rounds, heard them and came into Lucy's room.

"Betty, leave at once. You know you are not to go into each others' rooms."

"Please, Matron, I want to be with Lucy. She wanted to keep her baby Matron. Why couldn't she?" Betty spoke up bravely.

"It is none of your affairs Miss Betty. If you must know, Lucy has no means of supporting a child and would not be a fit mother. The child is better off where he is with two parents who can provide for him. It's no good raising a child on your own. Now go to your room."

Lucy was left to grieve alone.

Lucy remained isolated in her room and seldom came down for meals. Many days later, pale and listless she finally emerged. The young woman didn't speak or look at anyone, but glanced to the side or had her eyes cast down.

Then at breakfast one morning her chair was empty and remained so throughout the week. Matron could or would not give them any information about Lucy. The empty chair was the only reminder of the distraught young woman. Later, the girls heard the tragic news that Lucy had run away and had taken her own life.

Betty was disturbed by the tragic circumstances of Lucy's death. She didn't want the same fate for her child or for herself. It was already March and her baby was expected in May. Perhaps it was time to leave the shelter of three forty one Jarvis St. because it was feeling less like a shelter or place of safety. If her baby was premature, it could come anytime and Matron would insist that she sign adoption papers, or that awful Doctor might take her baby away under some other pretence. Lucy's wishes had been ignored. That was not going to happen to her baby.

"Yes", she thought to herself, "I have to go somewhere soon."

She needed a plan. The last time she made a major decision, it was to save the life of her child; this time it was to prevent her child from being taken away from her. Betty had an idea that she thought would work. She would excuse herself to go to the Ladies' room during a church service and slip out the side door. It wouldn't be easy getting home but she would walk if that was the only way.

It had been the coldest winter in Toronto on record and there was no letup to the weather extremes in March. The city was buried with record snowfalls in February and now, unrelenting winds and rain assaulted the city and sometimes it wasn't safe to go out. Trees were blown over on the streets and branches and small debris traveled through the air with the sudden gusts. City crews were working hard cleaning up the mess. Prisoners were brought from the jail to help with the cleanup. Any footwear that ventured out on the streets was soon soaked and the deep, cold slush chilled the wearer to the bone.

On the first Sunday in March, they were informed at breakfast that they would not go to church because of the conditions in the streets. The girls were instructed to have a quiet hour, from eleven to noon in their rooms. They could read the Bible or any of the religious tracts that had been given to them but nothing else. They might be wayward girls but they would respect the Lord's Day and "conduct themselves accordingly." Someone would be coming by during the morning to look in on them.

Betty's plan was thwarted.

She stood in her room and looked out the window at the horrible weather but she knew she still had a chance of getting away without being seen. She had made a decision to go home and today was the day. She chose not to call her father as he might insist that she stay to the end of her term. Betty would take her chances on the element of surprise and his love for her to be welcomed home again. There were three things she wanted to take with her, nothing else. Quickly Betty took her bag from the closet, slid in the three letters, then fastened the chain around her neck with her tiny cross, which she had not been allowed to wear and lastly, checked to make sure the precious box was still in the secret pocket. Her leather change purse was there too with about five dollars. She put on her second hand coat and tugged at it trying in vain to fasten it over her growing abdomen. Betty pulled her hat down on her forehead, yanked on her boots and laced them up, and with a furtive glance behind her, silently closed her door. She would have liked to say goodbye to her friends but there wasn't time; nor was it wise to give away her plan.

Quietly she tiptoed down the hall towards the uncarpeted back stair case which led to the kitchen and an outside door. She took her chances that no one would be in the kitchen and crept down the stairs being careful to avoid the creaky third step. Her heart was pounding and she was breathless as she maneuvered herself through the narrow door at the bottom of the stairs. She entered the kitchen and crossed the floor to the back door. No one was there. She turned the knob on the door and had to push hard to open it. The wind whistled through the opening and she feared the sound would alert someone. She held on tightly to keep the door from slamming shut which was sure to bring Matron racing to accost her. Betty stepped outside and the wind took her breath away, or was it the feeling of freedom? She clutched her ill fitting coat as if to shield her unborn child from the storm.

Betty waded through the slush to the side of the house and leaned against the wall in the alley to catch her breath. She pulled in a few deep breaths then straightened herself and plodded through the snow and icy water in the laneway to Jarvis St. She didn't dare look back at the house as someone might be watching.

It was about eight blocks to the Paris Café. She knew if the streets were passable she could make it there, have a hot drink, warm up, and then call a taxi to take her home.

With her head down she faced into the wind and began her journey home.

12. Escape Through the Storm

Icy water soaked through Betty's boots and numbed her feet before she reached the end of the laneway. Was someone watching her? Betty thought she saw a movement behind the curtains at the front window as she passed, but she didn't dare turn her head to look.

"Keep walking." she told herself. *"Don't look back."*

She pulled her coat around her in vain as the wind blew it open each time she tugged it around her stomach. Her weight gain was enough that she could no longer do up the buttons. The sidewalk was treacherous with ice beneath the snow and she had to concentrate on staying on her feet. She shuffled along as she had seen elderly women do as a precaution to prevent slipping, losing their balance and falling.

Work crews were busy shoveling the snow to clear the streets. Their shovels scraped along the ice on the road, sometimes hitting bare pavement making an unpleasant sound as they pushed the slush towards the storm sewers and heaved the heavy, water soaked snow that didn't drain away into large wooden carts. Jarvis Street was the worst it had been in years and Betty had heard Matron talking about the city refusing to spend money on a sand patrol and on the glare ice cars looped around two and three times and often crashed into a tree or another vehicle. Pedestrians had been injured too. Matron said that their Alderman asked the city to be responsible for the cost of any accident if the street had not been spread with sand or ashes.

Betty was heartened that the workmen were there and she was not alone and if at any time she felt it was unsafe to go further, there would be someone to help her. She was unaware that some of the men, who were working to clear the streets in Toronto, were from the prison and under the watchful eyes of their guards.

A small tree branch blew by, barely missing her.

"Watch out, Miss," one of the workmen called.

"You shouldn't be out on a day like today."

Betty plodded on, her sights set on the Paris Café, and the private booth that she and Clyde used to call their own. Some of the home owners had scattered ashes on the sidewalk and as Betty shuffled through them the black soot stuck to her boots. The streetcars were silenced by the storm and only the occasional motor car splashed slowly by with the driver hunched over the steering wheel, peering through the fogged windshield, ready to jerk the car away from sudden flying debris or out of a skid. Betty plodded on but it was slow, difficult walking. There were two more blocks to go and she was exhausted. Freezing cold from the wind and her wet clothing she could barely put one foot ahead of the other. But she must.

As she stepped down from the slippery curb to walk the last block to the Paris Café, her feet shot out from under her and she landed hard on her back in the icy water. Stunned for a moment Betty lay still, afraid that she might not be able to get up. Her concern was not only for herself but also her baby. Slowly, she rolled over on her hands and knees and awkwardly pushed herself up onto her feet.

Water dripped from every inch of her as she raised her aching body to a standing position. She had to have shelter and warmth soon or she would collapse.

Betty shivered uncontrollably as she made her way along the last block down Bloor Street. The wind blew and her clothes began to freeze and stiffen.

A few more painful steps and she was at the Paris Café which gave her a rush of warmth, welcoming and safety as she pulled open the door to this familiar, special place. She took a step towards the back of the café but she felt weak and dizzy. The room spun around and crazy coloured patterns swirled before her eyes as she crumpled to the floor from exhaustion and cold.

She could hear the voices of women standing over her; two women she thought. Looking up she could see the form of waitresses in their frilly aprons through a cloudy veil. Their far distant voices uttered words of apprehension. Betty listened to their conversation which sounded like a muted echo, something like the time she and James hollered into a rain barrel at the lake. One voice said,

"What should we do Effie?"

"We can't leave her on the floor, Inez. She's all wet and cold, poor thing."

"Do you think she's drunk?"

"I don't know, but I don't think so."

"Should we call the police?"

"Let's see if we can get her up first. She looks familiar, don't you think? Inez, is that woolen cloak still in the closet? We could use that to warm her. I'll get the cloak and would you make a pot of tea?"

Betty made motions of rousing and the waitresses hurried to assist her to her feet and to a chair.

"Let me help you out of your wet coat and hat, Miss. We have a woolen cape you can warm yourself in."

"What's your name Miss?" asked Effie.

"Betty, Betty Bicknell," she said.

"Betty Bicknell!" the waitresses echoed. "You are Betty Bicknell? I thought you looked familiar."

"Yes," Betty whispered, "I've been living at the Victor Home on Jarvis Street and I left there this morning. It was a longer walk than I thought and the streets are very dangerous."

"Oh, you poor dear. I remember you came here often with that charming man."

"Yes," said Betty in a faint, far away voice, "That was Clyde."

Effie rested one hand gently on Betty's shoulder and with the other pushed a lock of wet hair back from Betty's face.

"Miss Bicknell, you must get out of those wet clothes and get warm. You are shaking with the cold. May I pull off your boots?"

"Yes, please. I would appreciate that."

Effie knelt in front of Betty's chair, unlaced her frozen boots coated in ashes and pulled them from her feet, letting the water which had seeped inside cascade onto the floor.

"While you remove your stockings, Miss, I'll get a towel to dry your legs and feet,"

Betty watched as Effie walked deliberately to the café door, turned the lock, pulled down the blind on the door, hesitated, then reached under the blind and flipped over the *Open* sign to *Closed*.

Effie left Betty alone in the Café and soon returned with a hand towel and briskly rubbed Betty's feet and legs, then wrapped the towel around her feet to help warm them.

Inez returned with the cape and saw the window blind pulled and the *Closed* sign on the door. Betty listened as the drama unfolded between Effie and Inez. As Inez put the woolen cape around Betty's shoulders she said,

"Effie, you can't put the *Closed* sign on the door, or we'll get in trouble. Mr. Maurice will be furious if he finds out."

"Inez, he'll never know. Anyway, we have to help Miss Bicknell and there haven't been any customers all day. No one is going to go out for lunch or coffee on a day like today. I'll say I did it and you won't get into trouble."

Inez turned her attention to Betty.

"May I help you remove your wet dress Miss Bicknell? You can wear this cape to cover you and keep you warm."

Stripped of all feelings of pride and modesty, Betty gratefully accepted Inez' help. When the soggy dress was removed, Inez wrapped Betty in the woolen garment, then carefully pulled the hood over Betty's wet, blonde hair and squeezed her gently as she folded the soft, grey fabric over Betty's arms, leaving one hand free to drink the hot tea. It had been a long time since Betty had experienced any kind of warm personal caring.

"Thank you, Inez," she said as she reached out from her covering for Inez' hand and returned the squeeze.

Slowly Betty's numb body warmed. She nursed the tea, savoring each sip as though it was the finest beverage she had ever tasted. Inez carefully poured more tea when Betty's cup was empty.

Safe from the ravages of the storm, the three young women sat quietly together in the café. Betty was slowly drifting off when Effie broke the silence.

"My goodness," she said, "We haven't eaten anything. You must be starving Miss Bicknell."

"Please call me 'Betty', Effie. I'm very hungry and would love something to eat. You've both been so kind and I appreciate it. I would be glad to pay for a sandwich.

Effie went behind the counter and prepared ham and cheese sandwiches, made fresh coffee, cut generous slices of chocolate cake and returned with a tray of the goodies.

"Could we go and sit in the booth at the back please?" Betty asked.

"Yes, of course."

Betty gathered the large cape around her and walked in her bare feet to the special booth. Effie brought the towel and made a mat for her feet. The three young women enjoyed the food together and found conversation easy. Although they were curious about Betty, they were careful about asking too many personal questions. But Betty wanted to talk; it had been so long since she had been able to pour out her heart to anyone. Betty told them about leaving home and going to the Victor Home so she could keep her baby. She told them about Edna Damude and explained her reasons for leaving today, her fear that after the birth of her baby they might take it away. Effie and Inez were wide eyed and listened intently. They had read about Edna Damude and her baby in the paper.

Betty asked Inez and Effie about their families and listened to their stories.

The three women completed their lunch with amazing chocolate cake, smothered in thick creamy boiled icing and giggled as they licked the icing from their fingers. It had been a long time since Betty had giggled.

Strengthened by friendship and nourishment, Betty was feeling strong enough to make her next decision about going home. Calling a taxi was out of the question in her present condition, disheveled, wet, and with only a cape to wear and it would be impossible to pull on her wet, ill-fitting boots again.

Would her parents be at home? Sunday was their day to visit or receive friends and family but because of the storm they might have stayed home. Fred would most certainly be there. She would call Fred.

Betty excused herself from the table, pulled the cape around her and went over to the phone booth in the corner. She retrieved her change purse from her still damp bag and found ten cents, required for the call box and dropped it into the slot on the phone, then dialed the number for their butler and chauffeur, Fred.

Her heart raced as she heard the phone ring, one, two, three, four times.

"Oh, please be there, Fred," she thought.

Then, she heard a strong familiar voice.

"Hello, this is the Bicknell residence, Fred speaking."

When Betty heard Fred's voice, she couldn't speak at first. Then a faltering,

"Hello Fred. This is Betty."

"Betty, where are you?" Fred blurted out, forgetting his usual formal salutation of *Miss Bicknell.* "Your parents and brother aren't here right now. Your parents are at the Keachie residence and I'll be picking them up after dinner. I believe your brother is visiting a friend. Betty, it's so good to hear from you."

Betty spoke in a breathless litany.

"Fred, I'm glad you are there. Could you please come for me? I'm at the Paris Café. I left the Victor Home this morning and I've had an awful time. I had a bad fall and got soaked. Inez and Effie here at the café have helped me and have taken care of me. I need some shoes to go home. Could you find some shoes in my room and come for me?"

It warmed her heart to hear Fred eagerly reassuring her. "I'll be there as soon as possible, Miss Bicknell. I'll leave at once. Shall I phone your parents, Miss?"

"Thanks Fred, but no, please don't call my parents. I want to freshen up before they see me. Oh, thanks for coming for me."

Betty's knees felt weak after she hung up the phone. She also had a feeling of euphoria. "*I'm going home, I'm going home*," was Betty's endless stream of thought.

Inez and Enid stood on either side of Betty, at the door of the Paris Café watching for Fred's arrival, their arms around Betty's shoulders and waist in supportive gestures. Enid had raised the blind behind the curtain and turned over the *Closed* sign to *Open*.

Betty gasped and put her hands over her mouth when she saw the limousine slowly come to a stop in the slush. She watched as Fred jumped out and sprinted to the door carrying a blanket and footwear.

"Fred, oh, I'm so glad to see you."

Fred hid his overwhelming surprise when he saw Betty. He would not have recognized her had he met her on the street. He couldn't place the slim, vibrant young woman who disappeared from her home many months ago, in the body of the disheveled, pregnant woman now in front of him.

"Miss Bicknell, I'm so happy to see you too. Permit me to wrap you in this blanket and here are some warm boots you can slip your feet into."

Betty was glad to let Fred take over and after a teary "Goodbye" to Enid and Inez as well as the promise to return soon, Fred put his arm firmly around Betty and supported her as they walked to the car. When she was safely in the back seat he tucked the blanket around her and then slid behind the wheel for the risky trip home. Betty snuggled into the blanket and Fred gave all of his attention to the road. As the car nosed into the circular drive of Cluny Ave., Betty's pent up tears and emotions came flooding out. Fred half carried Betty into the house, and took her to the library where a warm fire glowed in the fireplace. He pulled a chair in front of the fire and tucked the blanket around her. Fred picked up the crystal brandy decanter from the table and poured a small amount of brandy in a goblet and without taking time to warm it he placed it in Betty's hands.

"Sip on this, Miss; it will help to warm you." Fred said as he placed the glass in Betty's shaking hand, holding his own hands over hers for a moment. "I'll find Marie and ask her to come and sit with you."

"Fred, is my brother James here? I so want to see him."

"He's visiting one of his friends, Miss, but will be here for dinner. Excuse me Miss Bicknell, I'll ask Marie to come and sit with you."

Betty snuggled deeper into the blanket and drank in the warmth of the fire and the security of being home. She closed her eyes and took in a long, deep breath and let it go, and then took a small sip of the brandy. It stung her throat and made her cough. Another sip went down smoothly and felt warm and pleasant.

Without asking her permission Fred went to the phone in the hallway to call the Bicknells and give them the news about their daughter's arrival home.

"Hello, Mr. Keachie, this is Fred, Mr. Bicknell's chauffeur. I'm sorry to disturb you but I have some urgent news for Mr. and Mrs. Bicknell. Is it possible for me to speak to Mr. Bicknell?"

Fred heard an affirmative reply and waited for Betty's father to come on the line.

"Hello, Fred. Morton said you had some urgent news."

"Mr. Bicknell, my apologies for disturbing you Sir, but Miss Bicknell has come home and she is in a bad way. She may require medical attention and I thought you should know immediately."

Fred heard the anxiety in Mr. Bicknell's voice as he replied, "God, Fred. Yes. Thank you. Betty is home? Yes, come for us right away. Is my daughter alright? Would it be better to call an ambulance? You could take us to the hospital. How did she get home Fred?"

"I picked her up Sir. It might be best if you come home and make the decision about the hospital yourself, Mr. Bicknell."

"Yes, Fred. Come for us, we'll be ready at the door."

"I'm leaving now, but the roads are icy and it will take longer than usual," Fred informed his employer.

James had already hung up and was probably relaying the news to his wife.

Fred left the Bicknell residence at once, leaving Betty in the care of Marie. The Bicknells were watching for their car when Fred drove up and very quickly they were on their way. Fred told them what he knew about Betty and her journey home. They would soon see for themselves and could welcome their daughter home.

"Fred, we thank you for your concern about Betty and also for taking the initiative to bring her home. It was appropriate for you to contact us, Fred. We appreciate your service as always."

The Bicknells arrived home and rushed into the library to greet their daughter.

Shock and dismay barely describe their feelings when they saw her.

Who is this disheveled young woman with matted blonde hair, wrapped in a grey, unbecoming cape? Surely it isn't our daughter. Bea was distraught and horrified.

My God, James thought, *she looks like some of the transient women that I've seen in the courtroom. Has our daughter sunk to that level of degradation?*

Betty saw her parents and sprang from the chair tripping over the long cape as she got up; new energy propelled her to them.

Betty fell into her mother's arms and it seemed their sobbing was endless. James stood by offering words of gratitude that Betty was home, muttered words of dismay at her condition and how she managed to walk so far in the storm.

"Betty, come here," James said, opening his arms. "We've missed you so much."

Betty left the shelter and comfort of her mother's embrace and went to her father. James enveloped his long absent daughter and held her close to him, saying over and over,

"Welcome home Princess, welcome home Princess."

He gently guided Betty back to the chair before the warmth of the fire, then pulled a chair on either side of Betty for Beatrice and for himself. James wrapped Betty in the blanket once more while he thought through what was best to do for Betty.

"Beatrice, do you think a warm bath and some fresh clothes might be helpful for Betty? I think we should have Doctor Brown come, but perhaps tomorrow would be alright. Betty, are you strong enough to go upstairs to your room?"

"Oh, Daddy, I'd love to. Could Marie draw me a bath? I don't want to go to the hospital, Daddy, I'll be fine here. I was just freezing cold and tired. I'll be fine when I have a bath and a sleep in my own bed. It's so wonderful to be home. I wish James would come home soon."

Her father left the room to ask Marie to prepare a bath and Betty's bed. Beatrice stayed close beside her daughter and didn't want to let her out of her sight.

Marie appeared at the door to say the bath was ready and Betty and her mother slowly ascended the stairs. The aroma of the glorious bath bubbles wafted through the air as she and her mother reached Betty's room. Betty tore off the cape, the blanket and her remaining undergarments and although she was still shaky, climbed into the deep tub and lowered herself into the foamy, warm water. She sat for a few moments absorbing the sensations of the warm water and perfumed soap which had been absent from her life for a long time, then slowly slid down into the tub letting the water cover her. Betty remained under the water as long as she could before emerging through the bubbles. A fragrant shampoo on the bathtub rack soon lathered Betty's dull hair, stripped of its sheen by the strong soap she had been using at the Victor Home. She splashed in the water and threw it down her back, then kicked her feet up and down.

"Are you alright dear?" her mother called, from Betty's room where she was waiting.

"I'm just fine, Mama, thanks. This is the most wonderful bath I've ever had."

Betty felt very relaxed and sleepy and carefully stepped out of the tub and wrapped herself in a big, fluffy towel. She rubbed her hair and her body and put on the warm gown Marie had laid out for her. When she stepped from the bath into her bedroom her mother saw a different person. HER Betty was back.

"Would you like some soup Betty, before you go to sleep?"

"No, thanks Mama; I'm too tired and I'm not hungry."

Beatrice helped her beautiful daughter into bed and pulled the covers over her. She bent down and kissed her cheeks lovingly.

"It' so wonderful to have you home, darling. We'll talk later. Sleep well."

Betty was almost asleep, but she murmured,

"Good night Mama. I love you. Please tell Jimmy I'm home," she whispered, calling her brother by his "pet" name, as she drifted into a deep sleep.

Bea went downstairs to the library where her husband was waiting.

"I've called Dr. Brown, Bea. He'll come to see Betty tomorrow. Then we'll talk about what to do."

"What do you mean, 'What to do?'James?"

"About the baby, Bea. I can't have Betty parading herself in front of my clients."

"James, she's just come home. Let her have some time to get well."

"We'll see what Dr. Brown thinks tomorrow. Is Betty asleep, Bea?"

"Yes, she is. She's totally exhausted and I expect she'll sleep until tomorrow. I'm very worried about her James. I just can't imagine what she went through today, walking all that distance and falling in her condition. I feel terrible too, that we let her stay in the Victor Home, James. She'll be fortunate if she doesn't get pneumonia."

"A restful sleep in her own bed is most important for her, Bea. I don't know how she managed to walk that distance either, without serious injury. The streets are so slippery and covered in cold slush, hmm, Bea, its fortunate that she found the café open and had shelter. The girls in the café must be rewarded for the assistance they gave her, Bea."

"Are you hungry James? Let's ask Marie, if she will make a supper for us. Would you like to eat here in the library?"

"That would be nice Bea."

The Bicknells settled into a quiet evening, glad that their daughter was safe and at home.

But Bea, was worried, very worried about what thoughts might be in James' mind. The days ahead would not be easy.

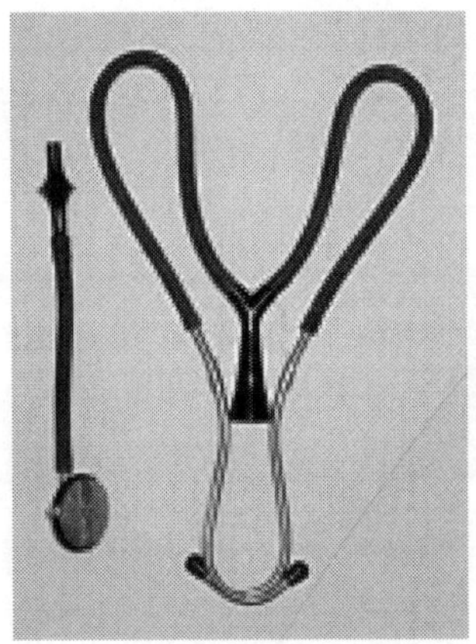

13. Edict

The late morning sun warmed Betty's body as she lay on her bed with the covers thrown back. Slowly she opened her eyes then reached for the familiar cover and drew it up under her chin.

Where am I? was her first thought. The events of the previous day flashed through her mind. Betty snuggled into the satin quilt as she recalled her horrendous experience on the journey home, but now she was safe and warm. Today, she didn't have to spring out of bed and go to the kitchen to do morning chores, but she thought about her friends at the Victor Home who were doing just that. Were they looking for her? Would Matron come and try to take her back? She half hoped Matron would arrive and be confronted by her father whom she felt sure would put Matron in her place.

Betty reached across her body and with her right hand pushed herself onto her back then saw her image reflected in the mirror of her dresser. Lying flat she couldn't see her toes but in this position she took in her full outline, her rising abdomen tapering off into a slimmer form. She tossed back the cover and took in the full view. Her hands lovingly caressed her stomach as thoughts of her baby and Clyde filled her heart. Betty closed her eyes, engulfed herself securely in the covers again and turned on her side. Sleep came swiftly and cradled her peacefully.

Her mother's voice wafted through her dream and gently called to her from far away. Bea touched her daughter and gradually the thin thread connecting the dream world to reality was separated and Betty surfaced to see her mother's smile.

"Good morning, dear. Did you have a restful sleep?"

"Oh yes, Mama, it is so wonderful to be home and in my own bed and to be able to sleep as long as I want. At the Home I had to get up early and help with the morning chores, Mama. I had to help set the table for breakfast at 7:00 o'clock in the morning when it was still dark outside. And after breakfast there was a mountain of dishes to wash and that awful oatmeal porridge pot to scrape clean."

As Betty recalled her recent life at the Victor Home her chapped hands became her focus. She reached for the lotion on her dresser and poured the creamy, soothing liquid on her rough skin.

Her brow furrowed into a look of pain. "Why didn't you come for me Mama? Why did you and Daddy just leave me there?"

Betty firmly massaged the lotion into her skin as she chided her mother.

Bea sat on the edge of her daughter's bed, took Betty's hands in hers and massaged the lotion into Betty's fingers. She stopped momentarily when she felt the chapped skin and the roughness of Betty's hands. She hadn't realized the full impact of Betty's life at the Victor Home for Girls, nor would she ever be able to do so. Bea embraced her daughter lovingly, and felt regret for the decisions that James made and that she allowed without questioning.

"I'm so sorry that we let you go through that, Betty," Bea said with sincerity. "You ran away Betty; it was your father, he …" Bea's voice trailed off and she didn't complete her thoughts because she hadn't done anything to help her daughter either. That would haunt her forever. They lingered in the safe embrace before Bea said,

"Betty, dear, Doctor Brown is here to see you. Do you feel like freshening up and then I'll bring him in?"

"Mama, is Jimmy here? Does he know I'm home?"

"Jimmy had to leave for school, sweetheart, but before he left he came into your room to see you but you were sound asleep and he didn't want to waken you. He's so looking forward to seeing you at dinner tonight."

"I wish he had wakened me. Mama, please give me some time before I see Doctor Brown. Could I have some breakfast in my room, please? That would be so special. Doctor Brown can visit with Daddy for an hour can't he?"

"I'll see, dear. I'll ask Marie to bring up your breakfast. Poached eggs on toast as usual?"

"That would be so grand, Mama. Could I have a glass of orange juice and coffee too, please? Thanks Mama. I'm so glad to be home." Water welled in Betty's eyes as she reached out to give her mother a warm hug and a rather wet kiss.

Was it only a day ago that she was living at the Victor Home where she was regimented, stripped of all decision making, told when, where and what to eat? As she lay in her warm bed cocooned in soft, sweet smelling bed linens she thought of her friends at the Home, and what she too had experienced there, sleeping between the harsh, disinfected sheets and wakening to Matron's caustic voice ordering them out of bed. When her bare feet came in contact with the frigid, bare floor it took her breath away. She shivered through the bathroom regimentation and getting dressed in her hand-me-down, ill-fitting clothing. Betty's body tensed as the march to the dining room, the silent breakfast and the dreaded kitchen duty came into her thoughts.

"I'm home; I'm warm and safe. I don't have to hurry or be silent. I can sing as I bathe with fragrant soap." Betty relaxed and snuggled into the covers.

A soft knock on Betty's bedroom broke her flash back and announced Marie's arrival with a splendid silver breakfast tray, complete with an exquisite pink rose in a crystal vase.

"Good morning, Miss Bicknell. It's so wonderful to have you home. I've missed you. Are you well?"

"Thank you, Marie. I am well and, oh, so pleased to be home again. Thank you for this beautiful breakfast and the rose. Betty sniffed the fragrance of the delicate flower.

"Hmm, so lovely. I haven't had breakfast in bed since I left home."

"I'm sorry, Miss. Mrs. Bicknell said to tell you the doctor would wait."

"Good, Marie. I'd like to take my time with this wonderful breakfast. Could you help me position the tray?"

Marie adjusted the tray beside Betty so she could sit in bed comfortably and enjoy her first meal at home in months.

"I'll come back for the tray later. I hope you enjoy your breakfast."

Betty slowly brought the fork to her mouth in anticipation of Marie's poached eggs cooked exactly three minutes. They were ever so tasty. When the last morsel had been consumed; when the last crumb had been retrieved; when the last drop of freshly squeezed orange juice had been savored, then and only then did Betty push back the covers on her bed. Her feet slowly found her fuzzy slippers and the young, pregnant woman took her time as she walked into her bathroom to do her ablutions in preparation for the visit from the family doctor whom she has kept waiting for over an hour.

This is a very difficult piece to write because of my deep compassion for my mother. I have vivid images of her, a young woman in a position of wealth and privilege who, because of her love for me, chose to run away from home to avoid an abortion. Now, she is about to learn that two people whom she loves and trusts are planning to take her baby, me, away at birth, in spite of her heroic efforts to keep me. This is real. It is heartbreaking. Betty misjudged her parents before; they let her down when she expected her father to allow her marriage to Clyde when she became pregnant; when she believed her parents would let her keep her baby but her father arranged for an abortion; when she ran away to the Victor Home for refuge to avoid the abortion and her parents didn't contact her. Once again she seems to be surprised at her father's decision that the baby must be adopted away. My mother's inner strength and courage was shown in so many ways, and yet, it seems, she was very naïve.

I feel as though my birth mother is on a rollercoaster, headed for a crash and I want to stop time and change the ending; but that's impossible. I want to leap into the pages of the book and rewrite my mother's life. The reality is, I know the conclusion and it's carved in stone.

I recall a futuristic black and white movie from the 60's, which had a similar theme, that of wanting to change the outcome of a situation. The movie begins in silence as the camera pans an empty street where a family comes into view. A father, a mother and their young daughter leave a restaurant and step into the street. The silence is broken by the roar of a speeding car which comes out of nowhere and we are horrified as the car bears down on the child. The father has the gift of freezing time and the scene stops at the frame where the car is inches away from the child.

The plot unfolds with scientists in a race against time trying to work out the correct formula to alter the conclusion of the scene and save the child's life. At the moment that each hour passes, the car moves one inch closer to the child. Suspense is heightened by a clock which counts down the seconds before the impact. The precise formula is found with a few seconds to spare and the outcome is changed; the ultimate success spares the child.

I want to freeze time, stop the frame in my mother's life because I know my grandfather's decision. I want to alter the outcome. I want to find the formula, but it is too late and this is not science fiction. Betty's life was real, not a product of my imagination. My life is genuine, although there were many occasions when I pleaded with the universe to tell me who I was. I'm sure we've all gazed at our reflection in a mirror for an extended period of time and asked the question over and over again; "Who am I? Who am I?"

The decisions of my grandfather Bicknell altered my mother's life and mine, forever. Whether for better or worse I will never know.

I am about to write the scene with Doctor Brown and my mother. How do I know the content of the conversation? I don't know for sure, do I? But, I was there in my mother's womb at the time and perhaps, just maybe, what if, I absorbed the distressing conversation into my memory cells? Could it be that what I'm writing comes from the recesses of my memory? It is fact that Doctor Alan Brown was the attending physician and I have the baby formula written in his hand for me.

It is commonly believed, proven, even that when people are in a coma they are able to hear conversations and respond with a squeeze of the hand or other gesture. I recently witnessed this while at the bedside of a friend who was dying.

A fetus responds to music and emotions and may retain memories of specific types of music. We cannot say with certainty what else a fetus may or may not remember. I have always loved jazz and was not exposed to that type of music while I was growing up. I tried to play something like jazz but I didn't have a name for it.

My passion for jazz came from somewhere; perhaps an inherited trait; perhaps I heard that wonderful music before I was born.

While doing research for this book I learned that my parents loved swing and jazz and that they were "regulars" on Saturday night in the Imperial Room at the Royal York Hotel where Moxie Whitney and his orchestra played for many years. Betty and Clyde developed a friendship with Moxie. Mr. Whitney was playing at the Chateau Laurier Hotel in Ottawa when I called to introduce myself. He invited my husband and me to be his guests at a dinner dance. It was a memorable evening. Moxie sat at our table and between sets told us what he remembered about my parents. They loved music and dancing and other couples often moved to the side of the dance floor to watch them. Moxie described my father as handsome, well informed and a skilled conversationalist; my mother as talented, athletic, beautiful and fun loving.

I've come to know my parents and have insight into their lives through others.

Sometimes I "choke up" as I try to write about my mother's life during her pregnancy. The panic attack was real as I wrote about my grandfather wanting to arrange my abortion. I felt scared, cold and hungry when my mother ran away to the Victor Home for Girls to evade the abortion and seek refuge. Through my research about The Victor Home for Girls at the time my mother lived there, I read about a young woman who killed her baby because of the ignorance, Victorian ideals and lack of support from society and the people who were supposed to be protecting her at the Victor Home. I grieve for the baby, the mother and the other young single pregnant women of that time. I felt anger as I read about the church's presumption of good in giving the residents, one of them my mother, "showers", at the Victor Home, but in the absence of the young women.

Take a deep breath, Margaret. Calm down. Brew some tea. Breathe in the calmness and beauty of this place.

I am in Omori, New Zealand as I write this piece. In this safe, stress-free, sun bathed environment, accompanied by the songs of birds, I am able to confront the questions I have and to accept the reality of the decisions that were made. There's no other choice, really.

Omori is fifteen treacherous miles from the nearest town of Turangi. Spectacular views and the sheer drop to the lake make driving here a breath-taking experience. The narrow, hilly road winds around the southern tip of Lake Taupo where active thermal hills spew out streams of misty, hot steam. Omori, in its isolation is a healing, meditative, environment. There is a walking path through the bush along the lake, alive with birds singing and taunting in the trees. As I write, Omori is much like a ghost settlement as most of the homes are vacant until Christmas when the settlement comes to life. I'm grateful for the friendship of Dave and Colleen the owners of Omori Store. Dave makes the most wonderful fish and chips on the planet.

But for now, doors are locked, shades are drawn, and the only signs and sounds of life, are the birds in the trees or strolling by and little rabbits that have left their hiding places to enjoy some fresh clover.

It is late December, the sun is dazzling and fathomless Lake Taupo, "as blue as," a New Zealand expression, beckons holiday makers and me. I've opened the double glass doors to my dear little writing haven, and hooked them back securely, giving me free access to the outdoors and the birds free access to my room. Screen doors are unnecessary as bugs and insects are scarce. But there is one gigantic bumble bee that I've named George who has sampled so many flowers he can scarcely fly. George buzzes in and out to keep me company. From atop the steep hill nearby I have a mind-altering view of the changing, volcanic Lake Taupo.

I breathe in slowly and deeply, filling my lungs with the pure, fragrant New Zealand air. The sun warms my body and soul. This wonderful place is so restorative.

A fresh pot of tea awaits and I'm ready to return to my mother's bedroom where Doctor Brown is about to give us the news of my grandfather's decision regarding my destiny.

Another sip of tea and I'm prepared to return to the story.

*

What Doctor Brown and James Bicknell discussed while Betty was enjoying her breakfast was the future of Betty's baby. James couldn't even imagine Betty keeping her child. What would she do? Where would she live? What about her debut party? Or, attending a finishing school like the Ontario Ladies' College in Whitby where her Aunt Muriel had attended. James had plans for Betty to travel with her young women friends as his sister had done when Muriel and Nan Gooch "took passage" on the Caronia to holiday in England. He wanted Betty to have a vacation in St. Moritz and he planned a trip for the family to enjoy a summer by the sea in Worthing, Sussex, England where Anne Caplin, Betty's great grandmother Bicknell grew up.

If his daughter completed her education, there would be banker's sons and young men of law who would be courting her. She must marry a young man in her social circle. It was simply impossible for any of these things to be achieved if Betty kept her child. James was adamant that adoption away was the only choice now.

Doctor Brown agreed to help James with the arrangements to be determined later. Ideally, the baby would be taken away at birth. If any of the doctor's patients were looking for a baby to adopt, Doctor Brown would contact James. The family would be carefully chosen. The other option was to contact the Children's Aid Society, not a choice as appealing to James; I believe because he would no longer have control.

And so without consulting Betty or even including her in the discussion, the fate of Betty's baby was decided. The child would be adopted away at birth.

Doctor Brown knocked gently on Betty's door.

"Come in," she said without enthusiasm.

Doctor Brown carefully removed his *Stethoscope*[8] *from the box and hung it around his neck.* He was kindly and gentle as he examined her. Betty had bruises on her shoulders, arms and back from her fall on the street. Doctor Brown positioned the arms of the stethoscope in his ears and placed the bell on her abdomen. She flinched as the cold metal bell of the Stethoscope touched her body.

"I'm sorry Betty, I'll warm this."

The doctor took the metal end and held it briefly in his hands, then repositioned the stethoscope to listen to the baby's heartbeat.

"The baby is in good health, Betty. I can feel the baby moving and there is a strong heart beat."

"Sometimes I can't get to sleep because the baby kicks so much. If it's a girl, and I think it is a girl, I'm going to call her Dorothy and if it's a boy he will be James William. James is for my father and brother and I like the name William."

Doctor Brown repositioned the stethoscope in one ear, paused and hesitantly said, "Betty, perhaps it's best if you don't name your baby. Your father and I have been talking and we think, for your sake and your child's, that you put your baby up for adoption. I'll find a good family for your child, Betty."

Betty was out of bed in a flash, almost knocking over Doctor Brown. She heard a yell as the stethoscope was ripped from the doctor's ear. Betty began to shake, her heart was racing and her breath was coming in short frequent gasps as she moved swiftly away from the doctor. Her arms cradled her stomach and she was bent over as though in pain.

Doctor Brown stood rooted to the floor, shocked by Betty's outburst.

As Betty's breathing returned to a more normal rhythm she placed her hands on her hips and leaned in toward Doctor Brown. Her large abdomen created a distance between them.

In teary defiance she shouted, "I'm not giving up my baby. So there."

"Betty, calm down, you'll upset yourself more. We can discuss this when you are stronger and feeling better."

"I don't want to calm down and I don't want to talk about it anymore. Clyde and I want this baby and he'll come back, I know he will. I won't let you take my baby away."

James and Bea heard the commotion and James ran up the stairs to Betty's room with Bea following close behind.

Bea reached out to take her daughter in her arms to try and bring comfort but Betty pushed her mother gently aside and remained defiant.

"You are not giving my baby away to anyone!"

"Betty, dear, calm down, it isn't good for you to be so upset. We'll talk later. Get dressed and come down for tea. Fred has lit a fire and it's cozy and warm, you can tell us all about the Victor Home. You father called the Home and let them know you are here."

"Who cares? You can't give my baby to someone else. Do you hear?"

Then, Bea changed the subject as though the life of the baby wasn't as important as the arrival of a parcel. Or was it that she thought the issue would just go away if she diverted the conversation?

"James, did Creeds Department Store send over a parcel?"

"Yes, Bea, they did. I'll have Marie bring it up."

"Goodbye for now, Betty," Doctor Brown offered his hand, "I'm sorry if I upset you."

Betty turned her back and did not accept Doctor Brown's hand.

"I'll see you out, Alan," James said as he waited for Doctor Brown to leave the room.

"Betty, your behavior is disappointing. It was very rude of you to speak to Doctor Brown in that manner."

Betty was left in the care of her mother as the men left to go the study where they continued their discussion of the future of Betty's baby.

Marie came to Betty's door all smiles as she presented the burgundy box with the gold lettering from Creeds.

"Here you are, Miss."

Betty's face was gradually returning to a more peaceful countenance but she was still shaking when Marie gave her the parcel.

She was temporarily distracted from the agony of the moment. "Thank you, Marie. Oh Mama, this is so nice," Betty said, in a calmer voice, but without her usual enthusiasm when a gift was offered.

"I ordered something for you to wear Sweetheart. I hope you like it," her mother told her, hoping to calm the waters.

A present, a parcel, a surprise, something new; it had been a long time since this had been a part of Betty's life.

Betty lifted the cover from the Creeds gift box and quickly peeled the tissue paper away from the garment inside. She caught her breath when she saw a French silk crepe, two- piece suit in a juniper green, a colour which Betty loved. The blouse featured a contrasting Georgette over-collar and cleverly cut sleeves with cuffs. The skirt had shirring on the front and gathering around the elastic waistband. A handsome ornament was clasped to the side of an all-around hip band on the blouse.

"Oh, Mama, I love it. Thank you, thank you." Betty gave her mother a hug and a kiss on the cheek.

"Betty, we'll have a seamstress make adjustments as you need them. In a day or two we can go to the store and you can look for other garments you like and have them tailored to fit you. Look in the bottom of the box, dear, there is another gift."

Betty took out the tissue paper and in the bottom of the box there was something else which she unwrapped then held up a strange garment. She looked shocked then burst out laughing.

"I'm not wearing this ugly thing, mother. You can take it back."

"Betty, it's a Gossard Maternity Corset. They are all the rage among pregnant women and they help support your back and stomach. It has lacing on the side which you can tighten and you won't even look pregnant."

Betty took the words in. She stared at her mother, at the gift.

"This is YOUR grandchild mother."

"Betty." Bea was taken off guard by Betty's statement. "*Yes, this is my grandchild,*" she thought. "*How can we give away our grandchild? Has James given this any thought? James loves children. Might he regret this decision?*" Bea was suddenly deep in thought.

Betty examined the maternity corset again briefly.

"Mama!"

"Sorry, Betty, I was thinking about something."

"Mama, I'm not wearing this thing. I'm not enduring the discomfort and constraint of being strapped into a corset. Take it back. And, do you know what? I want to look pregnant. I love the dress but I won't wear this." She threw the corset into the box and plunked on the lid.

Bea had never heard her daughter speak to her in that tone of voice and she was at a loss for words to respond to Betty.

"Whatever you think is best, dear. Why don't you get dressed in the new suit and come downstairs? I'll leave you alone now," she said in a low, almost whispered voice.

Bea kissed her daughter lightly on the forehead and left her to get dressed.

Betty sank into the soft chair in her room, her arms outstretched over the arms of the chair with her legs stretched straight out in front of her. She remained in that unladylike position for a long time pondering how she would get through the next few weeks before her baby was born. What new hoops would she have to jump through to convince her father that she was not giving her baby away?

What was she going to do? How could she find Clyde? Where could she go? Betty didn't have a plan and it disturbed her greatly. She really believed her father would give in and allow her to keep her baby when she came home. It was her expectation to live at home with her parents and her brother, James, until Clyde came back. How naïve she had been and she chided herself for her misunderstanding of her father.

In a few weeks she would be a mother.

"Please, Clyde, wherever you are, come for me and our baby."

Betty pulled herself upright and was engulfed by the soft cushions of the chair. In the silent luxury of her room she sat quietly staring into space.

14. A Spring Day in Rosedale
May 10, 1935

Marie has prepared a tasty lunch for me; a bowl of tomato soup and a ham sandwich. I often take a short nap in the afternoon, partly because there's nothing to do and the rest helps me to relax. Then, if the weather is favorable I go out for some exercise. I love walking and Mama says the fresh air is good for me. We've had a cold, rainy spring in Toronto and today the thermometer on the outside of the kitchen door was only up to sixty degrees. Even though it is overcast, I don't think it will rain.

Nap time; Ahh, it feels good to stretch. It's hard to rest but if I curl up on my right side I'm fairly comfortable.

I love my bedroom; my bed is so soft and I sink into the mattress and the bedclothes feel so cozy. It is entirely different from The Victor Home. Was I ever really there? It's like a bad dream. The room had faint memories of pale painted walls that had faded and cracked the colour dissipating into patches of dull yellow. Matron said we would have to do some papering in the spring and that would have been intolerable for me. These sheets are so soft and smell of lavender not like the ones at the Home that were worn thin and scratchy and smelled of bleach. Some even had holes that I'd catch my toes in. When I roll up in my satin comforter I feel so safe and the Home is far away…

What was that?

I was asleep … I was dreaming about the Victor Home and I thought Matron was knocking loudly on the door as though the world was coming to an end. It must have been a burst of wind banging the shutters.

I might as well get up. I'll push myself up and sit on the edge of the bed for a minute. I've got sharp pains. The baby moves around, poking and prodding and making me quite uncomfortable. I think it wants to get out of its cramped cocoon. No, no, not another stabbing pain. Now cramps. I'll support you in my hands. I'm glad I can talk to you, little one, as there's seldom anyone else with me. Remember that ridiculous Gossard Maternity Corset that Mama wanted me to wear? Do you think I should have kept it? Ha. Ha. It might ease my discomfort now. Please stop jabbing me. Settle down. I think you will be a star athlete and excel in the high jump. I did, you know. When you grow up I'll show you photos of all the things I did.

Let's go downstairs.

Okay, slowly, one step at a time. I'll grip the railing, my hand on my tummy helps. If I could see my feet it would be easier. The pain isn't as sharp now.

Why don't these dreadful cramps stop? I'm tired of them. They've been coming and going on for a couple of days. This morning I was full of energy and I felt on top of the world. I tidied my room, took the laundry down to Marie, put the silverware away in the mahogany chest, I had a wonderful warm bath and then arranged some books in Daddy's study. I wonder why I feel so awful.

Maybe if I have a little snack and after, go for a walk I'll feel better. I know there are some apples in a bowl in the kitchen. I love McIntosh apples. I'll have one of those. They're so juicy and crisp when they've just been picked. Daddy had them sent over from Elmer Lick's Family Orchard in Whitby. Daddy said to wash the apples before we eat them because Mr. Lick uses a spry to control the worms. Guess it works because this apple is perfect; shiny, red, crisp, juicy…it's running down my chin.

Now for "my constitutional" as Aunt Muriel would say. I wonder what she is doing today. Wish I could go for a walk with her and talk.

I'll wear my shawl and wrap it around me to keep us cozy and warm.

The air is refreshing on my face. It's cooler than I expected but not unpleasant. Let's walk. I'm glad Grandma Watson knitted the shawl in this lovely cobalt blue, a colour we both love. Grandma said she made it when I was in the Victor Home. She was thinking about me when I was there but I'm sad that I didn't know that. Why didn't she come to see me? Did she try to visit and Matron stopped her? So many questions and they may never be answered. Soon you'll be here with me, my baby, and we'll make a life together. I'm afraid though, because I don't know what Daddy and Doctor Brown may have decided to do. I won't let them take you away. If your Daddy would just come back everything would be perfect. Clyde, Clyde I need you so much. Your baby needs you.

Okay in there, settle down. You're drumming against me again. Ugh! Another cramp. I'll bend down and that may ease the pain. I hope it passes soon. It's similar to the pain you get when you have diarrhea or the flu. God that hurt. The pain is dreadful and makes it difficult to walk; it catches me and takes my breath away. I don't know if I can stand upright. I saw the patrol constable on his wonderful black horse and I hope he doesn't see me and come back. I'll walk faster if I can. It may be more of a waddle. Fast isn't in me. One…step…at…a…time. Deep breath in and out slowly…this helps when I have cramps from the flu. Nifty, there's a welcome sight, a park bench. Where are my cigarettes? My cigarettes? Are they in my coat pocket at home? In my purse? Here they are. I'm such a mess. Matches? Yes. I'm shaking so hard I can't light the darn thing. Is it lit? It's lit. A deep drag, inhale…exhale. My good old Players are helping. Baby settled down too. I feel alright now. I'm okay. I'm okay. A few more puffs.

It's so pretty here. The policeman is turning up the other street. Good, I don't want to chat with him today. I wonder if he grooms his own horse. I'd enjoy doing that. I love horses but Daddy says there's no place to keep one in Rosedale. I bet he could find a way. He can usually find a way to do almost anything as he did when Clyde and I told him I was pregnant. Within hours he had arranged for me to go somewhere to have my pregnancy ended, even though it's illegal. It was because of the possibility of losing my baby that I ran away. My thoughts are all over the place.

I love these streets with the curved walks and huge trees. Everything is becoming so green and luscious. The vibrant yellow forsythia in a garden on Crescent Road makes me feel so happy when I see it. I wonder if Daddy could have our gardener plant forsythia next year. I will bring my baby for walks with me in her push chair and my baby can enjoy the flowers and birds. It won't be long now until the baby is born, early in May I expect. Doctor Brown doesn't answer my questions. How will I know when it's my time? Are these labor pains I'm having? I read about false labor in a magazine. Is that what these pains are? Nurse Barclay at the Home talked about false pains too. Well, dears, the pain is real and there's nothing false about it. These cramps remind me of indigestion so I think I ate something that didn't agree with me, maybe the ham because the pain started shortly after lunch. Edna told me about the pains she had in the days before James Robert was born. Maybe I am going into labour.

I hope my baby is a girl.

I'm scared out of my wits. I'm scared about giving birth to my baby; Edna said it hurt like hell or worse and I don't know anything about having a baby. If only I knew more about what to expect. And Lucy said some of the nurses treat us as though we are trash because we aren't married. I'm scared because I don't know what I'll do without Clyde to help me and support me; I'm scared because I don't know what Daddy is going to do or if he'll let me live at home with the baby. Or will he try and take my baby away from me? I remember poor Lucy went to the hospital to have her baby and she never saw it again. They stole the baby at the hospital to give it to someone else. She didn't even know if she had a boy or a girl. I don't want to go to the Toronto General Hospital. Dr. Brown is at the Victoria Hospital so I'll ask if I can go there. But he wants to take my baby away too. Who's on my side? I haven't anyone to support me. I feel as if everyone is against me except Jimmy and he's on my side but he can't do anything for me.

Where is Clyde, damn it? Where are you Clyde? This is not fair at all. Clyde, if you were here I wouldn't feel so scared and lonely.

Clyde, you said you'd always love me and I love you but I haven't seen or heard from you for months and months. I'm exasperated with you. You left me in that horrible place, everyone did, but you are my baby's father and we planned this together. There's so much I don't understand. Now, you've made me cry again. Having your baby should be a happy time and instead I'm full of woe and frightened to death.

It hurts something awful. Maybe I've upset the baby. I wonder if the baby knows what I'm feeling and thinking? When I get angry the pains are worse. When I hear music the baby seems to settle down.

Daddy is in court and mother is at luncheon in the Royal York Hotel with some of her lady friends. I'm alone. I'm alone most of the time now because my friends don't invite me to their homes or the coffee shop anymore. I think their mothers have told them not to socialize with me. You'd think I had a dreaded disease that they could catch. There aren't many activities I can participate in. I can't go to the swimming pool or the ball diamond. Certainly I am not wanted at the dances or afternoon teas, nor do I want to be there. I'm lonesome. Last spring I was the fun-loving party girl. Now I'm the recluse. I still see Annie occasionally and she tells me about all of the things she's doing, ball practice, spring parties at Jarvis Collegiate and other things that she and her friends doing. We were always so close and I know we will be again. Today, Annie is at Varsity Arena with the girls of her Physical Training Class giving a demonstration of archery, basketball, tumbling and dancing. I ache to be there and see Annie. She told me about it but didn't suggest that I come to see her. The announcement was in *The Star* and I cut it out. The parents of the participants and the public are invited. Annie didn't invite me. I feel left out, even shunned. No one seems to realize how much I am hurting.

Sometimes Aunt Muriel comes to have afternoon tea with me or Fred drives me to Edgar Ave. to her home and that is always fun. Aunt Muriel used to take me to Simpsons for lunch or tea but now, we always have lunch at her house. She tries to cheer me up by telling me about all the mischief her boys get into. She has four boys between the ages of twenty-one and fourteen years of age and a daughter too, who is in nursing. The boys are always playing tricks on each other and their parents. Once, after everyone had gone to bed one of her sons, about twelve years old at the time, took the car out of the garage and drove it up and down Yonge Street. He got it back in the garage safely without his parents knowing about his escapade. Can you imagine? My brother Jimmy is fifteen and we have a good time together but one brother is enough. It would be fun to have a sister to talk to and go out with though.

I haven't gone to a concert or a movie for ages. I'd really enjoy seeing Jeannette MacDonald and Nelson Eddy in *Naughty Marietta* and its playing at *The Lowe,* Daddy's theatre so I can go in free. I may try to go to a matinee. Fred will take me.

Daddy and Mama don't take me with them when they go out. I guess they're ashamed and embarrassed to be with me. If I had a husband that they thought was suitable they would be overjoyed that I was with child. Why are girls who are in the family way always treated so badly? The women at St. Paul's are sure to spurn me so I can't attend. At the Victor Home I was accustomed to being ignored and put down but at church you'd think it would be different. Dr. Cody was always nice to me on Sundays but he hasn't come to see me since I've been home. I thought he was interested in me. Mama said he went to see Mrs. Broley when she came home from the hospital after she broke her leg. What's church and religion all about anyway?

I hear voices and giggling. It must be the junior girls coming home from school. I'll amble on down the path. I've had a good rest here on the bench.

I've been all through Rosedale. I went at a good pace for some of the time along Rosedale Road to Park Road, up Avondale Road and along the path to Cluny Drive and home. I see our house around the corner and just in time as the wind is getting up again and I feel rain in the air. Mama and Daddy don't approve of my walks because some of their friends might see me. They all know about the baby now so what does it matter? Daddy sees all of his clients at the law office now since the day I burst in on one of his meetings in the library. He was very embarrassed and so angry with me.

How does Fred anticipate the exact moment I arrive at the door?

"Thanks, Fred."

"May I take your wrap, Miss Betty?"

"Yes, Fred, I'm going into the library. Would you please have Marie make me some tea? I've got to sit down. I'm feeling a bit weak. Thanks so much."

Fred has made a fire to take off the chill that permeates the house. Daddy's desk calendar is at May tenth. We've hardly ever had a fire this late in the spring. I hope the weather warms up soon. I love the hot summer days but I guess I couldn't have walked on a hot day. It was great to get out in the fresh air.

Tonight, Daddy and Mama are going to a dinner party at Aunt Muriel and Uncle Mort's so I'll be enjoying my own company again. Annie will be basking in the success she had at Varsity Stadium and her parents will take her out for dinner. Wish I could be there. Annie is one of the best female athletes in her school. I'm so proud of her.

Ouch! These cramps are getting to me. Oh, oh, that was a bad one.

"Your tea, Miss. Your face is pale, Miss Betty. Are you feeling well?"

"I've got some stomach cramps, Marie. Probably something I ate."

"Call me if the pain worsens, Miss. It must be getting near you time. I'll be here all evening."

I'll try to snuggle into Mama's chair and relax for an hour and enjoy my tea. It's not easy to get my protruding stomach to snuggle. I love the dancing flames of the fire.

"Bye, Princess. Your mother and I are off to Uncle Mort and Aunt Muriel's for dinner. Muriel's birthday is on Monday and she and Mort and the children are going to Muskoka on Saturday, so the party is tonight. You know how your aunt loves a party. Is there something wrong? You're very pale."

"I'm fine Daddy. I'm tired from my long walk today. I saw some beautiful forsythia. Could we have some in our garden? They are a wonderful surprise of yellow amongst the green in the early spring"

"Sure, Princess."

"Betty, we are going now. Will you be alright alone?"

"Yes, Mama, I will. Marie and Fred are here. Give me a kiss before you go."

They've gone. I heard the door close and the car motor is running. I'll be glad when Fred gets back. It's reassuring to know he's here. Fred is always so kind and thoughtful. He never tells on me either. Ha, ha. When Clyde and I used to meet at the Paris Café, he knew about it but never said a word to Daddy or Mama. I wish I was there with Clyde right now.

I feel peculiar; sort of excited as though something is going to happen. Then I feel sad and lonely. My emotions are up and down like the roller coaster at Sunnyside Amusement Park.

Here's Mama's May issue of *Vogue Magazine*. I'll read it while I'm enjoying my tea. The cover is interesting. I love the artistic flair with each letter of VOGUE in a different colour in an almost child-like script. The outline drawing of a woman's eyes with one manicured hand applying eye make-up is a unique cover design. I'd love to do that type of work. Where would I go to study art I wonder? England? Paris? New York? What fun that would be.

I can't concentrate.

"Miss, will I serve your dinner in here?"

"Marie! I was deep I thought and didn't hear you come in."

"I didn't intend to startle you Miss Betty."

"I'm not at all hungry tonight. Some soup and a cookie or a piece of crumb cake if there is any left from yesterday, might be nice."

"It's eight o'clock, Miss. I'll make you a small supper and bring it in. You rest Miss."

The sharp pains are beginning again. It's as though they're coming in waves. One pain finishes and another begins. This is awful. I can't stand it much longer. My stomach is in spasms. The pain is excruciating.

Ahh. The pain's gone again. Ahh.

I'm afraid to move. What will I do?

"OUNCH..OUCH..MARIE, FRED"

Marie rushes to Betty's aid and holds her until the pain passes again.

"Miss, I think you are in labour. You have to get to the hospital."

"FRED, FRED," Marie calls loudly in a way she has been instructed to avoid.

Fred comes running into the room and takes in the scene; Marie is holding Betty who is writhing in pain in Marie's arms, a look of terror on her face, her eyes as big as saucers and her mouth wide open.

"I'll call Mr. Bicknell," Fred says without hesitation as he hurries over to the desk. Fred's hands are shaking as he picks up the cradle of the telephone, and with his index finger dials, RA 4666. After what seemed an eternity, Mr.Keachie answers the phone and Fred asks to speak to Mr. Bicknell.

Fred is talking to James on the phone to summon him home and get Betty to the hospital as quickly as possible, to give birth to her baby. James can choose whether to call an ambulance or go in the family car. Betty is in labor and in Marie's care.

My Great Aunt Muriel told me some of the circumstances of that night, the night Betty gave birth to her baby girl, whom she named "Dorothy."

Aunt Muriel and I sat in the old swing on the porch at the cottage in Port Sandfield on Lake Joseph, swaying back and forth, back and forth to the creak of the chains which held the swing and the rhythmic sound of the water lapping on the shore. Her memory for the details and dates of family events, births, marriages, baptisms and deaths was astounding. I loved her recitations of who attended functions and with whom and who stayed away and why. Her stories were interesting and new to me and through them, I learned about my family.

"You broke up a party at our house the night you were born, you know. We were having a party for my birthday which is on May 13th, Margaret."

"No, I didn't know, Aunt Muriel, tell me more about it, please," I said, moving closer, linking my arm through hers as we intertwined our fingers.

"We were having a party, we lived at 23 Edgar Avenue and your grandmother and grandfather came to the party but your mother remained at home. The phone rang and Mort didn't answer it at first but the ringing continued and when Mort answered, it was for your grandfather. I guess it was one of the help who called to say he thought your mother had gone into labor. Your grandmother and grandfather left immediately. I think Mort had someone drive them home so that they could get there as quickly as possible and it wasn't very far. You were born later that night. My brother, James, telephoned to tell us Betty had a little girl."[9]

15. The Singletons Search for a Child

A significant piece of my story is how my adoptive parents went about searching for a daughter which was quite an incredible undertaking for them in the 1930s living on a farm in rural Ontario. To create this episode which tells about their search for a child, I have woven together my adoptive mother's stories to me, together with the information in detailed letters and two documents which I found in a box in my mother's closet, after her death. As well, there were many hours of research. I marvel at the Singletons when I reflect on their steadfast journey over several years looking for just the right daughter.

"Mom, tell me how you got me."

I asked for that story over and over and my mother's recitation of facts was consistent. In my early years my mother and I squeezed into the rocking chair in the kitchen and I listened to the story while I was cradled and rocked. Sometimes we played with my dolls and my doll Brenda played the role of the baby going to a new home. At other times I would climb up on the stool at the kitchen table and sit on my knees so I could rock the stool back and forth as mother told me what she believed was appropriate for me to know about my adoption. As we talked I watched mother make the most wonderful tea biscuits in the universe. Tea biscuits were the medium for me to learn to read when I was four years of age. Mother taught me to sound out the words on the Baking Powder can and guests were invited to listen to me read.

I still love tea biscuits probably because of the pleasant association between the tea biscuits and those warm, loving times with my mother when she gave me just the tiniest glimpse of my lost birth family.

My mother knew much more than she ever revealed to me and my passion has been to find the missing information and to uncover the truth.

*

The Story
1934-1935

Without telling anyone except Florence's sister Lavenia, Stewart and Florence began planning for a daughter. This was a huge task for a couple living in a farm community, somewhat isolated, without the assistance of a solicitor and with few resources available to assist them in their search for a child. They had a telephone on a party line which meant that any calls they received could be enjoyed, discussed and commented upon by the entire community. Folks did "listen in." It was imperative to them that their search would be kept confidential.

They decided to find a "suitable" baby in a city three hundred dirt road, bumpy miles away and they kept the entire unfolding of the events confidential. I think it was amazing.

Florence had a cousin, Evelyn Braithwaite, who had been a nurse in Toronto General Hospital in Toronto and they asked her to help them. They couldn't have asked a better person. As a nurse, Evelyn came into contact with single women who were having babies "out of wedlock," and because of her position in the hospital she was able to obtain information about which infants were available for adoption. What I have learned from her letters is that it appears that deeply personal information was easily obtained. Evelyn left no stone unturned and contacted the organizations and homes in Toronto where babies were placed for adoption. Letters to my parents tell of Evelyn's visits to The Infants' home, The Protestant Girls' Home, meeting with a Miss Yeigh of the Children's Aid Society and visiting private homes where babies were boarded out. Evelyn also alerted doctors in the hospital that she was looking for a little girl available for adoption. It must have consumed a great deal of her time as her letters describe how she followed up on suggestions from doctors, whom she named. She visited many of the residences, both private and public to make her personal assessment of a baby. In her letters Evelyn described numerous children whom she visited over a period of months from the spring of 1934 until the fall of 1935. From Evelyn's correspondence I learned Florence had the responsibility of making the decision about the adoption.

I quote from a letter dated February 19, 1935.

"Now, Flo! As Stewart says, 'this is entirely your business and you are the only one who can make the decision.' "

The criteria for a "suitable" child astounded me as I read page after yellowed page of detailed, handwritten descriptions of baby girls in Toronto who were in Evelyn's words, "out for adoption." I quote from letters dated only from February 19th 1935 to April 14th 1935 describing some of the babies or their mothers.

"There was quite a favourable discussion amongst the Doctors at Sick Children's Hospital. All felt it was a perfect specimen."

"She (the mother) seems to come from a good family. They attend a United Church where Rev. Richard Roberts, the Moderator is pastor."

"It was sent over to the hospital for a blood test and Dr. Morgan saw it and if he had known anyone who wanted a baby he would have grabbed it then and there. Florence, you should see this one."

"The mother is not a nurse but in this hospital, they were just trained women apparently."

Later in the same letter she wrote, "Good news, Miss Yeigh called me re the baby and she says the mother is a graduate nurse after all, so you might want to consider it."

"Remember they don't expect you to take out final papers for two years and if you in that time decide you don't want to keep it you don't have to."

Babies with varied racial and religious backgrounds were discussed and their adoption was not considered further. The letters detailed criteria; the baby was too old and would not be a good companion for the couple's son Wallace, the mother wasn't educated, the baby had a poor background, the father was from another race, the mother was in ill health, the child seemed too quiet or the father was unknown. [10]

It is possible that Florence became discouraged because in March, 1935 Evelyn wrote to say,

"Dear Florence,

I have no definite news for you and I wanted to let you know that I have not forgotten you and also that I had received your two letters. You know Flo; more things are wrought by prayer than this world dreams of so let's pray, eh? That is a surer way to be guided to the right one if you are to have one.

Lovingly,

Evelyn"

Time seemed long to Florence that spring as she waited, but there were many things to occupy her time on the farm. She had a wringer washing machine with a hand crank and she washed the winter clothes, the sheets, pillow cases and other laundry and hung them outside on the clothesline. When the sheets were dry she brought them into the house, held them to her face and breathed in the clean, fresh smell. Stewart's long woolen underwear was flapping in the breeze for the last time this season and Wallace's mitts and woolen winter clothing were airing outside on the clothesline.

A quilt was in progress on the quilting frame in the parlor and once a month the women from the community gathered to add more tiny stitches to the double wedding ring quilt pattern. It was a social time for the farm women as they stitched their lives and stories into the exquisite bed cover.

As the women worked, their animated conversations were about the new spring catalogue from Eaton's, the young teacher in the one room school and how their children were growing. They were all delighted that the sap was running profusely so there would be lots of sweet, tasty maple syrup this year. Florence would make maple sugar for her family's porridge.

The joke of that spring was that Rev. Troup the minister in the United Church had a new black woolen suit and the trousers had a zipper.

"Have you ever heard the like?" asked Mrs. Jones?"

The women broke up with laughter. Mrs. Wood blushed and put her hand over her mouth.

"Upon my word," giggled Mrs. Myers.

"I'm going to get trousers with a zipper for Bill", announced Mrs. Lewis, with a bit of mischief in her voice.

"I don't think Stewart would wear them," Florence mused.

In late afternoon the women would disperse to their separate lives often not seeing each other again until their next quilting bee, except at church. Mrs. LaForty, who was the organist in the church had a car and drove the women home. Their husbands would usually bring them, some in a horse and buggy, but when it was time for the women to go home the men were busy with their chores.

One morning in late May, as the Singletons were having their usual breakfast of porridge, maple syrup, chunks of fresh cheese and bread browned on a wire frame toaster on top of the wood stove, Stewart asked Wallace if he would like a little sister. Stewart smiled to himself as Wallace nodded his head up and down indicating "yes", but he didn't say a word. Just as they were finishing breakfast, the phone rang, one long and two shorts. Florence let it ring once again before she walked over to answer it just to make sure it was their ring. Yes, one long and two shorts.

She pulled the receiver which was attached by a cord, up out of the hook and put it to her ear.

"Click"

"Click"

"Click" she heard, along with the definite sound of a radio in the background and thought it was the Garretts as they listened to their radio most of the day.

Yes, there were others on the line listening in.

"Hello", Florence said speaking into the mouthpiece that jutted out from the front of the oak phone box on the wall. The phone had been installed so high on the wall she had to stand on her tip toes to reach it.

"Hello, Florence, it's your cousin."

Florence recognized the voice as Evelyn's and sucked in her breath as her heart started to pound. She hoped Evelyn wouldn't say anything that would give away her secret.

"Evelyn", Florence cautioned, "we're not alone on the line."

"Florence, you know that parcel you ordered? Well, it has arrived."

Florence nearly fainted when she heard the news.

"Would you and Stewart be able to come and see it?"

Florence was completely taken off guard and could only stammer as she tried to take in the meaning of the message. She heard several clicks on the phone and knew someone had hung up to go and spread the news that the Singletons had a parcel of some kind being held by a cousin, somewhere. There were probably others still listening in on the party line. She had to be very guarded in what she said and she was grateful that Evelyn had worded the message so carefully.

The less said the better, she thought.

"I'll talk it over with Stewart and call you back tomorrow. Goodbye for now."

She ended the conversation abruptly before either she or Evelyn said something that would give away what they were doing. Florence placed the receiver back in the hook, slowly and quietly, with a far-away look in her eyes. *Was she finally to have a little girl? Were her prayers about to be answered?*

She told Stewart what Evelyn had said and they pondered the meaning of her message. Stewart said he thought Evelyn was saying she had found a suitable baby, just the right one and that's why Evelyn said, "The parcel has arrived". She seemed sure about this one. Her message also had a sense of urgency and she wanted them to come and see the child. There was only one other baby that Evelyn had urged them to visit but they didn't go. Why did she make a telephone call this time, instead of sending a letter? Yes, this was different.

In Toronto, Evelyn hung up the phone, turned to her husband Joe and said,

"Florence and Stewart should have this baby",

"Let them make their own decision," Joe said as he hitched up his trousers and walked over to the record cabinet to put a Gilbert and Sullivan record on the turntable.

In Soperton, Florence and Stewart could not concentrate on the daily chores. The cows had been milked and sent to the pasture but the stables still needed to be cleaned and the horses watered and taken outside to the barnyard. Stewart, his father Chalmers and Wallace all went to the barn and left Florence alone with her anxiety and silent planning. Ring, their large, black and white collie dog was still carrying his shaggy winter coat. He trotted beside Wallace then stopped abruptly and sat down. The men chatted about the spring work as they walked toward the barn and Wallace skipped along behind them trying to keep up. Ring remained still thumping his tail on the ground. His eyes darted from side to side, and then he stood up and trotted back to the house. Florence saw him coming and greeted him with pats and a hug. She was glad of his company and Ring relished the leftover porridge Florence ladled into his dish.

Thoughts tumbled through Florence's head. She wanted to know more about what Evelyn told her in her call. How would she make contact privately? Who would she confide in? It might be safe to call on the party line but there was always the chance someone on the same line would want to make a call and overhear her. She thought of going to her sister in North Augusta and calling from there but she also had a party line.

By the time Stewart came in from the barn Florence had a plan and she launched into it with excited anticipation before he had time to wash up for lunch.

"Stewart, do you remember the time you took me to the Revere Hotel in Brockville for tea? Well, didn't they have a public telephone in the lobby? I think you had to pay five cents which you put in a slot and then I probably give central Evelyn's number. The hotel manager can tell us how to do it. Couldn't we drive to Brockville tomorrow after church and use that telephone to call Evelyn?"

"What a good idea Florence. Yes, I guess so, we can do that. Father, can Wallace stay here with you or would you like to come for the drive?"

Chalmers was seventy eight now, getting frail and didn't "take to the city" so he declined the offer of a drive and agreed to look after his grandson. That way, Florence and Stewart could give their full attention to calling Evelyn and making any necessary plans.

Florence was very excited and hummed and sang for the rest of the day, as she went about her work.

Sunday morning Florence made a lunch for her father-in-law and Wallace and put it in the pantry. Egg sandwiches, cheese and pickles with pie for dessert would be just fine. Mr. Singleton could make himself a cup of tea. They dressed for church with extra care so they could leave for Brockville as soon as the service was over. Stewart suggested that he and his wife have lunch at the hotel as a treat.

The little black stone church stood in a field next to their farm. Chalmers had donated a parcel of land for the church and was very proud of how it had all turned out. The grain in the light maple pews was exquisite. The pews curved gracefully in three rows from the altar to the back of the church. The hanging gas lanterns hissed and gave a mysterious glow during the evening service.

In the summer and fall the women held suppers to raise money so they could purchase a pump organ. Most of the people in the community came after their evening chores; fathers, mothers, grandparents and children all sat at long tables created with planks set on saw horses outside on the grass. Just inside the fence at the side of the property Chalmers had suggested they build a shed as a shelter from the sun or the rain for the horses and buggies. On Sunday morning the slow strains of the last hymn signaled to the horses that they would soon be trotting home and they pulled at the reins, nodding their heads up and down as if keeping time with the music. Once, when it had rained during a supper, they moved the horses out of the shed and had the supper under the shelter of the shed roof.

Only a few people in the community had cars. The others either walked or came in a horse and buggy. The Singletons always walked over to the church and sat proudly in the second row from the front. They had their own leather bound hymn books. Florence's book had only the words of the hymns but and Stewart's had the music too. He loved music and sang with a strong true bass voice. Before he was married he played a coronet in a band in Newborough. Chalmers had a good voice too and he and his son lead the singing of the hymns from their place in the pew. Mrs. LaForty pumped and played the lovely organ with great skill. Once a mouse that had set up housekeeping in the organ jumped out when the first note sounded and everyone heard a muffled scream. Music filled the little church and the harder and faster the organist pumped the louder the music became. It was wonderful. On this day, Florence couldn't concentrate on the service and had trouble finding the psalm in her book. She just wanted it to be over but Rev. Troup droned on, longer than usual. When the strains of the last hymn faded and the benediction was pronounced, Florence left the church more quickly than usual mumbling something to her women friends about going for a drive with Stewart.

Later as they drove to Brockville, Stewart asked Florence what she had thought of the church service but she couldn't remember a single thing.

Stewart parked the car in front of the Revere Hotel on King Street, stepped out and opened the door for his wife. They entered the hotel and went directly to the dining room for lunch. A waitress greeted them and brought typed menus with several choices. Florence loved jellied chicken and it was on the menu. She would have that with some soup and tea later. Ice cream for dessert would be nice. Stewart chose soup, a hot beef sandwich and tea. He would have apple pie for dessert if it was on the dessert menu. They settled in to their special time together and enjoyed each other and the ambiance of the restaurant with white linen tablecloths, comfortable soft chairs and their unknown dining companions. The sun was streaming in through the elegantly dressed windows.

The waitress served their lunch and after they sampled a few appetizing bites they talked about what to say to Evelyn. Other people in the lobby might overhear Florence when she called Evelyn on the phone, so words needed to be chosen carefully. They leaned in toward each other to keep their conversation private.

"Stewart, maybe I'll just ask about the parcel and where it is. Evelyn will be able to talk freely on her end because she has a two-party line. It doesn't matter if someone overhears the conversation in Toronto."

"I'm sure that would be alright Florence. Find out when Evelyn wants us to come to Toronto. A Saturday and Sunday would be the best because of the chores. I'll ask Willy Howard if he can come and help father with the milking and feeding the cattle and horses. The rest can wait until I get home. I guess we'll be able to stay with Joe and Evelyn but could you ask about that?"

"Yes, I will and I'm sure that is what she intends. It's such a long way to Toronto Stewart. Will the car be alright? What if we have car trouble or run out of gas. Are there places to buy gas on Highway Two? Will the stations be open on a Sunday?"

"I think the car is o.k. for the journey, but getting gas to come home could be a problem. I'll fill the tank when we get to Toronto. I'll also fill the gas can and we can take it in the car with us.

I think those are the most important questions for now and we'll see what else Evelyn has to say when I call. I'm nervous Stewart."

"You'll do just fine, Florence."

They continued eating their lunch, each with their individual thoughts. Florence was thinking about what she was going to say to Evelyn and Stewart was mulling over in his mind all of the possibilities for trouble with their old Ford car.

The waitress came to clear the table and take their dessert order. Florence was delighted to hear there was Neopolitan ice cream and Stewart ordered the apple pie with a little ice cream on top. They savored their desserts chatting quietly together.

The waitress brought the check and Stewart looked it over thinking it was a little expensive, but they had both enjoyed themselves and he was pleased to treat his wife. On the way out of the dining room Stewart went to the man at the cash register and paid his bill of $2.40, then they walked into the lobby and over to the pay phone. The phone looked much like the one in their kitchen except it was black metal instead of oak and it had three slots at the top for coins. There was an opening at the bottom for the coins to return if you made a mistake or couldn't reach your party. Florence opened her purse and took out the paper that had Evelyn's phone number in Toronto, Hudson-80810. Carefully she removed the receiver from the hook and put it to her ear. Stewart dropped a nickel into the slot above the phone.

Florence heard Central's voice, "Hello, this is Central, what number do you want?"

"I want to call Toronto, Hudson -80810," said Florence.

"Just a minute please."

Florence heard the phone ringing short little rings, one, two, three and four. Oh, she hoped Evelyn was there.

"Hello", Florence knew Evelyn's voice.

"Please deposit five cents", Central instructed in her nasal, monotone voice. Stewart was ready with another coin and when Florence nodded to him, he dropped it into the slot. Stewart saw a chair close to the phone and went to sit there, so he could be at his wife's side in an instant if she needed to talk to him.

Florence continued with her conversation.

"Hello Evelyn, this is Florence. Stewart and I came to Brockville for lunch and I'm calling from the Revere hotel."

"Hello Florence. I thought you might call today. I went to church but hurried home in case you called. We've just finished eating lunch here."

"Evelyn, this is long distance so I'll get on with why I called. What about the parcel? We want to know more about it."

Evelyn loved to talk and the words tumbled out as she told Florence all about the baby she had found. Evelyn was very excited.

"Florence, I've made many connections in the last few months and I heard about a baby about to arrive in a very good family in Toronto. A friend of the family in question called me to let me know of the birth. He still isn't sure if the baby will be put up for adoption as the mother and grandmother want to keep it and also the baby has had an operation for a condition in her stomach."

"Evelyn, please tell me about the operation. Is it serious?"

"It was at the time, Florence, but she is getting along well now. It's called pyloric stenosis and I'll write to you about it but she may always be frail, Florence. I like this baby Flo because her family is of very good stock."

"Have you seen the baby Evelyn?"

"Yes, I called Miss Yeigh at the Children's Aid Society and asked for her assistance to make an appointment to see her. Because of her influence I knew she would be able to get some information, but I didn't know then that the baby was ill. When Miss Yeigh made enquiries she learned that the baby was in Sick Children's Hospital. I went to the hospital Flo, and the nurses let me see her. She's very tiny and pale but I think you and Stewart should come and see her. I know the nurses will let me in again and then if you are interested and the family do decide to let her be adopted you can be first in line. Baby girls are hard to find and Wallace is getting older and if you wait much longer a baby won't be any company for him."

Evelyn spoke quickly and was breathless when she finished.

Florence realized that although Evelyn was aware of the frailty of the baby who might require extra care, that she was totally besotted with the family and the baby's history. It was so much information to take in all at once.

"Evelyn, I want to talk this over with Stewart. I don't know what to think. I'm afraid to take a baby who is sick. I'm not a nurse like you, and I don't know anything about whatever it is the baby had the operation for. I'll write to you Evelyn."

"Don't delay too long Florence. If you decide to come to Toronto, bring Wallace with you. He should have a say in whether he likes the baby. If you take her, it's important that Wallace is involved for later on in life. Of course you can stay with us."

"Thanks, Evelyn. I'll write in a day or so. Goodbye for now"

"Goodbye, Florence. Joe says, 'Hello.' "

Florence slowly hung up the phone. Evelyn's voice reverberated in her head as she tried to understand the contradictions of the circumstances. What Florence understood was that a baby might be available for adoption, but she is ill. Evelyn was very enthusiastic about the background of the baby and doesn't seem too concerned about the infant's illness.

I'm worried about this, thought Florence.

"Stewart, I'll tell you what Evelyn told me on the way home in the car. We should get on the road and get home so your father can have a rest. He's been with Wallace for a few hours now."

"Father will be alright Florence. I'd like to go for a little drive around town and then drive to the river and sit there for a little while. Florence, you can tell me what Evelyn said. Would you like to do that?"

"If you think your father won't mind us being away so long, I would enjoy that Stewart."

They settled into the car and Florence was pleased when Stewart turned up Court House Ave. where the boulevard was lined with buildings in the ornate architecture of the 1800"s. At the entrance to the boulevard they passed the impressive granite War Memorial with an advancing soldier struck in bronze standing on the top, and then marveled at the architecture of Comstock Building, The Flint Block and others. The ornate white marble, Italian style fountain was spectacular. They had seen it at night when it was awash with lights shining on the ribbons of water cascading down from basin to basin and finally swirling in the bottom shell-like catchment. It was magical. They reached the top of the street and Florence remarked on Wall St. United Church which she saw on her right.

"I'd like to attend church there sometime."

"Let's do that, Florence. I'd love to hear the organ."

Stewart turned the car left and proceeded down the west side of the boulevard. The Fulford Block was impressive, built in sturdy red brick with ornate detail around the windows and doors. The wide boulevard opened to market square and went down the hill to the river providing a beautiful vista of the city. The St. Lawrence River sparkled in the sunshine with white caps forming on the choppy waves. Soon two familiar Steamers, the *SS Kingston* and the *SS Toronto* would be seen on the river carrying passengers on cruises up and down the river from Kingston to Quebec City.

"Stewart, it would really be nice to take your father and Wallace on a little excursion on the *Island Wanderer* this summer. It cruises around all the Islands in the Brockville area. It may even go as far as Gananoque, I'm not sure. I love an afternoon on the water. I could pack a picnic lunch and it would be pleasant."

"Father and Wallace would enjoy that I'm sure. Let's plan that on a Sunday sometime this summer Florence."

Stewart drove slowly down the hill to the river and they parked close to the water on Block Island. They sat silently for a few minutes just enjoying the view. The water pounded the breakers and splashed up on shore close to the car, the sea gulls swooped along the rocks looking for a morsel that might be thrown out of a car window and the sun was so bright on the water that Florence shielded her eyes with her hand. She was a little nervous so close to the water without any railings to protect them.

They sat back and in silence enjoyed the unfamiliar smells and sounds of the river and the rare feeling of not having to do anything at all.

Florence broke the silence to tell Stewart everything she could remember about the phone call to Evelyn. Words spilled out as she described how Evelyn found this baby, the baby's illness and the pressure to make a decision even though there was uncertainty about being able to adopt the child.

"Stewart, Evelyn wants us to come to Toronto to see the baby in the hospital. She thinks that that the nurses will let us see the baby because she has been there previously. It's such a long trip. And, she wants us to bring Wallace so he can be included in choosing his sister. What should we do Stewart?"

Stewart pulled on his bushy eyebrow as he thought about all that Florence had told him. *He hadn't planned on a trip to Toronto. It would be costly, it was a long drive and the car could break down. He would have to find someone to do the chores and they would be away at least three days.*

"It's a big decision Florence. We need to think about it and discuss it some more."

"Evelyn said the baby is from a very good family. There aren't as many baby girls for adoption and she is urging us to take this one.

She is also concerned that Wallace will be too old to be a companion for his sister if we wait much longer."

"We should go home now Florence. Father will be anxious if we are away too long."

Stewart, still deep in his own thoughts, turned the key and the car sputtered before the engine turned over. He released the clutch and as they jerked forward he steered the car up the hill toward the road home.

The drive to Soperton was interspersed with sporadic conversation as each shared a new thought about whether or not they could go to Toronto and if this baby was really one they should consider.

As they turned into the long laneway of their farm, Wallace appeared and ran toward them with Ring following close on his heels. Stewart stopped the car and Wallace opened the back door and climbed in for the ride to the house.

"Wallace did you and Grandpa have fun together?"

"We had pie and Grandpa took me for a walk to the woods. We saw some white snakes. They were ugly and I wanted to kill them but Grandpa wouldn't let me. Can I have some candy?"

The car came to a stop beside the house and Wallace jumped out without waiting for an answer regarding the candy and ran off toward the barn with Ring in pursuit.

Chalmers came out of the house to greet them and they walked to the chairs on the verandah to enjoy the peaceful day a little longer, until Stewart would have to go and get the cows from the pasture and bring them to the barn for milking. Chalmers sat in the old rocking chair and began to rock back and forth as Stewart and Florence shared the events of their day with him, their lunch in the hotel, the phone call to Evelyn, what they had learned about the baby and their concerns about the trip to Toronto. He listened intently to their story and their concerns. There was a pause in the conversation and Chalmers opened his mouth as if to speak, and then rocked a few more times.

"Stewart and Florence, I have some money, and if you decide you want to make this trip, even if it's just to see this child so you can decide whether or not she is suitable for you and Wallace, I can give you whatever sum you need. It is not a loan Stewart. I want you and Florence to have it as a gift. I've given your brother Chalmers and your sister Blanche a lot of money to go to University. I know you went to Guelph Agricultural College, but the cost didn't equal the amount of sending your brother and sister to Queens University. Let me know what you decide."

Chalmers stopped rocking, arose from his chair, stood in front of Stewart and gazed at him. He was very fond of this son who had given up an academic life to stay at home, work the farm and provide a home for he and his wife Mary Ann. Chalmers missed Mary Ann's company since her death two years ago. He was very glad he lived with his son and family.

"That's very kind, Father. Florence and I will discuss it further. Certainly your offer will make the decision easier. We are grateful to you."

The couple began an animated conversation as soon as Chalmers was out of site. With some financial assistance, Stewart was confident that they could make the trip. The cost of driving to Toronto and any unforeseen circumstances such as car trouble or eating in a restaurant could be covered.

"Florence, could you write to Evelyn tonight to ask her when we should come and make some plans for our visit?"

Florence was ecstatic and went into the house to begin preparing the supper. She had a new fondness for her father-in-law who wasn't always easy to please.

That night, after Wallace was in bed, Chalmers was engrossed in the Bible and Stewart was sitting beside the wood stove, reading

The Chemistry of the Soil, in his loud whisper, Florence pulled her writing paper out of the sideboard drawer, opened the ink bottle and pushed a new nib into the handle of her pen.

"Dear Evelyn," she wrote as she imagined herself with a little girl to dress in pretty clothes, to keep her company when the men were in the fields all day, a child to play with and to teach. She would show her how to knit, how to embroider tea towels and pillow cases. They would bake wonderful cakes, cookies and bread together. She would be so proud of her daughter and at their quilting bees, she would tell the women about all of her daughter's talents. Sometimes she felt left out when Mrs. White and Mrs. LaForty talked about their daughters.

Her reverie was broken by Stewart's voice.

"It's time for bed. Father, have you finished your reading? Florence, how is your letter coming along?"

Stewart waited a moment for his father and Florence to put away their work, and then reached for the lamp to lead the way up the dark stairs. The light faded behind them as they climbed to the top of the stairs. Mary Ann's needle work was proudly displayed in a frame centered over the top step. They each read it silently as they did every night.

"Christ is the head of this house

The quiet listener to every conversation

The unseen guest at every meal"

"Good night father."

"Have a good rest, Mr. Singleton"

"Good night."

Stewart and Florence went into their bedroom, undressed, put on their night attire and knelt beside their bed. They said their silent prayers of thanks for all they had been given that day. When Florence was snuggled under the covers, Stewart blew out the lamp and sank into bed beside his wife. He felt a new contentment and happiness.

16. Obstacles & Earthquakes

Slowly, I moved the paint brush along the last six inches of the baseboard in my study, drawing the chipmunk colour in a smooth, flowing line. One wall and the trim in the same hue blended well with the theme of the wallpaper, Montmartre, Paris. In the background is Bateau Lavoir, the name given to a strange conglomeration of studios where at the beginning of 20th century a group of outstanding writers and artists including Picasso lived. Now, I reasoned to myself, as I sat in *my* Lavoir I could feel the energy of previous authors and artists, peering out at me from those buildings. I could "kick some ass and write", to quote Natalie Goldberg in *Old Friends From Far Away.*

Carefully, holding a cloth under the paintbrush, I carried it to the kitchen sink to do the final cleanup. The decorating in my small fourth floor condominium apartment was finally finished to my satisfaction; the walls in the living room the rich red brick of a Turkish Market, the halls in the yellow-brown of Challah and the dining room a warm and inviting deep beige. I began cleaning the brush under the tap but the sound I heard was more of a cascade and downpour than just the tap running. The sound of boiling water coming from the back of the apartment caused me to drop the paintbrush and hurry to the laundry area to investigate. To my horror I was splashing through water flowing from some unknown source.

A frantic, incoherent call to the superintendent brought him swiftly to my door. He looked in disbelief at my disaster zone with the accompanying background sounds: water boiling, seemingly in the laundry room, gushing from under the baseboards onto the floors, splashing down the kitchen walls, dripping from a light fixture, and seeping under the maple floor boards, over the tiles in the hall and closets, flooding the small laundry room and then finding its way to the carpeted apartment corridor. I saw the superintendent open his mouth as if to say something but he hurried off, speechless, to locate the source of the water. Later, I learned that on the seventh floor a water tank overheated to boiling point, ruptured, destroyed that apartment and caused extensive damage to all of the apartments below.

I regretted having downsized the linen closet as my four bath towels were soon soaked. Water flowed for an hour and a half into my freshly decorated apartment.

Walls and floors had to be removed that day to alleviate the growth of mould. Drying machines blasted hot air into the interior framing and insulation in the walls and under the hard wood floor and dehumidifiers sucked the moisture and life out of the air.

It was impossible to live in the apartment and when an invitation came from friends I accepted it and left the city. One day I came home unexpectedly and was sitting at my computer when the apartment door opened and a workman walked in, glanced at me, muttered something and went to my bathroom. He left without saying anything, closed and locked my door. He had a key and goodness knows how many workmen were using my home for bathroom relief! A month passed before the work was completed and I was settled again and ready to resume my writing.

The devastation in my apartment was just one more obstacle I had to overcome since I began the search for my biological family and more recently began writing a memoir detailing the journey. But, I am a Taurean, a six on the Enneagram personality indicator and highly motivated to write my story, so, I took a deep breath, poured a glass of red wine, pushed some of the clutter from my desk which I had hastily piled there to keep dry, carefully lifted the plaster dust covered sheet from my computer and began to write.

It seems important to talk about the deterrents to my research and writing as this is part of life, meeting the challenges we face and finding ways of overcoming them and moving on. It isn't easy and it is often discouraging but I want to encourage others not to give up when set-backs occur. For many years I taught young children living with a variety of language learning and behavioral difficulties. When one method didn't seem to fit the needs of a child, I would say to myself or the child, *try another way.* I have repeated this refrain to myself countless times and acted upon it with success.

I also want to talk about the obstacles unwed mothers faced and the stigma attached to being an adopted person, no matter how loving the adoptive parents were. Parents are not always there to protect their children from the stinging arrows of derision from the uninformed.

While doing research for my book, *The History and Genealogy of the Bicknell Family*, the journey took me through hundreds of church records, on microfilm and microfiche dating between 1600 and 1800. I researched marriage, birth and death records, all of which revealed similar sentiments; mothers who gave birth out of wedlock were scorned and their children were referred to with very derogatory names such as *bastard child*, *illegitimate* and *ilegit.* Their children were refused baptism. If death occurred during child birth the mothers were buried outside church cemetery walls.

In 2006, in Ottawa, I had personal knowledge of a child who was refused baptism in the Roman Catholic Church because the mother was not married. Where was being God-like in that? I'm sure God wept.

Some of my experiences which were directly related to my adoption caused me pain and anxiety. When I was growing up, I was referred to as "illegitimate" and introduced as "Stewart Singleton's adopted daughter" numerous times. This was hurtful because being thought of as an adopted daughter didn't give me any identity, the indication being that I wasn't a Singleton. I didn't know my birth mother's name so I was an enigma. To have been introduced as Stewart Singleton's daughter would have taken on a whole different set of feelings. I was proud to be his daughter, proud of my name.

In the summer of 1955, I registered for an Ontario Ministry of Education course in Toronto. A list of possible boarding houses was provided and I selected one. When I arrived at the address, there were two other women in the boarding house. At the end of the first week the landlady said she was going to a wedding near my home town and in our conversation we discovered that we had some common acquaintances.

The landlady came back to Toronto late Sunday night and summoned me to the living room, where to my astonishment she addressed me with what felt like contempt. Her eyes pierced through me as she spit out her words.

"You can pack your bags and leave right now."

"Why?" I asked, totally bewildered. "What have I done?"

"Get out! The landlady said. "Because, at least I know who my parents are. While I was at the wedding I learned all about you."

I was baffled by her accusatory words and unable to comprehend the meaning of what she was saying. I skipped school once but surely that wasn't grounds for being evicted.

It took some time for that to sink in. By this time the other two women had come downstairs to hear what the commotion was. I still didn't understand why I was being evicted and the other boarders had to explain it to me! We talked together and then told our landlady that we would all be leaving, but not until morning. Our landlady was reported to the housing registry and she was immediately taken off the list of homes for students, but there was no other reprimand. Human Rights violations were not recognized or recorded at that time. I'm sure she was spreading her bigotry the next semester.

As recently as 2006 I experienced a similar incident of thoughtless, stinging words. My daughter Christine and I sat in the hospital talking gently and lovingly to our ninety-eight year old cousin with whom we were very close and who had a special place in our hearts and life. She was in a deep coma after a massive stroke, but I know she was still able to hear our words and sense our presence. We were holding our cousin's hands and speaking quietly to her, telling her how much she was loved. She squeezed Christine's hand in response to her words of comfort. A woman who had attached herself to this relative came into the hospital room and in an angry, authoritative tone, demanded that we leave.

"I'm her cousin and the hospital called me and asked me to come," I said through my anguish.

She looked at me with what I can only describe as disdain and said,

"You are not really her cousin."

Her words cut into my heart, the ultimate insult and in the presence of a dying woman who had been close to me all of my life; she had been my first visitor after I came to live with the Singletons.

It's difficult to believe that some still have archaic beliefs and attitudes about adoption and people who are adopted.

Below is a quote from Wikipedia which further explains my point.

"The language of adoption is changing and evolving, and it has become a controversial issue tied closely to adoption reform efforts. The controversy arises over the use of terms which, while designed to be more appealing or less offensive to some persons affected by adoption, may simultaneously cause offense or insult to others. This controversy illustrates the problematic nature of adoption, as well as the fact that coining new words and phrases to describe ancient social practices does not alter the feelings and experiences of those affected by them." (Taken from Wikipedia, *The Language of Adoption*, paragraph 129)

Perhaps I'm "home free," as far as obstacles are concerned.

I'm looking forward to doing my first reading from my book at a meeting of my writing group, *Ottawa Independent Writers*, at the Library and Archives. I've selected the piece and read it into the mirror, to my blackberry, to the birds flying by my balcony and to two friends. What I decided upon was a scene from the chapter, *Three Forty One Jarvis Street,* the Victor Home for Girls, in Toronto where my mother fled to avoid an abortion. My reading describes my mother trying to peel potatoes for the first time in her life and her feelings and reflections as she works.

My preparation has been worthwhile and I'm ready to do the reading.

In the afternoon, my house guest and I decided to go shopping for a new cell phone for her. We were in the Bell Mobility store at Carlingwood Shopping Plaza when the floor and walls began to shake and move. There was a loud crashing sound and I thought a truck had hit the side of the building.

"I'm out of here," I yelled above the loud rumbling noise and confusion as I fled from the store with dozens of others.

The news article below appeared in the *Ottawa Sun;*

"*Ottawa Sun,*

Laura Czekaj & Tony Spears

June 24, 2010

A moderate earthquake of a 5.0 magnitude rocked Ottawa and surrounding area on Wednesday afternoon, overwhelming emergency services and sending thousands of panicked people into downtown streets.

'It undermines your faith in all that is solid,' said a rattled Douglas Baum who fled the courthouse when the ground began to move. The rumbling and shaking began at 1:41 p.m. and radiated out from an epicenter near Val-des-Bois, QC, about 56 km northeast of Ottawa. The effects rippled outwards across Quebec, Ontario, and the eastern U.S. with reports streaming in from as far away as Boone, Iowa, more than 1,500 km away, according to the U.S. Geological Survey."

Soon after arriving home and turning on my computer I received an e-mail from my writing group saying the Library and Archives was closed, due to the earthquake. My reading had to wait.

Whether or not there are more obstacles and earthquakes in my life and in spite of the ones I've encountered while searching for my mother, the wonderful journey of finding my family and writing about the experience is accomplished.

17. The Apple Shed

My adoptive parents, Stewart and Florence Singleton made the decision to try fruit farming when I was two and a half years old and before my adoption became legal. In the fall of 1937 we moved from Soperton to a farm east of Brockville on the St. Lawrence River. There was a flourishing orchard of mature apple trees with several varieties, McIntosh, Russet, Talmon Sweet and a few crab apple trees. In later years, mother told me how excited she was about the move to Brockville and the distinctive new house in the architectural style of Folk Victorian. The house had wrap around verandahs and decorative gables. It was spacious with two marble fireplaces and a winding staircase to the second level where there were six bedrooms.

My memories of living there are vivid and as I write this I am looking at photos of the house and recalling the large, bright kitchen with windows on three sides where mother made those wonderful tea biscuits.

Mother made a "Play House" for me behind the kitchen and helped me to set up housekeeping with my dolls, dishes and pots and pans. I had a toy broom and dustpan and I swept vigorously. I have lovely memories of mother playing with me and my doll, Mary Lou and helping me tuck her into a cradle or my wicker doll carriage. The doll blankets and covers for the small down doll mattress and pillows were exquisite. My Aunt Sarah Bowser made a pink quilt for the carriage. Later I was given a coveted doll sleigh I saw in Mr. Phelps store in Delta, Ontario. I am fortunate that I still have these wonderful childhood treasures.

Our move to Brockville came just at the time the apples were ready for harvest. Dad hired a man to help him pick the fruit and pack it into barrels in preparation for delivery to stores in the town.

Mother had hired a woman to help her with the unpacking and household duties, and was busy getting settled in her beautiful new home. On one particular afternoon mother asked Wallace, my older brother, to look after me because my dad was away delivering apples and mother was busy unpacking boxes and organizing the kitchen shelves. Wallace was instructed to play with me and he was probably given a few choices; he could take me for a ride in his wagon, we could find a ball and play together or go for a walk down the tree-lined laneway. He was warned to stay away from the shed in the orchard where barrels, tools and equipment for picking apples and making apple cider were stored. The shed was an unsafe place to play.

Wallace grasped my hand and against my protests because I knew we were told not to go there, headed for the forbidden shed in the orchard with me in tow. The rusted metal hinges groaned as he unlatched and opened the weathered wooden door. We went in and when the door closed the latch clanked into place. The dirt encrusted windows and the webs left by busy spiders who had woven their magic, dimmed the light from the outside. A few flies buzzed their farewell to earth and joined their families scattered on the floor. When my eyes became accustomed to the light, I saw gadgets, farm implements, tools and containers hanging on the walls. The floor was scattered with leaves and sticks and there were apple barrels stacked in the corners and under the windows. I covered my nose because of the overpowering odour. The smell of rotting apples and fermenting juices permeated the air.

I was afraid at first, and wanted to leave but Wallace wanted to stay. I believe we played around with some of the less menacing paraphernalia first before Wallace experimented with a machine which could have been used to crush apples or corn cobs to be fed to the animals. We leaned into musty smelling barrels, shouted our names and listened for the echo; we stacked up dusty wooden boxes then climbed up and jumped off into an imaginary lake. The sticks on the floor caught our attention and became swords and guns and I was the conquered one in the game. By now my favorite blue dress was covered in dirt from sitting and falling on the floor. My blonde ringlets had sucked up dust and bits of leaves clung to the ends.

Then Wallace went to the crushing machine and told me where to stand. The smell of the damp, rusting metal of the machine mixed with the rank smell of rotting apples left behind seasons ago is still vivid in my memory. We took up our positions; I was at the side of the ominous machine and Wallace at the end where I remember there was a huge crank that activated the metal, spiked rollers which reduced everything that went through them to a pulp.

First I was told to push sticks of different sizes, into the machine's rollers. Next were the leaves on the floor and apples which spewed out the juice, skin and core as they were pulled into the jaws of the powerful rollers.

Then Wallace pointed and said, "That stick" and as I put it up to the rollers my index finger became entangled and drawn into the machine while Wallace continued to turn the crank. My poor vision had not been discovered at that time and I remember a blurry world until I had my first thick glasses at age four. Perhaps because of my vision I misjudged how close my fingers were to the machine.

No doubt I screamed from fear, panic and pain or in some way alerted Wallace that something was seriously wrong; or, I was shocked into silence from the trauma. The rollers came to a stop, too late.

My brother said he took me for a walk in a field hoping the bleeding would stop and mother wouldn't notice what had happened. Wallace was young and didn't understand the seriousness of the situation and may have been traumatized too. I must have been a shocking sight when Wallace finally took me to the house. My dress was soaked in blood and I had smeared blood over my face and arms. As the story was told to me, I wasn't crying when half carrying me by now, Wallace brought me to my mother. Given the trauma I had suffered, it's safe to assume I was in shock and weak from the loss of blood.

I can imagine my mother's horror when she saw me and Wallace told her what had happened. The girl whom mother had hired to help her, hid behind the wood stove in the kitchen and my mother, timid and filled with anxiety at the best of times was left to cope alone. She had no way of contacting my father. I'm sure she was frantic when she telephoned Dr. Bracken, our family doctor in Brockville.

Dr. Bracken drove immediately to our farm house on highway two which was under construction, being developed into a four-lane highway. Dr. Bracken instructed mother to fold some sheets to make an area suitable for him to operate on the kitchen table. The Brockville General Hospital was only two miles away and I've never understood why Dr. Bracken hastened to operate on our kitchen table, instead of taking me to the hospital. Perhaps, it was because of my loss of blood or more plausible the length of time which had elapsed since the accident. I was given an anesthetic with a mask over my nose and mouth and ether was dripped on the gauze of the mask until I was asleep. Dr. Bracken repaired and sewed my tiny hand as best he could in our farm kitchen that day. Given the conditions and the instruments he had available in his doctor's bag, I applaud him for his skill and stitchery.

I remember some things about the tragedy, and it was a tragedy for me, because it had a profound and lifelong impact on me. When I allow myself to go there and remember and I experience it all again, I see a small, frightened child in a blue woolen dress.

There are other things I remember; I remember my tearful plea to mother that she not cut off my favorite blue dress in the preparation for the surgery in the kitchen. I loved the blue, woolen dress which my cousin Jackie had given me when she outgrew it. It had a row of small white buttons on the elbow-length cuffs of the sleeves; I remember the smell of the ether; I remember being terrified of the ether mask on my face; I remember waking up alone, in the dark in my metal crib with the sides up and my hand pounding with pain and swathed in bandages; I remember the dread of having the stitches removed; I remember my horror when the bandages came off and I saw my disfigured hand with my finger gone; I remember the feel and the smell of the white kid gloves which mother gave me to wear to conceal my missing finger when we went to visit my parent's friends or when we went to church; I remember the index finger of the glove on my left hand stuffed with cotton, which made the finger of the glove stick straight out making it even more prominent; I remember feeling pain in my missing finger which no one could explain or make go away; I remember there were things I wanted to do and couldn't do as well as I might have, for example playing the piano and typing; and I remember creating one-handed finger plays for the kindergarten children I taught because my hand disturbed some of the children. Dining can be a huge embarrassment especially at a formal function because of my awkwardness in holding cutlery properly. The event in the apple shed impacted deeply on my life.

Photographs taken over the next few years document the extent of my trauma. In photographs previous to the fall of 1937, I was a smiling, happy little child; in the photographs over the next few years I am holding my finger or hiding my hand; I look sad and I'm standing apart from whoever else is in the photograph.

There are at least two exceptions which I want talk about because I have only happy memories and photographs of the times with my life-long friend Nancy Howard who lived across the road from me in Soperton and my cousin and special childhood friend, Eleanor Beaton. Besides, it will create lightheartedness in the story.

There is one special childhood memory of which Nancy and I still reminisce with great hilarity. During the Second World War the army carried out maneuvers at the back of the Howard farm and in the evening the soldiers would march behind the army trucks along the road past our farms. Nancy and I would sit on the grassy slope at the side of the road at the end of our laneway and sing, "You Are My Sunshine," I'm sure to the great amusement of the troops.

Eleanor and I are pictured in many photographs with my arm across her shoulders or we have our arms around each other, I think, showing the bond between us which remains. Eleanor and I played happily together during school holiday time and Monopoly games maneuvered with our own rules went on for months at a time. We loved our dolls that came to life and were "real" to us. In winter when we skied on the little hills in North Augusta we would tuck five cents into our pockets and pretend to buy a treat from an imaginary store on the snowy hill. Eleanor was skilled in figure skating and gymnastics and could emulate Barbara Ann Scott as well as do all kinds of wonderful things hanging from her knees upside down on the top bar of the swings. We put on a circus in the summer, complete with costumes, coloured crepe paper streamers and decorated bicycles and tricycles. We invited some of the local children to participate too and people from the community kindly came to see our high swing acts. I seem to recall a marching band too but have no recollection of the music. Probably I sang a marching type hymn! Once when we were in Athens we let my father's prize bull calf down the hay shoot by a rope around the poor little fellow's neck because we had planned that one of us would stand on the barn floor below and catch him and that didn't work out very well! Zeb, the bull calf survived.

Creativity in our play came from being allowed time to "lie in the hammock and dream." Although we had very little supervision in our activities, there were times that it might have been a good idea.

18. Musical Threads

In the previous chapter I wrote about my memories of the apple shed. I recalled the sounds and smells associated with the experience and the lifelong impact it's had on me, one of them being issues of trust and fear which have lingered long in my psyche.

When things are rough for me I cling to music as the thread which holds me together Music helps me to move on. Music of all types but especially classical, jazz and sacred music have sustained me through many difficult times.

The sounds of the music are external, but how the music affects me comes from within. Music is tightly woven into my spirituality. Music gives me sustenance when my spirit is impoverished following a disappointment or if I'm deeply concerned about someone or something. One way I can express outwardly what my inner spiritual being is feeling is to immerse myself in the music of the mood, often a Jazz piano tune. I reach for a composition by pianist, Jessica

Williams, who has a style that suits my needs. She has composed a wide variety of tunes, from strumming the piano strings to march beats. Music warmed me as I huddled in a damp, cold cathedral on a rainy day when far from home. It strengthened me and gave me hope after a terrible car crash which left me hospitalized for many weeks with a skull fracture and other broken bones as well as loss of language and memory. I listened to music when language failed me. Music on an old gramophone and wax record gave me courage when my father died and I was afraid.

Music stirs me to life and I want to dance and sing. One such time was when I was in New Orleans and a funeral was processing down Bourbon Street. The Funeral Band was playing, "When the Saints Go Marching In," a slow march beat. It stirred me. The members in the band moved and swayed as they played. Men with scarves and sashes in vibrant hues and women in flowing dresses and plumes waved frilly, colourful umbrellas. Black umbrellas trimmed with gold braid carried the name of the deceased printed in white as the mourners danced their grief in the funeral procession. A woman carried a large portrait of the departed one as the bereaved moved along the street past me. Horns played, whistles blew, ribbons streamed from tambourines and voices rang out as the people celebrated a life and expressed their grief through music and dance; it was the beginning of their healing.

Animals and birds join in our expressions of music and sound. Dogs thump their tails with a strong beat and wiggle their bodies to let us know their happiness; birds herald a new day with joyous notes and announce a pending rain storm with a different song. Music is all around us and each of us responds in a different way. Music is an integral part of who I am. Music is a way to communicate without words.

As I am writing it occurs to me that when I travel even though I haven't planned it in advance I find music. Either the music finds me or I am drawn to it.

I shall never forget sitting on the banks of the River Seine in Paris and being spellbound as dazzling, breathtaking fireworks rose and fell to the rhythm of the amplified, recorded voice of Maria Callas singing *The Queen of the Night*, from *The Magic Flute*. Her voice soared over the water and the city.

I have had the privilege of attending organ concerts in many of the world's magnificent cathedrals, abbeys and religious structures. In awe I heard the organist perform *Variations on Organ Themes* by Josef Haas in "Dom St. Stephan" on the largest organ in the world in Passau, Germany. Melk Abbey, a dominating Baroque convent, adorned with gold, is gigantic and spectacular and rests on a rocky perch overlooking the Danube River in the old town of Melk, Austria. In the Abbey surrounded by the spectacular golden pipes of the organ the full, rich tones of the instrument filled the space and engulfed me. Notre-Dame de Paris boasts an organ which is unique in design and history as well as the organists who have climbed to the top of the Cathedral and walked a tiny cat-walk to sit at the five manual organ console. The organ is located in front of the rose window at the western end of the cathedral. In St. Peter's Basilica in Rome I strained to hear the music as the organist competed with the noise of the irreverent tourists who jostled one another other as they continued their meaningless babble. On a rainy, cold day I attended an organ concert in St. Martin's Cathedral in Kalocsa, Hungary. I was feeling lonely. Perhaps the weather influenced my mood, but the rich, sustained notes of the full organ transformed my impoverished spirit. As I continued through the day the music accompanied me with every step. The church and the organ music were my refuge that day.

I met my first piano teacher, Mr. Thrasher, when I was six years old. He was our school music teacher, a gentle, interesting man who wore a monocle and I anticipated his arrival each week at our one-room country school in Soperton. His voice was soft when he invited us to sing together. I can still envision him sitting on the piano stool, his back erect but tilted slightly backwards as his long, bony fingers danced over the piano keyboard. I loved every minute of the music lesson he brought to us in our classroom. He couldn't seem to get the hang of writing with chalk and when he stood at the blackboard to teach basic music theory the chalk scraped in a way that made a spine chilling sound. I loved it when he played "Anchors Aweigh" and "It's a Long Way to Tiperary" as we marched around the schoolroom. Mr. Thrasher's visits were a happy time for me so I asked my parents if Mr. Thrasher could teach me piano lessons.

It was arranged and I looked forward to my piano teacher's visit to our farm home each week. He was never cross or unkind when my fingers found the incorrect keys because, with my index finger missing, it was impossible for me to play a chord with an F#, with my left hand or to play any black key for that matter. My lessons were a prescribed course with the *Royal Conservatory of Musi*c and I had to prepare for music exams. Everything was very precise; the fingering used on each note, the pieces I practiced, my posture as I sat at the piano and how I placed my hands on the keyboard.

Mr. Thrasher would say, "Mmm, that's difficult for you. Let's find another way." Mr. Thrasher accommodated my inability to fulfill some of the Conservatory requirements but teachers who followed him were less kindly.

I was ten years old when we moved to Athens, Ontario and I had to say "goodbye" to Mr. Thrasher. Two women piano teachers in succession followed Mr. Thrasher. They were both very strict about using correct fingering, but perhaps there was more at stake for them. They had a reputation to uphold which was based on the marks their students achieved and I didn't help them to advance their careers at all. One teacher with an outstanding record for her students' successes tapped my hand with a ruler when I made a mistake, often because the stub on my left hand was wide enough to play two white keys at once and I couldn't make the distinction between the piano keys. I would laugh to cover up my embarrassment but my teacher was cross with me. That same teacher was visibly absent when I participated in a piano recital for Conservatory students and although I played the piece well, the fingering for my left hand was not the prescribed one and I lost marks. The piano teacher never returned nor did she have the professionalism and courtesy to contact my parents and discuss it with them or with me.

Soon after that devastating experience I met Don Alberry, a wonderful piano teacher who suggested that I play tunes from musicals and more popular music in whatever way I could manage and forget about the Conservatory exams. He encouraged me and wrote complimentary comments in my music note book. Mr. Alberry approved the music credit towards my high school graduation diploma in Grade 13. I loved my piano lessons and would lose myself creating little jazz tunes and improvisations.

In later years, the Alberry house on Orchard Street in Brockville where I had taken piano lessons became *Pippins Restaurant.* Pippin is the name of classic English apple, often regarded as the finest of all dessert apples. Plaster panels between the sections of the original stone walls of the dining room were adorned with antique styled frescoes of robins and bluebirds in apple trees, painted in pastel colours. Decorative apples of all varieties adorned the tables, the deep stone window ledges and the menu. There were apples hanging on an artificial tree in the corner of the room. Of course there was an ample selection of apple desserts. Pippins became a favorite place to dine with my daughter, Christine and dear cousin, Helen Johns as well as other special friends. Pippins hosted two of our most festive family Christmas parties.

I'm amazed at the connecting threads of the apple shed, my music lessons with Don Alberry and later discovering the restaurant with an apple theme in the house where, finally I was given praise for what I *could* do in my piano lessons.

Going back to the apple shed, I asked Mother to tell me her memories of that day. I know she was devastated by what had happened to me and her fear was that she and Dad would not be approved as suitable parents and my adoption would not be approved by the court.

Because my father signed a document agreeing to certain conditions being met during the two years before my adoption could be legalized, it is no wonder that Mother was so fearful that I would be taken away. Who were "they" to whom Mother often referred? It had to have been my grandfather James Bicknell. My biological grandfather offered my adopting parents financial support for me, which they refused, and because of that I believe that my biological grandfather knew where I was. My biological grandmother delivered me personally to my parents, so my adoptive Mother had met my grandmother, if only briefly.

Since I began the research and writing of this story, I have a new understanding of why my Mother was such a worrier throughout her life. The anguish and anxiety my parents would have gone through in those first two years wondering if their child would be taken away; ever watchful of who might be observing them; fearful of a letter in the mail informing them of a decision that my birth mother wanted to take me back must have been dreadful.

When I was eleven years old I was invited to visit Evelyn Braithwaite in Toronto. Evelyn was the cousin who helped Mom and Dad Singleton search for a baby girl. Evelyn took me on a streetcar to Jarvis Street, in Toronto and from the streetcar stop at Gerard Street we walked to a house at 341 Jarvis Street named, *The Victor Home for Girls.* We stood in front of the house and Evelyn said, "That's where you were born."[11]

I remember being surprised and confused and I didn't know how to respond. How did she know I was born there? I took a photo of the house on my Brownie camera.

Soon after my visit to the *Victor Home*, the fact that I was adopted took on new meaning. Previously, although I had thoughts about who my mother was, I was satisfied just to know that Mother and Dad had "chosen" me. I was "special."

By the time I was in my teen years I became obsessed with thoughts about my birth and who I was. I wanted to know more.

Where was my birth Mother? Did she miss me? Why did she give me away? What was she doing? Did she like music? I didn't know who to talk to about my feelings and longings. I thought Mother was closed on the subject because when I asked her about my adoption she always told the same brief story that my grandmother brought me to Belleville in a chauffeur driven limousine, my grandfather had offered my Dad money, I cried a lot and my birth mother couldn't keep me. No other information was forthcoming.

In Grade ten my emotional health began to decline. I cried frequently, my grades took a downward swing and Mother and Dad finally took me to our local physician to find out "what ailed me." As I watched, the doctor mixed a wonderful concoction he called "Beef Iron and Wine" and poured it into an opaque yellow bottle. I loved the taste and willingly took the medicine. I'm sure the main ingredient was red wine, probably homemade, mixed with a little beef broth. I doubt that it had any impact on my mood swings but it was very tasty.

To add further to my emotional turmoil, there was a very inhumane custom in Athens High School while I was attending. After exams, the marks of every student in the school were published in long, horrible lists which appeared in the *Brockville Recorder and Times.* On one particular black day at the end of June, 1950, Mother grabbed the paper and her pencil in preparation for underlining my name, hopefully high on the list as she believed in miracles. I guess I neglected to bring home my report card to warn my parents in advance of the pending disgrace I was about to bring upon the family. The students were ordered in the paper according to our overall percentage of marks. Mother worked her way down the list reading aloud the names and the percentage that each of my scholarly classmates achieved. Mother ticked off person after person *as s*he continued down the Grade Ten column. There second from the last was, *Margaret Singleton, 47%.*

I had failed my year. Mother was inconsolable. I was pretty shaken up too but my feelings were secondary in this drama.

"What will people think?" Mother agonized, "What's wrong with you Margaret?"

I really didn't give a whit about what people would think. I was the one who was hurting. What about how I felt?

I knew what was wrong but I didn't have the language to articulate what I was feeling. I couldn't explain how in my thoughts I was constantly agonizing over who I was. When a History class or Math class ended I didn't know anything that the teacher had said. For the entire forty minutes I was away in my thoughts imagining my mother, wondering where she was, what she looked like and if she was looking for me, wondering, wondering. I longed for my birth mother. I don't know why, but it was difficult for me to say,

"I want to know who my Mother, is."

Usually, when I tried to say "Mother", I'd get a lump in my throat and I'd feel as though I was going to cry. I didn't know how to explain why I couldn't concentrate on my school work or how some days went by in a blur. But this particular day I blurted out,

"I want to know my real Mother." Tears streamed from my eyes.

The shock and hurt in Mother's eyes and the pain in her voice are still in my memory. I wished with all my heart and still do, that I could take the words back.

She was crying too, as she said,

"I'm your real Mother. I'm the only Mother you have ever known. Your father and I have provided a home for you and this is the thanks we get?"

I was fifteen years old and had neither the language nor the wisdom to articulate my anxieties and longings. I wanted to know more and for reasons unknown to me, my Mother and my Dad and whoever else might have had information wanted to keep the rest of the facts to themselves. I didn't mean to hurt my Mother, and of course I realized that she was the one who had cared for me and loved me and I was as grateful as an immature, emotionally upset fifteen year old can be. I loved her and I didn't mean to imply that I didn't think of her as my Mother.

The conversation was finished and Mother turned and sobbed her way to her refuge, the kitchen, and I called the dog and cried my way to my refuge, the woods. If we had been able to find a way to discuss what I was feeling and how my words hurt my mother the outcome might have been different. I'll never know what her fears were around revealing the truth, but perhaps it was that I might want to go to my birth mother, which was a strong possibility, given my immaturity, my longing and my unhappiness. Or, perhaps she had been instructed by the Bicknells not to reveal any information about them.

In my second year in grade ten my emotions settled down a little, I think because of the help of Mr. Hetanen, our high school principal who seemed to understand me better than anyone else. He allowed me to study Latin, which I loved and did well in instead of French, which I was failing. A gifted musician on the staff, Mr. Tuman, added a credit course in classical music to the curriculum for which I signed up right away. We were so fortunate because specialized courses were unheard of in small high schools. I began to achieve again and although my birth mother was still large in my thoughts and heart, I was able through grace, to move on.

There were other programs and activities which I became involved in which were bridges to moving forward. One organization which my Father encouraged me to join was Junior Farmers. It was and still is a grassroots organization run by farm youth to encourage future leadership in rural Ontario, through education, hands on projects, travel, fun and self help. We were each required to carry out a project and Dad built a wonderful brooder house to specifications so that I could raise chickens. The baby chickens were shipped by train to Brockville and Dad and I brought home the chirping, yellow day old chicks in large, flat cardboard boxes with round air holes. I carefully recorded the details of life in the brooder house and my self esteem was kicked up a few notches as I watched my chickens grow into beautiful Rhode Island Red hens.

Mother continued to scan the high school lists in the paper for my percentage position and circled my name in red when it was *near* the top which made us both happy. Unfortunately, I never gave her the joy of being number one. Once I came second with a mark of ninety eight on a Latin exam. Someone else knew all of the answers. I did excel in the music programs, both at school and in the community; the Glee Club, our yearly school Musical, and the church choir. I was sought after as a soloist at weddings, funerals and Women's groups. I absorbed Mother's praise like a sponge!

One sunny fall day I decided to skip school in the afternoon and hitchhike to Brockville to see a movie. "Singin' in the Rain", with Gene Kelly, Donald O'Connor and Debbie Reynolds was playing in the Capitol Theatre. I was full of anticipation for this adventure and for seeing a movie. I left school at noon and walked to the highway where I stuck out my thumb and waited. A car with a man and woman soon stopped and took me to Brockville. My heart was light and I felt a bit giddy as I strolled to the Capitol Theatre and bought my ticket. I ambled over to the food counter and asked for a large bag of buttered popcorn then nonchalantly settled into a seat, relishing my independence and freedom. I didn't want the film to end, ever. But it did end and I was faced with going home. The dancing and music from the movie filled me and as I sang out loud and danced my way to the Revere Hotel to get the local bus home, I didn't care who saw me.

I sat in the lobby of the hotel in a large cushy chair and watched the people. I knew there were people who lived at the hotel which I thought was very glamorous and I made a mental note of doing that one day. I bought my ticket and when the bus drew up to the front door I got on. The bus route passed by our farm but I continued on to the post office in the village and then walked the mile back home as though I was coming home from school. As I often either walked or rode my bicycle home instead of taking the school bus in order to take part in after school activities, my lateness did not arouse suspicions.

Our school had a policy that if we were late or absent, we must bring a signed, dated note from our parents explaining the tardiness or absence. How I was going to accomplish that I wasn't sure. I knew the format expected, so I composed a note in my terrible handwriting which bore no resemblance to either my Mother's or my Father's artistic penmanship. I signed the note with my Mother's name because I didn't have any hope of forging Dad's wonderful English script and rode my bike to school where I lined up, my knees shaking, in front of the office with the other students. Through the closed office door I could hear loud admonitions for some and a quiet word for others. I thought I was in deep trouble.

My turn came and I stood in front of Mr. Hetanen and handed him my note. I can still visualize Mr. Hetanen's face as he opened my note and read the words. *Margaret was ill yesterday afternoon so missed her classes.* A crooked smile crossed his face and he glanced up at me from behind his desk as he signed my note which allowed me to go back to my homeroom. I think he was glad that I had finally kicked over the traces and had broken a rule. I'm sure he knew what I had done.

When I was nineteen I enrolled in a Department of Education, Teacher Education summer course which allowed me to teach for two years after which I was required to attend Teachers' College for one year. Mother bought me a two-toned, green and beige Hillman Minx car, to encourage me to live at home and teach in a local school. That was an offer I couldn't refuse so for two years I had a full immersion into teaching in a one room school in MacIntosh Mills, with all eight grades. The school was across the road from an active saw mill and I competed daily with the noise, whines and buzz of the saws at the mill. Teaching in that community was a wonderful experience and I still remember every one of the children.

I chose to attend Toronto Teachers' College rather than the one in Ottawa which was much closer to our home and would have allowed me to come home week-ends. Finding my birth mother was still large in my thoughts and I was drawn to Toronto. The other factor in my decision was that Toronto Teachers' College was a modern state-of –the-art structure. Also, the leading educators of the day were the masters at the college and I was open to new ideas and methods; and it was time to leave home.

My Dad was not well during the year I was away at Teachers' College. I returned home for the summer to be with my parents as my plan was to move to Trenton in the fall of 1957 where I had been hired as a grade one teacher. My brother Wallace was being married that June and I was invited to be a bridesmaid, an honour which I was anticipating.

It was great to be home and with my car, Mother and I could go on day trips to North Augusta to visit her sister or have fun on shopping excursions in Brockville and beyond.

Dad was still unwell and the doctor suggested it was bronchitis although no tests were done and my Dad didn't seek another opinion. I guess that wasn't done then. It was wrongly assumed then, that doctors knew these things. Three days before my brother's wedding Dad complained of severe chest pains. I don't know why we didn't call the ambulance. We helped Dad into the car and Wallace drove us to a hospital in Brockville. It seemed like the slowest trip I've ever had in a car. Dad died before we reached the hospital.

Dad's death had an unexpected kind of grief and loss for me. I was inconsolable. His death left me feeling that not only had I lost my champion but that I had lost my connection to the Singleton family. Whether it was true or not, my link to the Singletons felt tenuous. Dad had given me my surname, the only one I knew even if it wasn't genetically mine. I was proud to be a Singleton and I didn't want to lose the only identity I had. I was grief-stricken; my sobbing went on and on.

Dad's wake and funeral were held in our home. I lay on my bed in deep sorrow and it was my high school singing teacher, Mrs. Ray who came to comfort me. It had been three years since my graduation from high school but somehow, she cared and understood. Perhaps she had experienced something similar. I shall always remember her coming to be with me, sitting on my bed and talking in a soft soothing voice as I sobbed. Whatever her words of comfort were they were just right.

Dad's death left my Mother devastated. She and Dad were soul mates, companions and best friends. She wasn't able to find a way to live fully after the loss of her life partner and although the birth of her granddaughter, Joan, gave her new joy and a renewed interest in living she still grieved, deeply, for her husband.

I went to Trenton, Ontario that fall and taught in North Trenton Public School, a new elementary school, just constructed. I remember the Director of Education came to visit me before the school was opened and asked if there was anything else I would like for my classroom.

"It would be wonderful to have a piano for my grade one pupils," I said.

The next day a piano arrived. I was so fortunate to be a part of the educational system then when teachers mattered, programs were important and school systems were small enough to address the needs of the individual children.

In 1958 I was married and we moved to Ottawa where my husband and I taught for the Ottawa Board of Education. Mother visited us in our small apartment and encouraged us to buy a house which she helped to make possible. We chose a bungalow in City View as our first home and I'm so glad she was able to visit us there and see us in our home. Mother helped me plan a large garden, plant the seeds and later enjoy some of the harvest. With my Aunt Lavenia Beaton, we dug up little pine trees in my uncle's wood lot and planted them in a row across the front of the property. Fifty years later they are reaching for the sky, totally blocking the view to the back of the lot. My husband made a wonderful wooden seat around the huge maple tree and we sat on it to watch Sputnik in the night sky. Our daughter, Christine was born while we lived in that lovely little house. It was a good time in my life.

On Easter Sunday, April 02, 1961 Mother became ill during the church service. She was driven home and a doctor came and pronounced "A little indigestion." She suffered dreadfully that night and the next day. The doctor came again, was unconcerned and insisted it was indigestion. In the afternoon I called the local ambulance.

It had been eleven years since I had hurt my Mother so deeply with my words, "I want to know my real mother;" Eleven years since we had spoken again about my adoption. I was in the ambulance with Mother on the way to Kingston General Hospital. My heart and body ached with anxiety as I held her hand and tried to reassure her and let her know how much I cared for her. Mother looked at me and said,

"Margaret, some day you might want to find your real mother. There are some papers and letters in that old, green, wooden box in my closet."

What secrets was she letting go of at last? I felt a deep love for her and once again that big lump came into my throat and interfered with what I wanted to say.

Mother was admitted to Kingston General Hospital and was diagnosed with a massive heart attack. The misdiagnosis, indifference and pompous attitude of her family doctor angered me. "It's just a *little* indigestion." Wallace and his wife Dorothy had joined us at the hospital and when we were given some hope that Mother might get through the attack, they left to do farm chores and look after their young daughter.

A few hours later, as I sat on the edge of her hospital bed, Mother struggled for life. Gasping for breath in her oxygen tent, she sat up, reached out for me and I grasped her hands in mine unable to cradle her in my arms because of the contraption surrounding her. Death overcame my Mother suddenly, before the nurse and doctor answered my frantic call.

"Uh," A sound came from my throat. In stunned silence I watched in awe as an elongated, opaque, silver mist rose from Mother's head and floated silently towards the ceiling before dissipating slowly, into the air. I believe I witnessed Mother's soul ascending to another level of consciousness. Still holding tightly to her delicate hands as though trying to prevent her from leaving me I stroked her smooth, soft, silky skin with my thumbs. At this moment she was my only Mother, the special one who had loved and cared for me. She was my Mother. Now resting peacefully, the last brief struggle for life was over and whatever else my Mother, Florence, might have wanted in life was now unimportant.

The doctor and nurse bustled in too late and motioned in a "shoo-like" gesture for me to leave Mother's side. I stood at the foot of the bed unable to speak as they tried to resuscitate her lifeless body, injecting her and pummeling her chest. I waited for the misty substance to return to her body and give her life again. Mother was gone.

I was asked to leave the room.

No time to be alone with my Mother.

No time to whisper how much I loved her, with my face close to hers.

No time to be with her departed spirit and feel that peaceful presence.

No time to say goodbye.

Mother was only sixty-eight.

It was two o'clock in the morning when I called my brother Wallace to give him the news that Mother was gone. Wallace said he'd come to Kingston for me in the morning. I was alone, alone to cope with my numbness and an endless night. My husband was with his parents and had no way of coming to be with me; I didn't call him.

A nurse took me to a lounge, somewhere in the hospital, for the remainder of the night, where I sat silently at a table, in shock, unable to cry or feel any emotion. The same kindly nurse checked in on me from time to time, bringing me tea, biscuits and words of comfort.

Mother's longing for a daughter led her to me. Growing up with the Singleton family shaped my life and influenced who I became.

My daughter, Christine was born three years after Mother's death. I resigned from teaching not just because of the archaic law which required me to do so but because I wanted to be a full- time Mother, to experience and enjoy every moment of my new daughter's life. As I reflect on those years, I cherish the memory of each morning when I walked into my baby's room and received her beautiful smile, her outstretched arms and her body in motion with an enthusiastic greeting. Against everyone's advice, I rocked my baby to sleep each night, often with music playing on the record player. We listened to everything from *Brahms's Lullaby* to *We Shall Overcome* with Joan Baez. My life became forever enriched with my beautiful daughter.

The longing for my birth Mother was still with me but it would be a few more years before I could begin a focused search for my birth family.[12]

19. The King Edward Hotel Clyde Returns

"What is REAL?" asked the Rabbit one day..."Does it mean having things buzz inside you and a stick-out handle?"

"Real isn't how you are made," said the Skin Horse, "It's a thing that happens to you. When a child loves you for a long, long time not just to play with but REALLY loves you, then you become Real."

"Does it hurt?"asked the Rabbit.

"Sometimes," said the Skin Horse, for he was always truthful. "When you are Real you don't mind being hurt."13

Clyde admired his well-groomed image which was reflected in the large oval mirror of the mahogany dresser in his hotel room. He smiled and straightened his shoulders as he imagined all of the medals he would be awarded in his new career as a soldier with the Irish Regiment of Canada. He had recently enlisted and was very proud of the uniform; the saffron tartan kilt, caubeen & hackle headgear and a green cut-away tunic. If this didn't turn the ladies' heads then the dress uniform with feather bonnet and white plume and the scarlet tunic was sure to stop them dead in their tracks.

"Clyde Elder, you are a fine figure of a man," he said out loud.

His self-admiration was brief. It was letting his mind wander to other ladies that brought down the guillotine of guilt and remorse. Memories of Betty tore into his heart and body; the fun-filled times they had shared, the way she pushed her body into his when they walked together, her beautiful smile and hearty laugh, how she held her cigarette so gracefully with her little finger curled in, these were all vivid in Clyde's mind. His love for Betty was alive; the only passionate love he had ever known. He ached to be with her. *We had a child*, he agonized, letting himself feel the heaviness of the pain like a cold stone in his gut. It wouldn't go away.

What kind of coward had he been? James Bicknell had threatened him with jail if he tried to contact Betty again and he had been accosted by a mysterious man on a dark street. The stranger had scared him and said Clyde would come to bodily harm if he didn't leave town. Then an envelope with a large sum of money was thrust into his hands. Clyde had moved to Northern Ontario to work in the mines and perhaps forget; he couldn't forget. He couldn't forget the pain, he couldn't forget Betty and he couldn't forget his child.

What had happened to their baby? He had tried to find information but was blocked at every turn. He called all of the hospitals but there was no record of the birth. There was no record anywhere of a birth to Betty Bicknell. Did the infant live? If so, was the child living with Betty? Did the Bicknells send Betty away to another city to have the baby? Or, even to another country. Was the baby adopted away at birth? James Bicknell would do anything to protect his name and status in the legal and social milieu.

I'll bet he's handsome like his father.

Perhaps the baby was a girl; a beautiful little girl with captivating blue eyes like her mother's sparkling eyes.

Clyde had more than one regret nibbling at his conscience. Impulsively, he had married someone else, but the marriage had been brief and they had separated.

Starting a new career was a good decision; a clean slate. He believed that he had a future with the prestigious Irish Regiment and that might impress James Bicknell and be the trump card which would influence James to allow Clyde to see Betty again. Betty would be old enough now to make her own decisions without her father's consent, but the consequences could be losing her substantial inheritance and also her status in the prestigious Rosedale community. And how might Betty react to the news of his marriage to someone else, thus admitting to being unfaithful to their love?

Clyde's regiment would be leaving Toronto very soon and the call could come at any time to move on. Today might be his only opportunity to contact Betty. He would do it. Yes, this was the day to call Betty. Just the thought of talking to Betty gave him a feeling of happiness.

He took one more glace at himself before heading for the Gentleman's Café and Bar on the ground floor of the hotel. He turned the key in the lock of room number 237, heard the "click" of the lock, then in a gesture of playfulness, tossed the key in the air, caught it and dropped it into his pocket. Clyde felt lighter now that he had made a firm promise to himself to call Betty.

Clyde stepped into the elevator and descended to the first floor. The door opened to the elevator lobby in the Rotunda, and Clyde emerged into the hub of the hotel. Stylish guests were milling about the spacious elegance. There was a buzz of voices as they greeted one another with a handshake, a nod of the head or a slight bow. He hesitated at first, absorbing the opulence and also looking for the

Café. Clyde shared Betty's interest and enjoyment of architecture and this was a superbly designed building, the tallest in Toronto.

The golden marble columns surrounding the two-storied, glazed atrium, took his attention. In the center of the atrium a wonderful Oriental sculpture encircled by upholstered seating was very inviting, but he couldn't have a drink there. This area was reserved for reading the paper, visiting with friends or sitting quietly. Scattered throughout this light filled space there were rugs which he believed were Persian and Turkish, dark coloured leather and wooden chairs, benches and spectacular potted palms from far-away places. Clyde looked up and marveled at the large, globular chandelier which hung from the ornamental ceiling.

He observed that the main office was resplendent in its cast-iron grillwork. Where was the Café?

Clyde took in a deep breath then continued his walk through the Rotunda. Two women swept by him giggling and gave him a provocative look. He touched his hat in a sort of salute. His eyes wandered further but not after the women. Off the Rotunda was the European Restaurant which was the main Dining Room. It took his eye and he strolled over and peered in the door. No waiters were there so he dared to step inside. He probably wouldn't be dining here. It was highly decorative, with ivory-coloured plaster work on the ceiling which complemented the soft green silk wall coverings. He smiled as he remembered the time he and Betty were at the "The Grill" and as he was cutting his roast beef, smothered in gravy thc piece flew off the plate and hit the wall. They broke up laughing. The waitress brought a wet cloth and the mess was soon taken care of. What if that happened here? Roast beef and gravy on silk wall coverings would not be taken care of so easily. Nor, would the staff be amused.

He'd love to share this place with Betty, but it was beyond what he could afford. No doubt, her parents have already brought her here, he mused.

He stopped his reverie and walked out of the dining room and towards the reception desk on the far side of the Rotunda. The manager would direct him to the Café. Just to the right of the long, curved mahogany desk there was a notice board announcing the evening's main event.

Clyde came to an abrupt halt and stared. He caught his breath as he read the words which were written on the board.

JAMES BICKNELL SUPPER-DANCE IN THE CRYSTAL BALLROOM
LUIGI ROMANELLI ORCHESTRA
TIME: 7:00 P.M.
GUESTS PLEASE ANNOUNCE YOUR ARRIVAL AT THE RECEPTION DESK

As if frozen to the floor, Clyde read the words over and over.

"My, God!" he said out loud. People walking by stared at him. Then he heard a voice beside him; "May I help you, Sir?" It was the desk clerk.

Clyde was quick with his answer, "No, thank you, I was on my way to the Café and stopped to read the Bicknell announcement. Do you know how many are in their party?"

"No, I'm sorry, I can't say, Sir. The Café is that way, Sir," he said pointing behind them.

The clerk went back to the desk and Clyde regained his composure. Questions raced through his mind. Would Betty be here? If he remained here in the Rotunda, might he see her? What would James's reaction be when he saw him here in the hotel? Surely, respect towards him when he observed Clyde in his stunning new uniform; and I'm doing my duty for my country. Yes, he thought, I have a few things in my favor.

What was the best strategy? He had learned about strategies in his training with the Irish Regiment. Where should he wait?

The Gentleman's Café was the logical place. He would continue with that plan.

As he entered the Café and searched the area carefully for the most suitable table for his lookout, he was thinking of Betty rather than the decorating and design which had previously engrossed his attention. He did notice that the Gentleman's Café had the dignity of an old baronial hall and the high, paneled wainscoting reminded him of James Bicknell's library. A familiar aroma of wood and leather brought back memories; reminiscences of the last time he was in that library played in his mind like a second-rate movie. Clyde was so absorbed in his thoughts that he scarcely noticed the murals above the wainscoting done on hand-tooled horse-hide leather.

He chose one of the round-backed chairs which were grouped around small tables and hoped no one would come to join him. Any other time he would welcome someone to talk to but tonight he wanted to be alone without any distraction. From this vantage place he could observe the entrance and the arrival of the Bicknell party. Clyde's heart raced with excitement and some apprehension.

If Betty came, and without an escort, he would make himself known. How to accomplish that, he decided would be a spur–of-the-moment decision.

"I'll have a Single Malt Scotch, please," he said when the waiter came to take his order. "Do you have Singleton Scotch?"

"Yes, we do, Sir. It's a good choice to complement your regimental colours."

"Scotch is just right for this occasion," Clyde replied.

Usually, when he went for a drink he sat at the bar, but tonight he settled into a chair where he could observe the people arriving. He adjusted his kilt as he was still not entirely comfortable in the new attire. But he did enjoy the attention which came his way when he was wearing his uniform. The waiter brought his drink and he inhaled the aromas before savoring a sip of the fine, rare scotch.

It had been a long time since Clyde had felt these overwhelming feelings of excitement, but there was also apprehension.

He was breathing in the richness of the scotch when there was a flurry of activity at the entrance. A limousine had come to a smooth stop in front of the ornate, canopied, dark green metal entrance porch. Who would step out?

"Good God, it's Fred." He recognized the Bicknell's chauffeur who opened the back door of the limousine.

An elegant young woman emerged gracefully. She was wearing a long, dark blue satin coat which swirled around her shapely legs as she moved. When he saw her it evoked sensual feelings and memories; his fingers caressing her blond hair, now long and pulled back away from her face in loose rolls on the sides; running together, hand in hand to catch a streetcar; snuggling together in the back row of the Lowe Theatre; parties on the beach at Presqu'ile. Betty was so beautiful.

Clyde could scarcely breathe. The love of his life was entering the hotel.

He jumped to his feet clutching his glass.

Clyde sucked in his breath and held it.

He was struck dumb. He couldn't move.

She came closer to him as she entered the hotel but didn't look his way. Betty was between her parents as they walked to the desk and announced their arrival to the receptionist. A smartly uniformed escort acknowledged the group and motioned for Mr. Bicknell to follow him. They would be escorted to the Crystal Ballroom.

Clyde's eyes followed the Bicknell family as they moved over the patterned, marble floor of the elevator lobby as though in a dance. Their escort pushed the shiny brass button to summon the car which would take them to the Crystal Ballroom on the 17th floor. Spontaneously, with a flip of her head, Betty twirled in a pirouette in the elegant lobby. As she did so her distinctive Cartier perfume wafted across the space and into Clyde's nostrils and brought him back to reality. He couldn't let her go, no matter the consequences.

"Betty," he blurted out as he strode towards her, his kilt moving in time with his quickening step.

She swung around and looked at him, stunned. It was Clyde's voice but she was taken by surprise. Where was he? For only a fleeting instant she didn't recognize him in the uniform.

Each stared at the other in disbelief.

When reality struck, Betty screamed his name and threw herself into his arms. They remained in a blissful embrace and whispered each other's names over and over.

Clyde gently pushed Betty back to gaze at her and then pulled her close to his body again. They were totally oblivious to the Bicknell parents. Some of the hotel guests around them stared and made "tisk, tisk" sounds at the inappropriate public display of affection.

Betty was breathless and in tears as she said, "Clyde, I can't believe it's you. Oh, Clyde, I'm overjoyed to see you."

"Betty, Betty, me too, I never dreamed you'd be here. But I did plan to call you today. Can you believe that? What a marvelous coincidence." He held her closer for a moment then took Betty's face in his hands and kissed her with as much passion as he dared in this place. He knew in his heart that he would never let her go again.

Betty showered Clyde with tears as she clung to him, saying his name over and over as if to make him real, just like the Velveteen Rabbit.

"Clyde, Clyde, is it really you? Clyde, where have you been? When did you join the army? Why are you here in this hotel? Clyde, I've missed you so much, don't you know that?"

Betty blurted out question after question which made Clyde uncomfortable. Her parents stood, uneasy and still not acknowledged by Clyde.

James and Beatrice were shocked and for a moment, James was uncharacteristically speechless. Then, James found his voice.

"Where, did he come from?" James said to his wife, not expecting an answer.

"He's joined the forces, James. I wonder why he's in this hotel."

James wanted to break up the embrace.

"Well, well, young man, it's been a long time. I see you've joined the Irish Regiment. That's an honorable thing to do in these times of anxiety." James didn't seem to be making much impression on Clyde who continued to be lost in his embrace with Betty.

"Clyde," Beatrice gushed, but with sincerity, "I'm so surprised to see you. I never expected to see you here. Where did you go, Clyde?" Betty never stops talking about you, do you dear?"

James continued to try and get Clyde's attention and spoke in a voice with more authority as he said, "Our son, James, Betty's brother, is thinking of training to be a pilot with the R.C.A.F." James offered his hand for a greeting.

Clyde and Betty continued to cling to each other but over Betty's shoulder Clyde could see Mr. Bicknell's extended hand. Clyde kept one arm around Betty and let go of her with the other arm just long enough to shake James' hand and then greet Beatrice.

"Mr. Bicknell, I'm glad to see you again." Clyde lied. "My regiment placed me here for a few days until we ship out to Halifax. This hotel is a place where we army guys get together to share stories and have a drink or two. I'll be leaving soon."

When the couple turned and faced James he saw Betty and Clyde flushed with excitement. Betty's arm was wrapped around her soldier and with hesitant resolve James decided that for tonight at least, he would allow Betty to have the pleasure of Clyde's company. If Clyde was shipped out soon he wouldn't be a threat as a suitor. Besides, to have a soldier in uniform at his table tonight, would give his party additional attention and prestige, something James sought.

"Excuse me, please," James said and walked back to the reception area. "There will be one more person at the Bicknell table tonight," he told the manager. "Clyde Elder who is with the Irish Regiment is joining us for dinner. Please add his name to our guest list."

As she clung to Clyde and waited for her father to return, Betty's mind was flooded with all that she had to tell Clyde; her life at the Victor Home, the birth of their baby and the falsified birth record and why she had to part with their daughter. She was also desperate to know where Clyde had been. There were many things to be discussed and Betty would not let him go again. She reached into her evening bag and felt the small velvet box she had been carrying for years. Dare she hope that tonight, Clyde would slip the ring which was inside on her finger; this time forever.

James returned to the elevator and the Bicknell family and Clyde stepped inside. The door closed behind them and onlookers in the lobby watched the dial light over the doors indicate their floor by floor assent and arrival at the Crystal Ballroom, the room at the top of the hotel which was one of the tallest buildings in the city.

The elevator doors slid open and they walked through the short corridor to the entrance of the Crystal Ballroom. Two sets of large double glass doors opened to the magnificent Ballroom. Betty and Clyde chose the ones on the right and emerged into one of the city's most refined spaces, the centre of Toronto's social life which attracted rich and famous socialites and movie stars. Tall windows provided sweeping views, south, east and west of the surrounding city. Clyde caught his breath when he saw the classically styled Ballroom with ornate golden patterned plaster cornices and long crystal chandeliers.

With Betty on his arm, in this prestigious setting, Clyde was where he wanted to be.

The next day the Social Notes of *The Toronto Daily Star* carried an article about the Bicknell's Supper Dance at the King Edward Hotel. The guests included Miss Betty Bicknell and Cpl. Clyde Elder.

20. My Search for My Birth Mother

A longing for my birth mother since I was a very young child along with the mystery and intrigue imbedded in what I knew of my story, pushed me towards a life-long journey to find the truth, the whole story of my birth and adoption. By the time I was in my teen years it had become an all-consuming passion for me to find my mother, to know who she was and to be close to her. I also wanted to know who I was. It was as though there was a piece of me missing. My obsession was so intense that I failed grade ten in high school; my thoughts were consumed with my birth mother.

I imagined that my mother was young, had blonde curly hair and lived in a city. I could visualize her pretty clothes; I heard her laugh and I often talked to her.

I am including this chapter detailing how I went about searching for my identity to encourage others who may be disheartened. I kept on trekking even though I had very little information but I found important bits along the way which led to other discoveries. It's amazing how things come together when you least expect it. I followed leads, wrote down names I overheard, interviewed people and searched in newspapers and city directories.

The Access to Information Act had not yet come into law and there were no "family find" organizations to help me. I was on my own.

My search began with what I knew. Information on a document that I had, possibly given to my adoptive parents during their search for a child indicated that my grandfather was born in 1893, had attended St. Andrew's College and Osgoode Hall and in 1935 was practicing as a barrister in Toronto. My grandmother attended Model School and a private school. My grandmother's father owned a well known Candy Factory in Toronto. No names were on the document.

My birth mother was described in this way:

"She is 5'2" tall, has an oval face, blonde hair and large blue eyes. She has good features and is dainty and attractive in appearance. She attended a private girl's school in Toronto. She has taken dancing and is fond of all physical activity. She sings and plays and is said to have definite musical talent. She was in excellent health during her pregnancy. Her health has been good apart from childhood illnesses and an operation for appendicitis.

She is a member of St. Paul's Anglican Church

There is also a younger brother in the family."

The document also revealed information about the putative father:

"Canadian, twenty-one years of age. He is working as a reporter for a well known daily paper. In appearance he is tall and handsome with blue eyes and fair curly hair. He is described as gentlemanly, attractive, all-round young man, fond of sports.

He has a brother employed in the mines in Northern Ontario."

The second document in my possession was a Court Order for what I assumed was my adoption but the name of the adoptee on the Court order was not mine, or so I thought. The document was a mystery to me. How could I use this meager information to build a search?

Our family lawyer was admired and respected in Ottawa. He had a reputation of humanitarianism and working tirelessly for his clients and the community. At the time I am writing about, he had not yet entered politics. In the summer of 1968, I summoned my courage and made an appointment to see him. It took courage because I always felt intimidated when in the company of lawyers. My intuition was bang on. Although my intention was to talk about my intended search for my mother I didn't inform the secretary of the reason for making the appointment.

I arrived at the address on Lisgar Street in Ottawa and was shown into my lawyer's office and directed to a large chair near the desk. Soon the lawyer came in, we exchanged greetings and then I pulled my papers out of a small leather case and began to explain the reason for my visit. I was seeking his help in finding my birth mother.

I explained that the Court Order for my adoption was very confusing to me and I hoped he could help me to understand the information. The names Dorothy Watson Bicknell on the Court Order seemed to be for someone else and the document was dated over two years from the time my adoptive parents had told me that I came to live with them. There were mysteries to be solved. I asked if he could interpret the information for me and if I could use the Court Order to trace my family. I knew that my lawyer had attended Osgoode Hall in 1953, much later than my grandfather, but still I felt there might be a connection, an "Old Boys Club," sort of thing. Perhaps the names on the document would be familiar. He would have access to the law journals and ledgers and with his influence he might be able to move my search along.

It was many years later that I learned anyone could go to the Osgoode Hall Library and search the records. I also discovered that my great grandfather had written extensively in the law books which my lawyer would have studied. My cousin Jim Keachie, also a lawyer, took me to the library at Osgoode Hall where we enjoyed many meaningful hours together in research for the Bicknell Genealogy which I was writing. We used the Law Journals to bring to life the work of a great, great uncle, Harry Bicknell who was a lawyer in Toronto in the early 1900's.

I sensed anger and disapproval from the one from whom I was seeking advice as I explained my intention to find my birth family. He raised his voice as he berated me for wanting to find my biological family. He towered over me when he stood to make the point that my parents had adopted me, given me a new name and a home and it was unclear to him why I needed to find my biological mother. He cited a person close to him who had been adopted and said he wouldn't want to think of that person trying to find his/her birth parents.

"You have a family," he said. "You already have a mother."

I later discovered that some of the members of my adoptive family felt that way too, but not all. It wasn't that they didn't accept me, it was just that they didn't understand my need to know who I was, to learn what genetic issues might be lurking in my background and that it was possible that my mother might be waiting for me to contact her.

Without warning, the lawyer leaned across his huge, orderly, wooden desk and literally snatched my documents from me. He read them silently, stoically, shuffling the papers one behind the other. He sat down and reached into a desk drawer and pulled out a large brown envelope into which he stuffed the papers. He licked the envelope and pressed it shut, stamping it with his fist. He wrote my name on the envelope as he informed me that what I was doing was illegal, he would not help me and he was confiscating my documents.

My heart stopped, I think literally. I sat motionless, frozen in the moment on the hard chair. I felt small and insignificant as though I was being punished for something I didn't understand was wrong. He had no right to assault my dignity and self esteem.

Why did I come? I lamented to myself. Tears wouldn't come and the pressure began to build up inside my pounding head even though I seldom had headaches. In a weak voice, I asked for my papers back but the answer was a resounding;

"No, they will be sealed and filed as it is illegal in Ontario for anyone to search for or contact their birth parents. You should not have been given these documents. Where did you get them?"

"They were in my adoptive mother's things when she died. They are mine. Could you make a copy of the papers for me? They are all I have." I pleaded.

The man stood to make his point sink in and said;

"You could be charged with breaking the law so I suggest that you let the matter drop.

Goodbye, Mrs. Bresee."

(Bresee was my married name. After my divorce in 1982, I reclaimed the surname of my adoptive parents, "Singleton.")

Would my weak wobbly legs carry me out of his office? I was very definitely being dismissed. I would have reached over his desk and snatched the envelope away but my strength and will were gone.

My hopes were dashed and my psyche crushed but I knew I wasn't finished with Mr. Legal Man.

I walked out of his office into the brilliant sunshine of the summer day, temporarily defeated but I knew I would not give up.

Months passed by and I talked to many people about what had happened. My friends were astounded by the lawyer's action and encouraged me to keep trying to have the documents returned. Several times I called his office in an attempt to retrieve my precious papers, my life-line to my unknown family, but without success. I confirmed, however, that an adoptee searching for birth parents was illegal"[14] but I didn't care. I intended to find my mother one way or another. I had to know who I was for my own emotional health.

As a person who was adopted I had experienced personal insults and verbal abuse. Never, from my adoptive parents which I must make very clear. They were loving parents.

In the autumn of 1969 I called my lawyer's office and spoke to his secretary. After identifying myself and providing a brief background to my call, I enquired once again about my documents and demanded to have them returned.

"Oh", the secretary informed me, "The office has been moved and all of those documents were burned".

"Burned," I screamed at her, "No, you had no right to do that".

I slammed the receiver down.

I was stunned. Why was this happening? What was in those papers to cause this lawyer to try and prevent them from getting back into my hands? What was the trigger which caused him to over-react so vehemently?

The details of the next few days are a bit hazy and violence may have crossed my mind.

I limped along heartbroken and angry with myself for having gone to seek advice at all. Without the documents I had nothing to help me in my search for my mother. Then, as I thought more about it, I felt it was extremely unlikely that a law firm would burn sealed documents. Why had I been told they were destroyed? What could I do?

Undaunted and angry, on December 8th, 1969, I wrote a letter to my lawyer demanding the return of the documents. I threatened to seek legal counsel if necessary to obtain my documents, or if they had indeed been burned, to sue his law firm. According to my former lawyer's tardy reply to my letter, more than a month later, I "pleaded for them."

Soon after January 15th, 1970 my documents arrived intact, in the mail, along with a letter from the lawyer in question (now on file in my personal archives) saying he hoped I hadn't been inconvenienced by any delay in returning the documents. The papers had been in his possession since the summer of 1968. His tone had completely changed, and the letter was signed;

"Kindest personal regards,

Yours very truly,

xxx

Another two years passed before time and circumstances came together for me to search for my biological family.

August 19, 1972, became a very important date in my search for my family. The Week-End Magazine of the *Ottawa Journal* ran a full feature on St. Paul's Anglican Church, Bloor St, Toronto, written by Hartley Steward, a Toronto freelance writer.

Where have I heard about that church before? I thought. *The name of that church is very familiar.* Most people have experienced that sort of thing at one time or another.

I read the magazine article and was very impressed with The Venerable Robert P. Dann, Archdeacon of Toronto East and the Rector of St. Paul's. He had a vision for change in the church and encountered opposition when he tried to establish youth programs and a youth hostel. There was an outreach program in place, sending out hampers of food and serving supper to indigent people at Christmas. After reading the article I chucked the magazine out with the rest of the papers, but I held the information in my mind.

Days later, a light dawned and I went to get the old letter which was sent to my parents many years before. I gasped as I read that my birth mother attended St. Paul's Anglican Church in Toronto, the same church that the magazine had featured. I dove into the box of papers in the garage and for once I was glad that my husband had been slow in throwing out the old newspapers. I retrieved the magazine and clutched it to me as I walked into my sunny, yellow sitting room and sank into my favorite chair letting it engulf me, still holding the magazine to my heart.

My heart was beating wildly as I read every word on the cover, then again, before slowly opening the magazine to read the feature article again and again, taking in the compassionate, gentle qualities of Archdeacon Dann, all the while searching the right side of my brain for some creative way to tap into this story. The information in this article could be the key to finding my mother.

Many ideas flashed by; I could go to the church and go up and down the aisles to see if anyone looked like me; I might ask from the pulpit if anyone was missing a daughter; I could hand out little cards with my birth date that said, "Does this date mean anything to you?" No, I wouldn't do any of those things.

I learned from Mr. Steward's article that Archdeacon Dann came from United Empire Loyalist farming stock and that he milked the cows on his father's New Brunswick farm. He was approachable, soft and kindly. He listened to the complaints of widows, was compassionate to drunks and street people and took communion to the homes of those unable to come to church.

Oh, I liked him.

It seemed that Archdeacon Dann at St. Paul's Church was the link I was looking for. I felt comfortable about giving him copies of my documents and composed a letter. As I recall I told him my story and explained how important it was for me to find my birth family. I made it clear that my adopting parents were good parents and described how much they had done for me. I enclosed a copy of the September 1935 letter and the court order for my adoption. That was all I had to begin a search. Would he help me? If by some chance he found my mother, would he be the one to make contact with the family?

I received an immediate reply from Archdeacon Dann that he would love to help me find my mother. He would do what he could, but it would take time.

My primary interest was in finding my mother but, in that same letter there was the information that my father was a reporter for one of the daily newspapers in Toronto.

I quote from the letter, "The putative father …works as a reporter for a well known daily paper."

Not much to go on but I reasoned to myself, if I had the names from the payroll records of newspapers in Toronto, they might provide a clue. There was a name which was unfamiliar to me on the Court Order for my adoption. Perhaps I could match a name on the payroll record to the name I had. Someone might remember something or have information.

I wrote to *The Toronto Star*, *The Globe and Mail*, and *The Toronto Sun* and asked for their payroll records and the names of reporters working for the newspapers in 1934 and 1935. In replies from *The Toronto Star* and *The Globe and Mail*, I learned that the newspaper records were not available from that long ago and that editorial staff from1934 and 1935 who might have been able to provide information, understandably, were no longer on staff. The paymaster from *The Toronto Sun* replied and informed me that the newspaper did not begin publication until 1971. I didn't pursue the search for my father.

Several months after my first contact with Rev. Dann, I received a letter from him with details of the names and birth and baptismal records of a family. The dear man had gone back through years of church records and matched a family, father, mother, sister and brother with the information which I had sent to him. He also wrote that he was searching for my baptismal record. He felt sure I would have been baptized because of what he knew of the family and their involvement with St. Paul's. Although they had at one time been regular supporters of St. Paul's they were no longer members there. He had contacted a member of my grandmother's family, the Watsons, who still attended St. Paul's but wasn't able to get any information.

"I think this is your family," he wrote. "I am very sure you are a Bicknell and that your mother is Beatrice Louise Bicknell."

I read the letter over and over.

I was overjoyed to know my biological name.

"I'm a Bicknell, I'm a Bicknell," I sang over and over as I danced around my sitting room after I had digested the astounding letter. I had a biological name.

I had asked Archdeacon Dann to make the first contact with the family or my mother to find out if she was willing to meet me. Perhaps it would not be appropriate for my mother to meet me if she had married; or it was possible that she wasn't interested in meeting me regardless of her status. I understood that. I had no idea of her situation or why she gave me up for adoption. There were numerous circumstances to be considered and I confided my concerns to Rev. Dann. I also promised that if, for any reason my mother did not want to meet me I would not pursue my search any further. Rejection was a possibility that I had to face, but in my heart I felt that if I could find my mother she would welcome me.

My first idea was to place an ad which I talked about earlier, in the personal column of *The Globe,* in 1974 on my birthday, May 10th. There were no respondents.

How do we proceed? More letters and phone calls went back and forth between us, but Rev. Dann couldn't uncover any more information.

Then, I had an inspired idea, but before doing anything I wanted to discuss it with Rev. Dann.

Genealogy was an interest of mine and I had worked on the family history of my adoptive family, the Singletons, so why not write the Bickenll genealogy? I had some skills in research and a good knowledge of how to do genealogy. It would be a way of contacting people without saying who I thought I was. I called Rev. Dann to talk to him about my idea and ask his advice. We discussed the pros and cons of writing a Bicknell genealogy and Rev. Dann encouraged me as he thought it was worth a try, although he had some doubts about me being able to find information about the Bicknells with so little information.

The first thing I did was to obtain a copy of the 1976 Toronto Phone Directory and remove the pages with *Bicknell* and *Watson* for easy access to the names and addresses. There were only about twenty Bicknells listed in the Toronto phone directory in 1976. It seemed that the logical order was to write to all of the lawyers first as it was already established that my grandfather was a lawyer. What responses I would receive was unknown.

The list of Watsons, my grandmother's maiden name, in the directory was daunting, so I randomly chose a few names.

Now, how to proceed?

Computers and e-mail were foreign to my life then. I did have a rented electric typewriter for which I had little skill and my first draft was a typewritten form letter which I photocopied on our school copy machine. There was a specific type of grayish, coated paper used in the copy machines then which reproduced in a very poor quality. The result was so inferior that I discarded the typewritten multiple copy form letter in favor of hand written letters on my personal stationery. With a personal letter I could request specific information if required.

I began by hand writing letters to *all* of the Bicknells who were listed in the Toronto Telephone Directory.

I included a self addressed, stamped envelope for a return reply.

Box 5510, Station F.
Ottawa, Ontario
K2C 3M1
November 15. 1977

Dear Sir or Madame,

I am trying to locate Beatrice Louise Bicknell, born April 03, 1918. She had a brother James Bicknell, born July 1st, 1920.

They were the children of James and Beatrice Bicknell. The Bicknells were members of St. Paul's Anglican Church on Bloor St. E.

Any information you can provide about the family would be appreciated. I am working on the Bicknell genealogy.

Sincerely,

Margaret R. Bresee

Most of the Bicknell families who received a letter of enquiry sent a reply, whether or not they had pertinent information. There were only a few replies from the Watsons, perhaps because of the randomly chosen names which may not have had any relevance to the people to whom I wrote. All of the letters are a treasured inclusion in my personal archives.

I should say here, that my husband was not supportive of the idea of me searching for my birth family; perhaps he feared that I would get hurt, or he may have had other reasons which he was never able to articulate, or chose not to discuss. I was on a very important journey, determined to search for my family, so secretly I rented a postal box for the replies and waited.

The letters flowed into Box 5510. On November 6, 1977, I received a letter from Edith Bicknell which opened doors to my search and it was also the beginning of a wonderful friendship between us which has recently expanded to include her daughter and her family.

20 Avoca Ave, #303
Toronto, Nov. 6/77.

Dear Mrs M. R. Breece:

I believe the James & Beatrice Bicknell to whom you refer were cousins of my husband (A. Bertram Bicknell, son of Alfred).

James & Beatrice had two children – James (who was born on July 1st but I do not know what year) and a girl called "Betty". Possibly this was a nickname. She died some years ago. I did not know her.

Sincerely,
Edith Bicknell

When I read that Betty had died, at first I was saddened, but then, I thought, perhaps Edith had incorrect information. I replied to her note and she suggested that I contact Muriel Bicknell, my grandfather's sister.

Muriel Bicknell's married name was Keachie. I wrote to Mrs. Keachie immediately and her son James Keachie replied with a five page family history of the immediate Bicknell family. He said he was delighted that someone was updating the family genealogy. *The Bicknell Genealogy,* by Thomas W. Bicknell, had been published in 1913. James Keachie had a copy of the book and said he would be delighted to let me see it. He invited me to come to Toronto to meet his family and see the book.

One line in James' letter crushed my hopes and dreams when I read that my mother, Beatrice Louise Bicknell had died on April 03, 1964. I was shattered. I read it over and over, hoping I had made an error in interpreting the information. It could be another Beatrice Bicknell. I didn't want to believe that my mother was dead after all the years of trying to find her. Sitting in the car alone at the postal centre where I picked up my mail, I sobbed and sobbed. There was no one to share my grief.

It seemed that so many people that I had loved had been taken away from me. My parents who adopted me had been dead for many years, my first love died in a car crash on his way to visit me and my family for a week-end. I had lost classmates, aunts, uncles, cousins and even two dear kindergarten students who were very special in my life. Even though I had a husband and daughter whom I loved, at that moment I felt very much alone.

I had finally found my beloved birth mother only to learn that she had died too soon.

Would I continue? Of course I would. I had decided that I would to write the Bicknell family history as a way of finding not only my birth mother but my family of origin, so, although my mother was my motivation I would continue my journey.

I decided it was time to introduce myself to the Keachie family and tell them who I thought I was.

Provided that the Keachies thought that it was appropriate, it would be wonderful for me to meet Muriel Bicknell, who I concluded from the information sent to me by her son James Keachie, was my great aunt, my grandfather's sister. Now, I had to decide how to introduce myself to the Keachie family.

I planned my introduction. I would carefully choose someone to write a letter of introduction for me which would accompany copies of my documents and my own personal letter and photographs.

There were many people I could have approached, to write this crucial letter. I've been asked why I didn't choose a person in a position of authority or prestige and there were such persons I could have called upon but it was more than just writing something about me, it had to be someone who understood the confidential and very personal nature of my request. Whoever was entrusted with this task had to know me well and be able to convey the sacred nature of my interest in meeting my family, specifically, to the woman I believed to be my Great Aunt Muriel.

I considered very carefully about who knew me well enough and would have the interest and skill to capture my highly charged emotional interest but non-threatening approach to meeting my family and could introduce me by way of written communication. I decided Carl and Dorothy Steele were those special people.

The Steeles knew my husband and I and our daughter Christine through our work together in our church. They were dear friends, articulate, interesting and greatly respected in the community and in our church. I called them and asked if I could come to talk about something important to me. They agreed and listened intently as I told them about my search for my birth mother and what I had found out thus far. They read the letter from James Keachie and we discussed it together. They shared my sadness that my birth mother had died; they shared my joy with tears and laughter at having, at last, found my birth family. I explained that I wanted to meet my family, especially Muriel Keachie, and asked Carl and Dorothy if they would write a letter of introduction for me to accompany my own letter. I knew it would be perfect.

Dorothy and Carl wrote a flattering introduction, a copy also in my archives, and I sent their letter, along with mine, a letter from Archdeacon Dann and copies of my authenticating documents and some photos of my husband Del, Christine and I, to James Keachie, in Toronto. I thanked him for his letter, and confessed that I had a specific reason for writing a Bicknell genealogy. I believed Beatrice Bicknell was my mother, and expressed my sadness that my mother had died. I asked if he thought it was appropriate for me to meet his mother, Mrs. Muriel Keachie. She was the closest living relative to my mother, or so I thought. I said that if he felt it was not appropriate, that I would not pursue my search any further.

The letter was mailed, this time with a phone number instead of a self-addressed, stamped envelope.

A few days later as I was preparing supper the phone rang in the kitchen.

"Hello," I said still focused on stirring a sauce.

"Hello, Margaret?" I heard a strong, warm voice that I didn't recognize.

"Yes, this is Margaret."

"This is Jim Keachie in Toronto. I've just called to welcome you to the family."

When my feet returned to the floor and my heart started beating again I stammered and blurted my way through the conversation. Then I heard Jim's wife, Kay's soft, musical voice, also saying how glad she was that I had contacted them. Jim came back on the phone and invited me to come to meet them. I'll always remember Jim's voice welcoming me to the family.

It's one of the most wonderful invitations I've ever had.

I hung up the phone.

"Who was that dear?" My husband asked.

Okay, what do I do now? I had to tell my husband what I had been up to and understandably, he was not pleased and as you can imagine a few awkward, even unpleasant hours ensued. I won't delve into that any further. Eventually he became caught up in my excitement and he and Christine were fully included in all of the plans.

In the next few weeks, many telephone calls and notes passed between the Keachies and me. They encouraged us to come to Toronto to meet them. On the day after Christmas, 1978, we made that momentous trip on our way home from visiting with my Aunt Lavenia Beaton, her daughter Eleanor and family in Wingham, Ontario. It turned out that Eleanor's husband Jim Ward knew Edith Bicknell who was one of the people who so kindly took the time to reply to my seeking letter. Edith Bicknell and Jim Ward's mother had been good friends for many years. Neither of us knew of this connection previously. It really is a small world.

An account of my first visit with Aunt Muriel is written in another chapter of my memoir.

When I returned from meeting my Great Aunt Muriel and her family, I was in a euphoric state which I cannot describe. I learned that my parents had married six years after my adoption and that I had a brother and three sisters. I was anxious to meet them and to get to know them. I wanted to hear their stories about growing up with my mother and to see photos of my mother and my family. I wanted to know everything all at once! My new found family was all I wanted to talk about.

The word spread throughout the Bicknell family that "Betty's child has turned up," and family members wrote and called, wanting to know all about me. A recurring question was,

"Have you had a good life Margaret? Were your parents good to you?"

It warmed my heart that they were interested in me and concerned.

I easily answered, "Yes."

My school principal didn't know how to cope with my heightened excitement about my new-found family and invited the school psychiatrist, to come to visit me. She wasn't long recognizing that the classroom wasn't the place for me during this exciting time.

Her advice was, "You must go to your family and stay until you know within your heart that it's time to come home. I'm approving compassionate leave, starting today."

I left my classroom at noon that day for an extended absence. I shall always be grateful to the Ottawa Board of Education for their understanding and kindness, not only then but throughout my career.

And so, on January 23, 1979, with the full support of my husband and daughter, I climbed on the train in Ottawa and traveled to Toronto for one of the most wonderful and emotionally charged visits of my life. I was going to get to know my birth family, at last.

*

After conveying the news to my Singleton family that I had found my biological family, the first letter I received was from Freda (Singleton) McElroy. The letter was beautifully written and conveyed her delight and happiness for me. That letter was quickly followed by others from her sisters, Jackie (Singleton) McRobert and Rae (Singleton) Darling, now deceased who were equally excited for me. It means a great deal to me.

21. Meeting My Great Aunt Muriel

The table was beautifully laid with a linen cloth, sterling silver cutlery and exquisite crystal glasses. On the dark walnut buffet I saw the dessert dishes, delicate cups and saucers and a tray of liqueur glasses carefully placed for later. Aunt Muriel was on my left still holding my hand so tightly that it was getting prickly from lack of circulation. She had taken my hand as we entered the house less than an hour ago when we met for the very first time.

Cast into my memory forever is the image of that dear, elegant woman standing on the verandah with her arms outstretched, gracefully waving an ivory cigarette holder while she waited impatiently for me to climb the few steps to reach her. As I stepped on to the verandah she had engulfed me in a warm, firm embrace.

"I'm your Great Aunt Muriel", she said in her strong, low voice. "My brother James was your grandfather".

Then she placed her hands firmly on my shoulders still brandishing the cigarette holder and pushed me back at arm's length, looked into my face and in a tone of disapproval but with a twinkle in her eyes, she said,

"Your mother was a bad girl."

I had found my family and it was overwhelmingly wonderful. It was the day after Christmas, 1978, a sunny day, but numbingly cold, so we didn't linger long outside. How wonderful of them to have come outside to greet us. They must have been watching for our arrival from the window.

Warm introductions to Muriel's sons Bill and Jim and Jim's wife Kay were made to me, my husband Del and our daughter Christine, then Jim ushered us into the house out of the cold. Our coats and outer clothing were taken and we were guided into the formal living room. It could have been so awkward for them and for us but Jim and Kay were welcoming and warm.

Sherry was served, greetings and toasts were offered and I sat spellbound, overwhelmed and almost incapable of taking in the conversations. Over and over I kept thinking, *this is my family, these people are my family.*

I could feel the brilliant red of my flushed face and skin as I stammered answers to very simple questions.

"Did you have a good Christmas?" asked Jim

"Yes thanks." I said

"Who was it you were visiting"? he continued.

"We had Christmas with my adoptive mother's sister, Lavenia Beaton and her family in Wingham".

"Was it a long drive from Wingham? Were the roads plowed?"

This time Del jumped into the conversation and answered,

"The roads were snow covered and icy in spots but we didn't have any trouble. And it was interesting to see the Mennonite families wrapped in warm blankets driving along the shoulder of the road in their horse and buggies."

"Mom," Jim glanced at his mother, "Do you remember that Pop called me 'Horse' and when I married Kay he called her 'Buggy'? Pop had a nickname for everyone. Pop was my dad, Margaret."

I have a spontaneous laugh that is hearty and comes deep from within me and my laugh overcame my feelings of insecurity.

"My God," said Jim, "There's no denying you are James Bicknell's granddaughter. Your laugh is just like his. You could easily pick James out of a crowd by his laugh. Kay, isn't Margaret's laugh just like Uncle Jim's?"

"Yes, I guess, but I didn't know him well. I was thinking how much she is like your sister Clare, Jim. Not just her looks but her manner too. Clare was just few years older than Betty, Margaret's mother."

"Clare was my daughter," said Aunt Muriel, squeezing my hand, "She was a beautiful person and died of cancer a few years ago. We were very close and I miss her. Kay, we must introduce Margaret to Clare's daughter, Lesley."

This was amazing to me. I was already placed in the family and made to feel that I belonged through a suggestion that I meet another family member. My excitement rose as the day progressed.

Jim turned his attention to Christine.

"And you, my dear girl, what do you enjoy doing? You have a cast on your leg. What happened there?

"I was running down the stairs and jumped that last few steps and tore the ligaments in my knee."

I'm sorry to hear that, Christine. I hope it isn't too painful."

"It's not too bad."

"That's great, my girl. I expect you have lots of friends in Ottawa."

"My best friend is Wanda and she lives in the house next door. She was adopted, just like my Mom."

"Oh, was she. And what sports or activities do you like, Christine?"

Christine and Jim had a conversation about her favourite activities and interests while other conversations filled the room. A little "buzz," of sorts.

"Margaret, you are a teacher in Ottawa, you said. What grade do you teach?"

"I'm a kindergarten teacher for both four and five year old children. I'm presently working on a project to create a Special Education Program for kindergarten aged children."

"Why would young children need a special program?" Bill asked.

"In the Ottawa Board of Education children must fail grade one and two before they are given any special help and by then many children have a very poor self image and often behaviour problems develop as a result. It is important for children to have successes rather than failures and not just in a school environment but at home and in other activities as well. In the special program which I am creating, each child would have an individual program designed for his or her success. I will work closely with the parents and families of the children."

I could have talked longer about the program because it was something I was passionate about, but it wasn't the right time or place. Sometimes I get carried away in my enthusiasm.

"That sounds very exciting Margaret", said Bill.

"It is," I replied.

Kay made numerous appearances from the kitchen as she tried to be a part of the conversation as she prepared the lunch. Through the years I learned that she was a master of this art. She appeared once again in the doorway and announced that lunch was ready. I don't remember if I offered to help her with the preparation of the meal but I expect that I didn't. I was too overwhelmed by the emotions surging through me to think of anything beyond soaking in the warmth and closeness I felt as my "new" Aunt Muriel sat close to me and cradled my hand in hers.

Jim invited us to the table.

"Mom, down your sherry," he laughed, "we'll have wine at the table."

Aunt Muriel had been too busy attending to me to drink her sherry, but she put the glass to her lips and finished it, then peered into the glass to make sure there wasn't any more.

We walked into the formal dining room and Del and Christine were seated at the far side of the table away from the door, Aunt Muriel and I opposite them and Bill on my right leaving me between mother and son. Bill smiled at me and leaned in to bump my shoulder with his. Jim was at the head of the table and Kay at the other end closest to the kitchen for convenience in serving.

Aunt Muriel, on my left continued to grasp my hand.

"Bill, would you pour the wine please?" Jim asked.

"Oh, I'd be delighted to do that," Bill said as he stood to reach the bottle.

The wine bottle covered in gold mesh indicated a very fine wine. The wine had already been uncorked and wrapped with a white linen serviette which partially covered a distinguishing blue and gold label. Bill carefully poured wine for Jim to taste and asked for his approval which he gave with lively enthusiasm. We were then each offered the full bodied red wine. As the meal progressed Bill was attentive to our wine needs, topping up each glass. I wasn't very knowledgeable about wine then, but I knew this was a superb one. Bill offered Christine a variety of juices or soft drinks to choose from.

Kay had chosen to serve a roast beef dinner at noon as we had a long drive home to Ottawa later in the day and she thought we might need something substantial. Jim carved the tender, rare roast beef at the table and served each plate. Bill placed the vegetables carefully on the side and then handed the plates to Kay who added the mashed potatoes. When the gravy and other condiments began circling the table, Bill could see I was having difficulty and admonished his mother in a kindly, fun loving way.

"Mother, maybe you could free Margaret's hand so she can serve herself some gravy!"

My freedom was short lived and as soon as I had poured the gravy, Aunt Muriel found my hand again and gave it a squeeze. The meal continued with my hand alternating from immobility to use. Aunt Muriel who used her right hand exclusively made awkward attempts to lift her fork to her mouth with her left hand to the great delight of her sons.

She finally gave up on her attempts to eat with her non-dominate hand and just concentrated on drinking her wine.

"Jim, could I have some more wine please".

"Yes, mother, but just sip it to get the fullness of the flavour.

I was growing fond of my new cousins and in the first few hours of getting to know my family I began to understand their sense of fun, their affection for their mother and for each other.

Aunt Muriel drew closer to me and the stories of my unknown birth family began to tumble out as she tried to fill in forty four missing years for me, in one afternoon.

"You know who your father was," she announced, waving her wine glass precariously at me and diving right into the subject.

"Mother, be careful," Bill admonished.

"No, I don't know who my father was," I said, realizing she was speaking as though he was already dead. I really never thought much about my father."

My intense interest had been focused on my mother. The chance of finding my father seemed remote as it had taken so many years to get this far in my search.

"Your father was Clyde Elder," Aunt Muriel said with authority. She was a woman who at the age of eighty- seven still had a keen mind for the details of her immediate and extended family's lives. She knew the birth and marriage dates of everyone close to her, the details of her grandchildren and great grand-children's lives, what they enjoyed and who their friends were. She was a skillful story teller and remembered the particulars of events, long forgotten by other family members. Over the years it was Aunt Muriel who brought to life many of the people I missed knowing in person.

"You know you have a brother and three sisters and you have twin sisters. I attended their christening and I was also a guest at all of their weddings." Aunt Muriel informed me.

"I went too," said Kay. "Jim didn't go though, did you Jim?"

"No," said Jim, "I leave those functions to you women to attend and represent the family".

I was excited to hear more about my siblings. How could this be? *Probably a half brother and half sisters*, I thought. I shuddered when I recalled how my search was almost aborted ten years earlier because of the incident when my documents were confiscated by a lawyer.

Aunt Muriel let go of my hand and stroked my hair, sending shivers of delight up my back and also jolted me out of my silent reflection.

“Please tell me more about my brothers and sisters.”

Aunt Muriel finished her glass of wine and held it out for more. Her son obliged but poured just a little.

“Well”, she continued, “Your mother Betty Bicknell had you when she was still in school. She had to leave Branksome Hall. I’ll tell you the story of how she met your father Clyde Elder and why she got pregnant when we are alone sometime. When your grandfather, James Bicknell, found out that she was pregnant he arranged for Betty to have an abortion. But Betty wanted to keep you and I think your grandmother did too. In Betty’s headstrong way, she ran away from home and went to the *Victor Home for Girls*, a home that the Massey family established in Toronto for wayward girls. She lived there for a few months and then came home a couple of months before you were born. It upset your grandfather because she would parade herself in front of your grandfather’s most important clients.”

Tears surfaced as I tried to imagine my mother, a young woman of privilege, recently a student at Branksome Hall, pregnant and alone in the Victor Home for Girls.

When I was about eleven years of age I had a wonderful adventure when my parents put me on the train in Brockville to go and visit a relative in Toronto. While I was in Toronto my cousin Evelyn took me to see the house where my mother lived during most of the time she was pregnant.

“This is where you were born,” she said.

My Brownie camera captured a photo of the brick house with the large front verandah. It was The Victor Home for Girls.

The afternoon progressed in a blur. So many questions to be asked, so much to learn and I couldn’t take it all in. Jim brought the Bicknell Genealogy which had been published in 1912 to show me and we talked about my progress in the one I was writing which was still just an idea really. It had been a way of contacting Bicknells and finding my family and I knew I had to complete the project.

As the evening approached we said out good-byes and left Toronto to return home to Ottawa. I was invited to return as soon as I could so that I could meet more of the family. Aunt Muriel was very anxious for me to meet my brother and sisters, but I'm sure her excitement didn't match mine.

22. A Conversation with Grandfather Bicknell

Hello, Grandfather, it's me, Dorothy. Remember me? In spite of your elaborate schemes and illegalities to erase me from all records, even to the extent of altering my birth registration, I have found you. I'm not sure if you will be proud or angry that I discovered ways to sift through years of locked drawers, sealed documents, secrecy and closed mouths to find you and my mother in order to claim who I am. Even a pretentious lawyer succumbed to my demands and returned essential documents to me. I'm peering back through time trying to understand your motivation for the decisions you made when you learned that your daughter was pregnant. I also have questions about my birth. Your decisions affected many of your loved ones but specifically, your daughter, Betty who is my mother. Your decisions changed my life. Grandfather, even though I have come to know you as a very powerful man, I also see a soft and loving side of your personality.

You seem so far away but I have an idea that I'm quite sure will allow me to see you more clearly, a way that will to bring us closer together for this little chat.

When your sister, Muriel, died, among her possessions was your exquisite Paris opera glasses, engraved with your name *James Bicknell,* in script and, Grandfather, I am the fortunate one who received this precious gift. Do you know that I take these beautiful glasses with me when I attend the opera? I imagine you sitting beside me and after the performance we have a lively discussion. I have them in my hands and I'm gently pushing up the clasp on the lid of the worn, shaped, black leather case. Now, I carefully slide the shimmering mother of pearl opera glasses out of their fuchsia coloured velvet lining. I lift the lovely glasses to my eyes and adjust the lens.

You are coming into focus, Grandfather.

You look very comfortable there in the library relaxed in your leather chair with its aged patina. Your brow is furrowed and it appears something is troubling you. The recent issues of *Time Magazine, Film Weekly* and *The New York Times* are waiting, unopened, for your attention. Your faithful butler, Fred, is still with you and has just brought you your evening drink, I see.

I love the patent leather shoes and silk socks. You are always so perfectly attired. I've looked at dozens of photographs of you and your wardrobe is extensive. Guess that's where my fashion gene comes from.

May I come in? Could we talk, please? There are a number of things on my heart that I want to discuss with you; so many unanswered questions to be addressed.

Thank you, Grandfather.

Yes, thanks, I'd like a drink. I'll sit here close to you in Grandmother's place if I may.

Scotch will be perfect. Over ice, please.

Thank you, Fred.

This isn't easy for me, Grandfather and I've spent a great deal of time thinking about what I want to say. I want to ask about some of the decisions you made and which I wish to challenge, but, I am keeping an open mind.

First of all I want you to think about how heart wrenching it had to have been for my mother to say goodbye to me when I was seven months old. When my own daughter was a baby I hadn't yet found you, and knew nothing of the circumstances of my birth, although I always knew I was adopted into the Singleton family. As I held my baby I thought about my mother giving me away and wondered how I would ever cope if I had to give my child to a stranger and never see her again. Is it any wonder that Betty developed stomach ulcers which were the cause of her early death? I grieve that I hadn't found a way to begin my search earlier and if I had, might she have lived beyond her forties? Were her ulcers a result of her pain and heartbrokenness in giving up her baby?

Indeed Grandfather, I realize it was embarrassing for you when important clients came to the house and saw Betty expecting a child. By then the whispering and whatever else you feared had already happened. Aunt Muriel told me about your embarrassment when Betty ran away from the Victor Home for Girls and returned home so visibly pregnant to you and Grandmother and as Aunt Muriel said,

"Betty paraded herself in front of your Grandfather's most important clients."

Even though Betty was young you could have let she and Clyde marry. They did anyway, soon after your death. If you'll pardon me for this, it sort of amused me to see Clyde's signature on the second line of the visitor's book at the Funeral Home where many came to visit you for the last time. Grandfather, Clyde was a pall bearer too.

I know about the reunion between Betty and Clyde at the King Edward Hotel. You had a deep love for Betty, your "Princess" and you saw how much she loved Clyde even though he wasn't your choice of suitor.

They didn't marry until after your death Grandfather, a few years after that meeting at the King Edward.

I'm sorry about your untimely death, Grandfather and if you hadn't sent me away we might have become quite close in the six years we would have had together. I have tears, thinking about how I was deprived time with you and getting to know you when I was a child. You might have read to me as we curled up together in that big chair. That's a dream which can never be. Aunt Muriel told me about your love of fun and your distinctive laugh. I've been told that my laugh is like yours. I too, love fun and laughter so we have those things in common.

Let's go back to the Victor Home for Girls for a moment. Betty was so brave to go there and I doubt that she had any idea of what she was going to experience. I think that you quickly traced her there but left your daughter in that place without any emotional or family support. Did you want to punish Betty in the same manner as the rest of society? Betty could have died and certainly my life was in danger too. Betty was lonely; she was looked down on and without proper nutrition or even suitable clothing. How could you abandon her like that? What was grandmother's reaction? Surely it wouldn't have been her choice to leave her daughter there. It makes me so angry and perturbed when I think about it. You had wealth, prestige, connections and power, everything you needed to help your daughter to have a wonderful, safe, healthy life during her pregnancy. And another thing that just makes me steam. It terrifies me, actually. Why did you arrange for my mother to have an abortion? That's why she ran away. She wanted to give birth to the baby she and her lover, Clyde, had planned.

I'll pour another drink if that's agreeable to you, because I need one. Fred's gone out. Oh, I know, women don't pour the drinks but it's something I know how to do so just deal with it. This is a lovely crystal decanter, Grandfather. I have your sterling silver sugar shaker, the one you always had on your dining room table. It was a gift from Aunt Muriel the day we met for the first time. It's another of my special treasures; another reminder of you and Grandmother and my family, lost.

I wept as I was researching the Victor Home and living my mother's life there through writing her story.

I'm sure it made you angry that Betty had disobeyed you when you had already arranged the abortion. It was embarrassing for you to have to tell your friends where Betty was so I expect you just told them she was on a trip. You decided that she had "made her bed and she could lie in it." You would wash your hands of the whole situation. Once, you called the Home and Matron said you couldn't see Betty, it was against their policy.

But Grandfather, you must have sent money to the Victor Home otherwise Betty could not have stayed. They took in "wayward girls" as they were referred to and many of the girls were destitute but Betty was from a position of prestige in society and Matron would know that and I'm sure demand money from you if Betty was to be allowed to stay on as a resident. I think you left your daughter there alone to fend for herself because you were exercising your control and disapproval and punishing Betty for her "sins." An attitude of, "You dare to disobey me, I'll show you who's in control here!"

Grandfather, I'm incensed about the fallacious records of my birth. You, a prominent lawyer falsified your daughter's name and mine on my birth registration which is a legal document. You were so determined to bury my identity and yet, when I needed emergency surgery at birth you found the most skilled surgeon and against all odds, I lived. I am very grateful to you for the decisions you made then and I want to talk more about that later.

I searched for years for my birth registration and only recently received the document from Service Ontario.

Dr. Louis Scheck, your uncle by marriage to your Aunt Ellen Bicknell, delivered me into this world. Grandfather, Dr. Scheck was eighty-four years old, for goodness sake. I'm appalled. As I'm writing this a person who is eighty-four is not thought of as old, but in 1935 a person who lived to eighty-four was ancient. I doubt there are any doctors over the age of seventy years delivering babies even in this era. Were you so focused on keeping my birth a secret that you arranged for that old man to be my mother's physician knowing you could control what he recorded on the birth registration? We were both at risk for death or injury. Dr. Allan Brown was my subsequent baby doctor and I know that because I have the baby formula he wrote for me which has his signature. He was your friend too, and he was the one who examined my mother after she escaped from the Victor Home. Why would you not have had Dr. Brown deliver me? I was astounded when I recently found this new information about Dr. Scheck. The positive outcome is that I learned that his wife was my great Aunt Ellen, after years of searching records for the Bicknell genealogy for her, to no avail. When I traced Dr. Scheck' family history I discovered his marriage to Ellen Bicknell, in 1911. You kept it all in the family. I'm appalled at your conniving ways. I'm convinced that you chose Dr. Scheck so that you could have the records changed.

Dr. Brown would have refused to alter the names on the birth registration as he was at the pinnacle of his career and it would have had severe consequences had he been found out. For Dr. Louis Scheck, it didn't matter. He had already left his practice but you arranged for him to be at the Victoria Hospital when it was Betty's time to deliver her baby. I'm heartsick for my mother too, having that old man deliver her baby.

The power and influence you had just boggles my mind. It also makes me mad as hell that you could get away with this to the detriment of other people. It seems to me that you didn't think of others, just yourself. How did that impact on my mother? She had to sign a document using another name that was not hers. Were you and Dr. Scheck standing over her? Did she hesitate and refuse at first? There is an error on my birth registration, an answer scratched out and rewritten and I wonder if it is because she was distraught, under pressure. She named me and although my first name was on the birth registration, my surname and hers is incorrect. When I began my search for my birth family the falsified name on the Court Order for my adoption threw me totally off track.

"Dorothy Watson." Who in the world is that?

I wonder if the falsified birth registration had anything to do with my lawyer's strange behavior in confiscating my documents because he realized they had been altered. Did he actually know you? He would have recognized the name Bicknell on the court order. The Old Boys Club was protecting one of its members, perhaps. I wonder.

But, Grandfather, I found you in spite of all of your efforts to conceal my very existence.

But, it's too late Grandfather. It's too late and I lament not knowing my mother or you and Grandmother.

The other piece in my birth story I want to talk about is my illness. I give you accolades with this one! You arranged an abortion and when my mother outsmarted you and avoided the procedure you orchestrated an elaborate cover-up of my birth. But then when I was only two days old I required immediate surgery for pyloric stenosis and your response is, in my mind, out of character. You found the best surgeon and medical care for me that was available. Would it not have been easy to let me die? You could have called old doctor Scheck who probably had trembling hands and poor eyesight by then and he might have done me in quite naturally, without any question or autopsy. You could have. In 1935, most babies died during that surgery. From what I have learned about you, that would have been your logical course. Am I judging you too harshly?

Grandfather, I found the surgeon who assisted at my surgery. She was the Medical Officer of Health in Ottawa at one time. Her internship was at Sick Children's Hospital and she remembered the surgery because, first of all, it was rare for girls to have the condition and secondly, most girls died. Boys had a better chance of survival for some reason. The doctor asked me if she could see my scar, and when she saw it laughed heartily and said I should sue the medical profession for the botched job in stitching me together. Grandfather, I'm very grateful for my life. Thank you for doing the right thing that time.

I want to believe that after you saw me everything changed and you felt a bond with me because I was Betty's, child and your granddaughter. But, you still couldn't let her keep me because of the social stigma for Betty, her brother James and for you and your wife, Bea, as well as the extended family. You would have wanted Betty to finish school and to find a suitable young man to marry, perhaps a doctor or a lawyer in her social circle. In your view, Clyde was not the right man for her and she was too young to understand the consequences of marrying beneath her. Betty wouldn't be accepted in Rosedale as a single unwed mother. What a stigma for Bea, her mother to endure. Bea was looking forward to Betty's "Coming Out Party." Betty couldn't do any of the things young women were expected to do if she had a child, even with a nurse to care for the baby.

I wish I knew more about how you looked for parents for me. I know the full story of how my adoptive parents searched for a child. That day, in late November, 1935, when Fred drove the Limousine to Belleville with me cradled in my Grandmother's arms, to give me away to strangers, it must have been utterly heart rendering for grandmother and for my mother. How did Betty get through that day? Why didn't you all come with me, Grandfather? Did you ever think about how I felt? Did you not realize how terrified I was? I cried for days and days. People didn't know that babies felt emotions of abandonment and fear when they were adopted away. Think about it. At seven and a half months of age I was suddenly in unusual surroundings with strange people; the car was completely unfamiliar; the farm smells must have been bizarre maybe even repulsive; the spoken language and voice intonation was different. When we arrived in Soperton, and my new home, even the dog waiting for us was terrifying, bigger and more active than my mother's little Jack Russell and he smelled bad! There was nothing comforting or familiar about the house. I was cold at first and everything was unknown; my bed, my clothes, the diapers, the person who held me and fed me, the songs she sang, the young boy who peered in at me. And that big, black thing they called a wood-stove, once they got it going, belched out heat and it was frightening.

Don't you understand Grandfather? My new parents did everything they knew how to do and never understood why I was so distraught for so many days. They changed my name to Margaret, too and I didn't recognize the name as mine. Few people in the family understood my longing, sadness, anger and discontent as I was growing up. Once when I was sent to my room for being so cranky, I was often sent to my room, my Uncle Ed Harney came upstairs to talk to me. He told me that if I didn't stop being so cross I would never have any friends. I was only about four years of age then, but I remember that incident vividly and how I worked at overcoming those feelings that I didn't understand. I did try not to be so grouchy but I still had longings and sadness.

The Singletons were good parents and I loved them. They cared well for me and I experienced a healthy and remarkable life on the farm. Remarkable in comparison to how farmers are often portrayed. The Singletons were well educated but led a strict Victorian life-style. Activities such as dancing, cards, cigarettes and alcohol were taboo! However, they took me to concerts, sent me for piano and voice lessons, bought books for me to read and encouraged me to go to University, which I did in my adult years after their deaths. I'm sure they made sacrifices in order to do things for me. Even with their love I longed for my birth mother and could think of little else, with the result that I failed a year in high school. I was really "messed up," Grandfather.

My personality was worlds apart from my adoptive brother. My parents believed strongly that environment was more important than heredity. How wrong they and psychologists of the time were and I can attest to that without any doubt. I longed to go to dances, to sing in a concert hall not just in church or in school productions. I wanted to be a journalist and secretly applied and was accepted at Ryerson College in Toronto. I wasn't allowed to attend the program. The professions considered appropriate for me were teaching or nursing. I felt I belonged in the city which beckoned to me but I couldn't leave and disappoint my adoptive parents. Grandfather, I lived at home until I had the courage, to announce that I planned to attend Teacher's College in Toronto after I had taught for two years in a rural school. I had earned enough money to support myself in Toronto. Grandfather, you might not have allowed me to go into any profession. You would probably have wanted me to marry well and entertain at teas and be seen at gala functions and that wouldn't have suited me. My adoptive parents strongly believed in getting an education and having a profession, although selected from a short list, "To fall back on," my mom used to say. I'm happy I had those opportunities.

Sorry, Grandfather, I didn't intend to go on like that. I guess I've been holding on to that for a long time. Whew, it's good to get my thoughts and feelings out into the open and let it go.

Now, my dear Grandfather, I want to tell you that it is due to the wonderful, loving reception of my biological family and through writing this story that I am healing from the trauma of being adopted away and overcoming the sadness of my detachment from my birth mother.

Do you remember Betty's friend Annie German, Grandfather? She told me that when I contacted the Keachies a cousin who was a friend of Annie's said, "Guess who turned up?" That speaks volumes in that I know you were not totally successful in hiding the fact of my birth. Some members of the family knew of my birth and wondered what had become of me.

If my adoptive parents and others who had information had shared what they knew, all of our lives would have been different.

Whether that would have been good or bad we'll never know. I'm thankful that the Singletons were my parents and in retrospect many of the experiences I had living in the country enriched my life. But, I continue to regret that I didn't know my mother, Betty Bicknell, my grandmother and you, grandfather. My other sadness is that I didn't grow up with my sisters and my brother. But, it's a joy to know them now.

The letters and documents were all in the box in the closet.

Grandfather, don't cry. May I kiss you on the cheek?

I love you and forgive you, Grandfather.

23. Epilogue

When James Bicknell refused to allow his daughter Betty to marry Clyde Elder, James believed it was the best decision. I have been able to establish that Clyde Elder married someone else after he was banished from Betty Bicknell's life. After the death of James Bicknell, Clyde divorced his wife and married Betty Bicknell. Their marriage certificate is dated March 6th, 1943. Clyde and Betty had four more children, twin girls, a third girl and a boy.

24. Acknowledgments

Many people were involved in the journey of this book. Heather Menzies, author and friend, nudged and encouraged me to write my story and walked the journey with me from the exploration of the mosquito infested woods of my childhood to search for a lost special place, to our visit to the historic King Edward Hotel in Toronto where we stood in awe of the magnificent Crystal Ballroom of the past.

I am indebted to Rita Donovan, author, mentor and editor who read my unfolding stories and critiqued with humour, patience and creative vignettes and helped me to mold my tale into a book. When my confidence faded, her optimistic faith in me and my story, cheered me on.

My daughter, Christine Bresee, a nurse by profession, researched the medical instruments and procedures used in the thirties. She dove into Canadian Medical Archives of the past and found fascinating films about pregnancy and birthing. I deeply appreciate her skilled research, literary knowledge and support.

It is always a delight to meet Cousin Susan Norwich, who has shared family stories and assisted me with dates and timelines. Cousin Lesley Crysler consulted her attic treasure trove of albums and found rare photographs, one of an electric car owned by a great grandmother. She also gifted to me my grandfather's precious Paris opera glasses. My birth brother Jim Elder, his wife Nancy and my birth sister Donna Liggitt and her husband John provided documents and photographs and continue to give acceptance, love and friendship.

My birth mother's friend Annie German is an astonishing woman. She shared stories of my mother, their friendship and schooldays and their life in Rosedale in the 1930s. I appreciate Annie allowing me to record our conversations and to reveal some of that discourse in the public realm.

Others who gave willingly of their time and expertise are; my brother and sister-in-law Wallace and Dorothy Singleton, who spent time with me going through family albums, as Wallace and I talked about our lives together on the farm, cousin Eleanor Ward for photos and family stories, Ag O'Neill who listened to my stories and plans from the very beginning of my search, Karen Hill who helped with typing when my computer was whirring it's last gigabyte, Sister Rosemary O'Toole for her instantaneous intuitive wisdom and spiritual guidance, my dear friends Rosemary and Graham Takarangi in Wanganui, New Zealand for offering their lovely vacation Bach in Omori, New Zealand so that I could write in an idyllic setting, Dave and Colleen Colling at Omori Store, for their friendship, food, trips into Turangi and to Taupo and also for generously allowing me to use their internet while I was in Omori.

When including names there's always a chance that someone will be left out and if that has happened, I do apologize. It was unintentional.

25. Index of Photographs & Illustrations

26. Reference Books

Dorothea Brande, *Becoming a Writer*, J.P. Tarcher, Inc., Los Angeles, 1981.

Ted Cate, Adrian G., *Brockville, A Pictorial History*. Kingston-Hanson, *1972*.

Michael William Charles, *City of Bellville History*. Picton Gazette, 1943.

C.S. Clark, *Of Toronto the Good, The Queen City of Canada as it is*. The Toronto Publishing Company. 1898. Reprinted Coles, 1970.

Bess Hillery Crawford, *Rosedale*. Boston Mills Press, Erin, Ontario, 2000.

Natalie Goldberg: *Writing Down the Bones, Freeing the Writer Within*. Shambhala Publications, 2005.

Natalie Goldberg: *Old Friend from Far Away, The Practice of Writing Memoir.* Free Press, New York, 2007.

Ted Loder, *Prayers For The Battle*, Page 17, *Guide Me into an Unclenched Moment*, Innisfree Press, Philadelphia, PA, 1984.

Heather Menzies, *Enter Mourning*, Key Porter Books, Toronto, Ontario. 2009.

Mika, *Historic Belleville*, Mika Publishing Co., Bellville, 1977.

By Mika, *Mosaic of Belleville; An Illustrated History of the City.* Miko Publishing Co., 1966.

C. Pelham Mulvany, *Toronto Past and Present Until 1882, Illustrated.* W.E. Caiger, Publisher, Toronto, Ontario, 1884, Reprint, Ontario Reprint Press, Toronto, 1970.

Colleen Sell, Editor: *A Cup of Support for Writers.* Adams Media, Avon, MA, USA, 2007.

Brockville, The River City. Published by Toronto Natural History/ Natural History, 1977.

Websites of Interest

Adoption Council of Ontario; http://www.adoption.on.ca/

British Isles Family History Society; Ottawa; http://www.bifhsgo.ca/

Bicknell website; http://familytreemaker.genealogy.com/users/s/i/n/ Margaret-Singleton-ON/

Church of Latter Day Saints, Family History Centre; https://www.familysearch.org/

Domestic Public Adoption; Adoption Resource Central; http://www.familyhelper.net/arc/pub.html

Family Tree Records and Research; Ancestry.ca; http://www.ancestry.ca/

Ottawa Branch Ontario Genealogical Society; http://ogsottawa.on.ca/

Ontario Genealogical Society; http://www.ogs.on.ca/

Ottawa Independent Writers; http://www.oiw.ca/

Searching for Adoption Records in Ontario; http://www.mcss.gov.on.ca/en/mcss/programs/community/records/index.aspx

Jessica Williams: http://www.jessicawilliams.com/d

27. Music to Support Writing

I like to have quiet music in the background when I am writing. The keyboard skills of Jessica Williams playing solo piano help me go beyond the mundane. Her tunes are creative, interpretive, mystical and sometimes haunting.

All Alone, 2003, Jessica Williams: I often begin my writing with this recording; it speaks to me. "Alone, I meet myself, without guile, ornament or ego." Jessica Williams.

Aloneness does not necessarily translate into sadness; sometimes being alone gives one the privacy and space to be creative and call out new thoughts and ideas and also to go into the depths of oneself.

Jessica Williams, *Intuition*, 1995, Jazz Focus Records, Calgary, Alberta, Canada.

Jessica Williams, *It's Jessica's Time*, 1999, Solo Piano live at Jazz Alley, Seattle, WA. Red and Blue Recordings, CA.

Jessica Williams, *Some Ballads, Some Blues*, 2001. Jazz Focus Records, Calgary, Alberta.

Jessica Williams, *Unity,* Live in Concert, 2006. Produced by Jessica Williams, Red & Blue Recordings, CA.

Jessica Williams, *Resolution*, 2006, Recorded live at The Triple Door, Seattle, WA. Red and Blue Recordings, Jessica Williams.

Jessica Williams, *Prophets,* 2007, Produced by Jessica Williams, Red and Blue, Olympia, WA.

Jessica Williams, *Songs for a New Century*, 2008, Produced by Jessica Williams.

Jessica Williams, *Touch*, 2010, Live at the Triple Door, Seattle, WA.

Angela Hewitt, Solo Piano, *BACH arrangements*, 2001, Hyperion, London, U.K. Any live concert or recording by Angela Hewitt is awe-inspiring and conducive to writing and also, meditation.

Oliver Jones, *From Lush to Lively*, 1995, Justin Time, Montreal, Quebec.

Oscar Peterson, *The Oscar Peterson Trio, Canadiana Suite*, 1965. Polygram Records, Quebec.

One Sound, 2000, Traditional Buddhist Music, Ellipsis Arts, New York.

These are but a few suggestions; you can choose music which is special to you and which compliments your mood and writing style.

28. A Word About the Format

The Box in the Closet is written in the format of a creative non-fiction memoir. Documents, stories, photos and interviews, personal experience and research from newspapers were sources of information I sought to weave the story, along with my book *The History and Genealogy of the Bicknell Family.* I cannot say that the scenes and conversations which I have recreated are verbatim but they are within the realm of possibility.

Memory creates a huge controversy in writing memoirs since everyone remembers an occurrence differently. Each person's account of an incident is told according to his/her perception of the event.

29. Endnotes

1 *Elizabeth Kubler-Ross, Brainy Quotes,* Internet: *http://www.goodreads.com/author/quotes/1506.Elisabeth_K_bler_Ross,* 2011 Public domain.

2 Singleton, Margaret R. (Margaret Rose), 1935-History and Genealogy of the Bicknell family in Canada : whose ancestors came from Normandy and Great Britain / Margaret R. Singleton -- Ottawa : M.R. Singleton, 2006. ISBN 0973404000 -- AMICUS No. 32172646

3 Aunt Muriel's description to me was that "A family battle raged on while your grandfather came to a decision. Your grandfather wanted you to be adopted away and your mother and grandmother wanted to keep you. In the end your grandfather won."

Chapter 5

[4] In 1931, Pablum, an infant cereal containing necessary minerals and vitamins for children's health, became available in Canada and the United States. The food was heralded as an excellent cereal addition to the infant's diet and remains a popular infant food today. It was three Canadian doctors - Frederick Tisdall (1893-1949), Theodore Drake (1891-1959), and Alan Brown (1887-1960) - who developed Pablum at the Hospital for Sick Children in Toronto.

iv. The continuance of the pregnancy would not involve greater risk to her life than termination, and there was not substantial risk that, if the pregnancy were not terminated the child would suffer from such physical or mental abnormalities as to be seriously handicapped

[5] Cousin Helen became one of my dearest and closest friends and loved telling me this story as she punctuated the fact that she was my first visitor. Helen would end her story by giggling as she said, "You've improved in looks over the years, Margaret." When my adoptive mother, Florence, died, Helen came to visit me and said, "Now that you don't have a mother, I will give you advice." Over the years, she did so, kindly and creatively.

Helen had a delightful sense of humour and we shared time, laughter and many stories and adventures together. At one time we lived close to each other in Ottawa and she took delight in tending my flower garden, often gift wrapping the dead blooms and leaving the parcel between my doors for me to find when I arrived home from school. One of our favourite things to do was antiquing and we had many sleuthing adventures looking for glass, dolls and furniture. Her death in 2005, at the age of 98, left a huge void in my life.

Chapter 9

6 Each month a parcel arrived at the Victor Home for Girls, from one of the United Church women's groups in the city; the Women's Association, the Women's Missionary Society or the Women's Christian Temperance Union. The meetings of the organizations and the gifts were all reported each month in the *Toronto Star*. Bloor St, Urskine, Bathurst, Humbercrest, Carleton St., Detonia Park, Windermere, Hope, Howard Park, Fairlawn, United Churches all contributed to the Victor Home for Girls. One church reported having given 234 gifts to the Victor Home in one year.

7 At each of their meetings one of the women gave a report of the "splendid work being done at the Victor Home for Girls." "Showers" with different themes were held at the meetings and the gifts were distributed to the residents of the Victor Home. The young women were never invited to one of these "showers", perhaps because one would expect them to be embarrassed by their condition. In principle it was a kind and thoughtful act by the women's groups but it set the young women apart and was not inclusive.

Miss Gertrude Aikenhead, superintendent and Miss Barclay, the nurse at the Victor Home attended the women's groups and made regular "interesting reports" of the difficulties and problems facing both the Victor Home and the girls in residence, who were described as "not too strong morally." By whose assessment and standard the *Toronto Star* does not report. Mrs. Moat, president of the Victor Home reported that "Miss Aikenhead is winning the girls back to decent and normal living."

Chapter 13

8 "A Bowles Stethoscope is likely to have been the one used. The practical diaphragm stethoscope was developed and patented by Dr. Robert C.M. Bowles in 1894. The original version had a flat diaphragm chest piece that could be used with or without a short rod that screwed into the diaphragm in order to localize heart sounds. The chest piece could be connected to a typical Cammann type binaural ear piece or, alternatively, could simply be used by applying the ear directly to the hollow opening of the chest piece. Early versions of his stethoscope had only the diaphragm chest piece, but later models had both a bell and diaphragm interchangeable in the same chest piece, which was usually referred to as a combination stethoscope. The sole manufacturer of the Bowles stethoscopes in America during the first half of the 20th century was George P. Pilling Son Co. of Philadelphia. This was the first type of combination bell and diaphragm stethoscope."

Taken from Medical Antiques: http://www.antiquemed.com/20th_century.htm

Chapter 14

9 THE CERTIFICATE OF REGISTRATION OF BIRTH shows Victoria Memorial Hospital, Toronto, as the place of birth for Dorothy Watson., May 10, 1935, only daughter of Beatrice Watson (Bicknell). Dr. W.S. Scheck was the attending physician. Dated; Toronto, July 13, 1935. When I received my original birth registration, I was astounded to see that my mother signed a false name on the birth registration certificate and registered me under a false name. Dr. Scheck, the attending physician, was the husband of Betty's great Aunt Ellen Bicknell

Chapter 15

10 In today's society with our numerous options for adoption in Canada those conditions would not even be on the table. There are many different ways to adopt a child now and as people begin to explore their options and learn more about the children who need families their original thoughts and plans may change. Some of the options available to singles, couples both straight and gay and lesbian, are public adoption, international adoption, private adoption, Canada's waiting children's program, Adopt Ontario and open adoption. Many people also choose child sponsoring programs as a way to assist children in Canada and other countries.

Chapter 18

11 I later learned that I was not born there but my birth-mother sought refuge at the *Victor Home for Girls* when she was pregnant and she lived there for several months. When I was eleven years old I took a photo of the house on my Brownie camera which I treasure, as the house has been torn down and replaced with a neighborhood park.

In July, 2010 I received my original birth registration from Service Ontario with the information that I was born in Victoria Hospital in Toronto, May 10, 1935.

12 These dates are interesting to me.

> My adoptive Mother, Florence Mildred (Hough) Singleton died on April 03, 1961.
>
> My birth Mother, Beatrice Louise (Bicknell) Elder was born on April 03, 1918 and died on April 7, 1964.
>
> My daughter Christine Elizabeth Bresee was born on August 31, 1964.

Chapter 19

[13] *The Velveteen Rabbit,* 1922, Williams, Margery, Running Press, Philadelphia, Pennsylvania, page 14. In the public domain.

Chapter 20

[14] *The Freedom of Information Act* had not yet been passed by Parliament. Mr. Walter Baker introduced the first ever *Access to Information Bill* which died on the order paper with the Tory government. However, much of his Bill became part of the eventual *Access to Information Act* which came into force under the Pierre Trudeau government, and was introduced by Liberal Solicitor-General Francis Fox in 1983. It permitted Canadians to retrieve information from government files, establishing what information could be accessed and mandating timelines for response. It was passed by Parliament into law in 1983. It, quite simply put, gives the public a right to access records, a right to request correction of personal information and prevents the unauthorized collection, use or disclosure of personal information by public bodies.

[15] Glen Road bridge Photo: http://www.toronto photoarchives.ca/ Toronto